SECRET INVASION

HOME INVASION

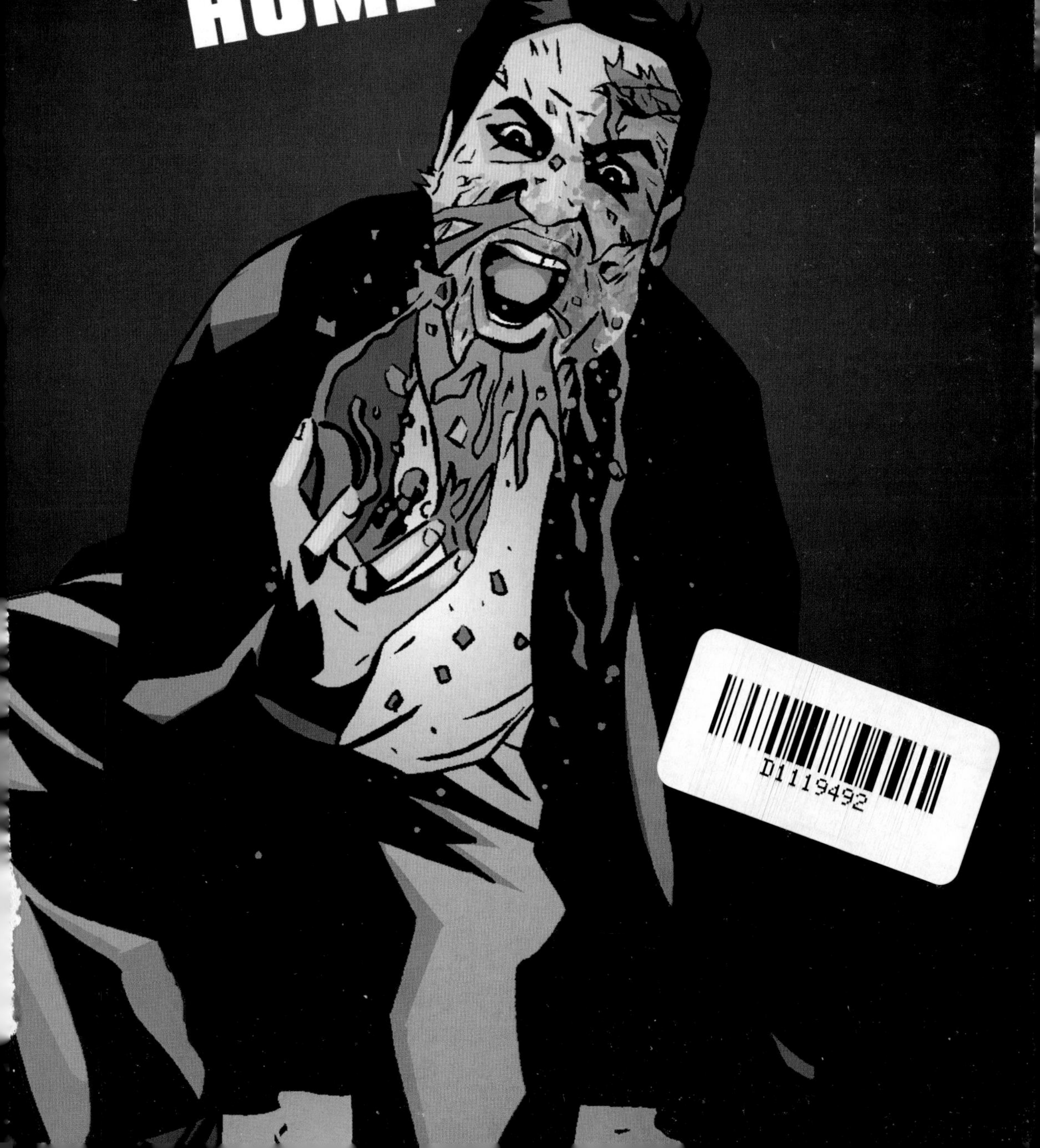

SECRET INVASION
HOME INVASION

Writer: IVAN BRANDON
Artist: NICK POSTIC
Colors: SOTOCOLOR'S J. BROWN
Letters: DAVE SHARPE
Assistant Editor: MICHAEL HORWITZ
Editor: JOHN BARBER

SPECIAL SKRULLY THANKS TO

Jim McCann, Ben Morse, Sam Walker, Ryan Penagos,
Jeff Suter, John Cerilli, Tim Smith, Taylor Esposito and Harry Go

Collection Editor: JENNIFER GRÜNWALD
Editorial Assistant: ALEX STARBUCK
Assistant Editors: CORY LEVINE & JOHN DENNING
Editor, Special Projects: MARK D. BEAZLEY
Senior Editor, Special Projects: JEFF YOUNGQUIST
Senior Vice President Of Sales: DAVID GABRIEL
Book Designer: SPRING HOTELING

Editor In Chief: JOE QUESADA
Publisher: DAN BUCKLEY

PREVIOUSLY IN THE KINSEY WALDEN VIDEO BLOG:

Kinsey Walden was a typical high-school senior.

With her parents out of town, she should have spent the last few days enjoying herself – playing soccer or shopping for the perfect prom dress. Or doing anything other than what she has been doing: spying on her brother, Hank, who's been acting a little stranger than normal recently.

"Strange" as in writing notes to himself in a made-up language and keeping maps of Manhattan hidden under his mattress. Kinsey believes something is seriously wrong with Hank, and when she decides to confront him with her suspicions, he... turns green.

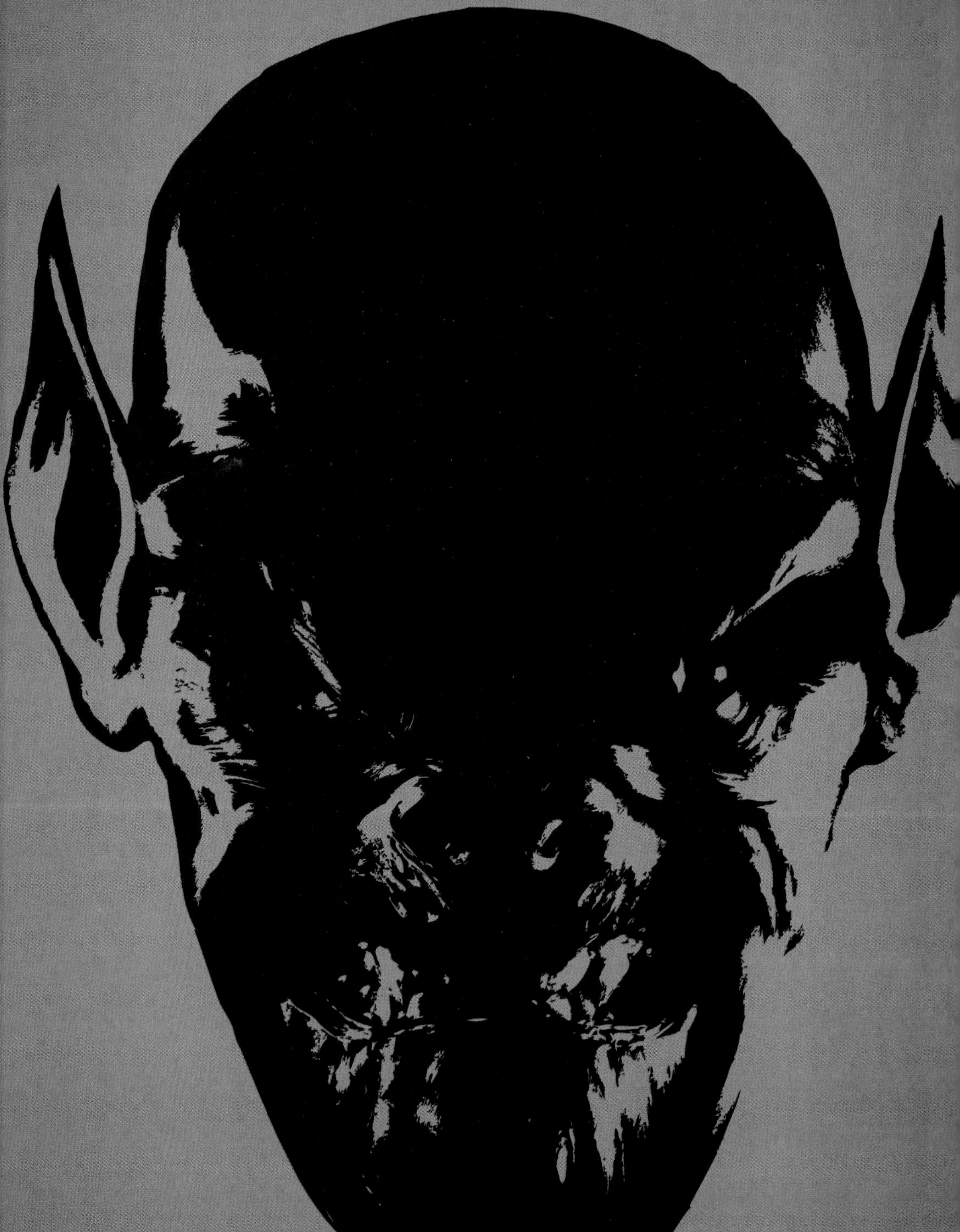

CHAPTER 1

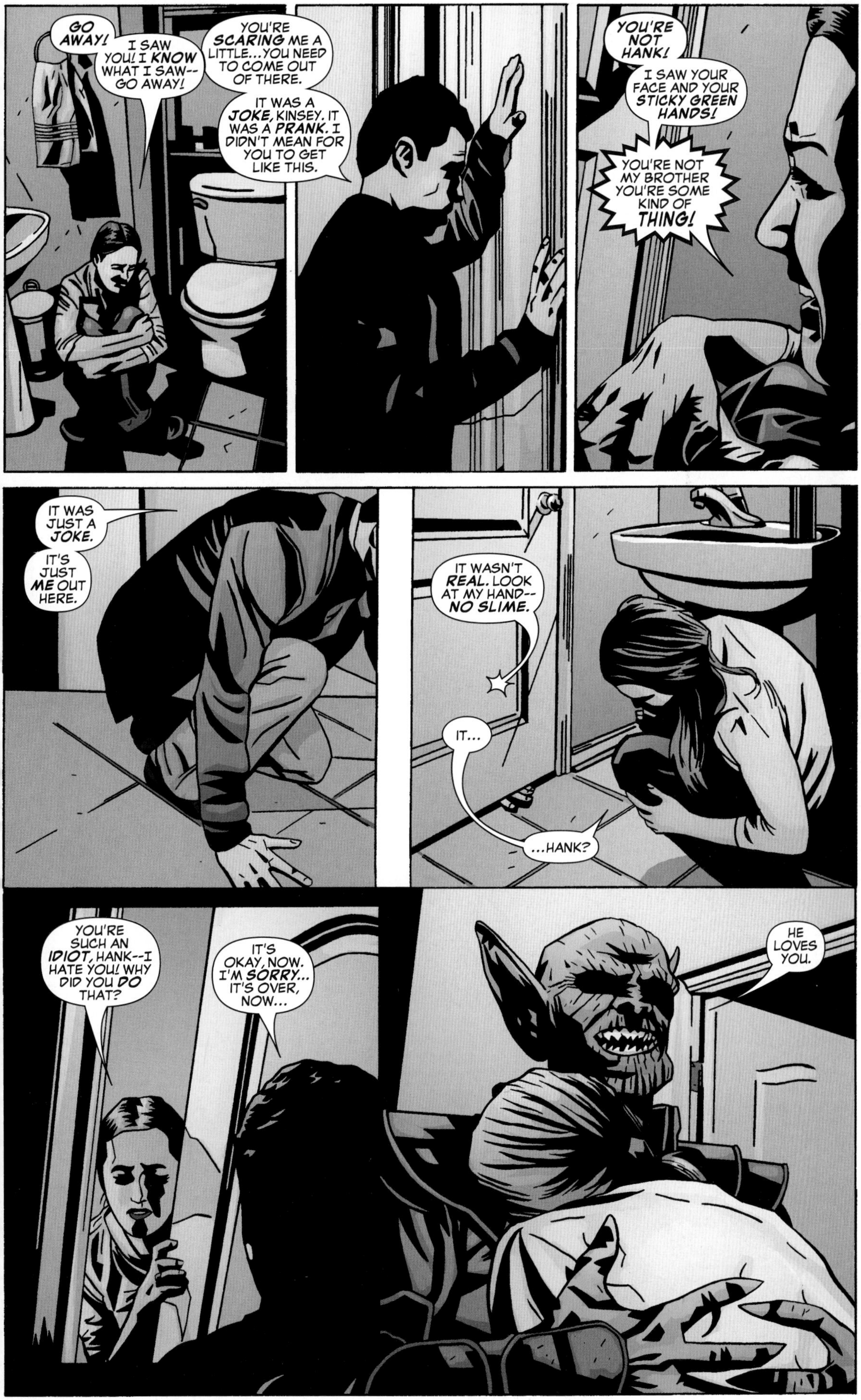
GO AWAY!
I SAW YOU! I KNOW WHAT I SAW-- GO AWAY!
YOU'RE SCARING ME A LITTLE...YOU NEED TO COME OUT OF THERE.
IT WAS A JOKE, KINSEY. IT WAS A PRANK. I DIDN'T MEAN FOR YOU TO GET LIKE THIS.
YOU'RE NOT HANK!
I SAW YOUR FACE AND YOUR STICKY GREEN HANDS!
YOU'RE NOT MY BROTHER YOU'RE SOME KIND OF THING!
IT WAS JUST A JOKE.
IT'S JUST ME OUT HERE.
IT WASN'T REAL. LOOK AT MY HAND-- NO SLIME.
IT...
...HANK?
YOU'RE SUCH AN IDIOT, HANK--I HATE YOU! WHY DID YOU DO THAT?
IT'S OKAY, NOW. I'M SORRY... IT'S OVER, NOW...
HE LOVES YOU.

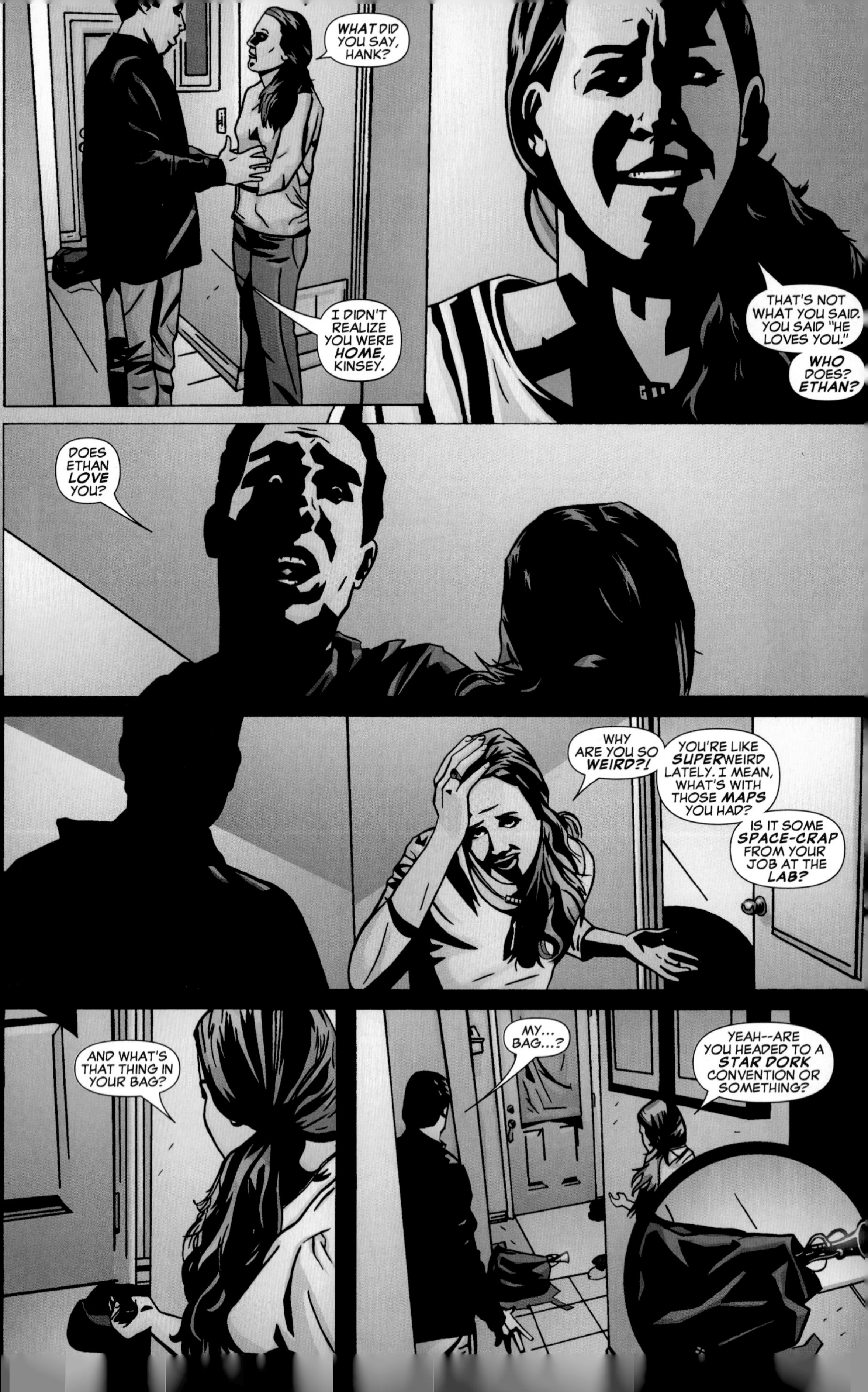
WHAT DID YOU SAY, HANK?
I DIDN'T REALIZE YOU WERE HOME, KINSEY.
THAT'S NOT WHAT YOU SAID. YOU SAID "HE LOVES YOU."
WHO DOES? ETHAN?
DOES ETHAN LOVE YOU?
WHY ARE YOU SO WEIRD?!
YOU'RE LIKE SUPERWEIRD LATELY. I MEAN, WHAT'S WITH THOSE MAPS YOU HAD?
IS IT SOME SPACE-CRAP FROM YOUR JOB AT THE LAB?
AND WHAT'S THAT THING IN YOUR BAG?
MY... BAG...?
YEAH--ARE YOU HEADED TO A STAR DORK CONVENTION OR SOMETHING?

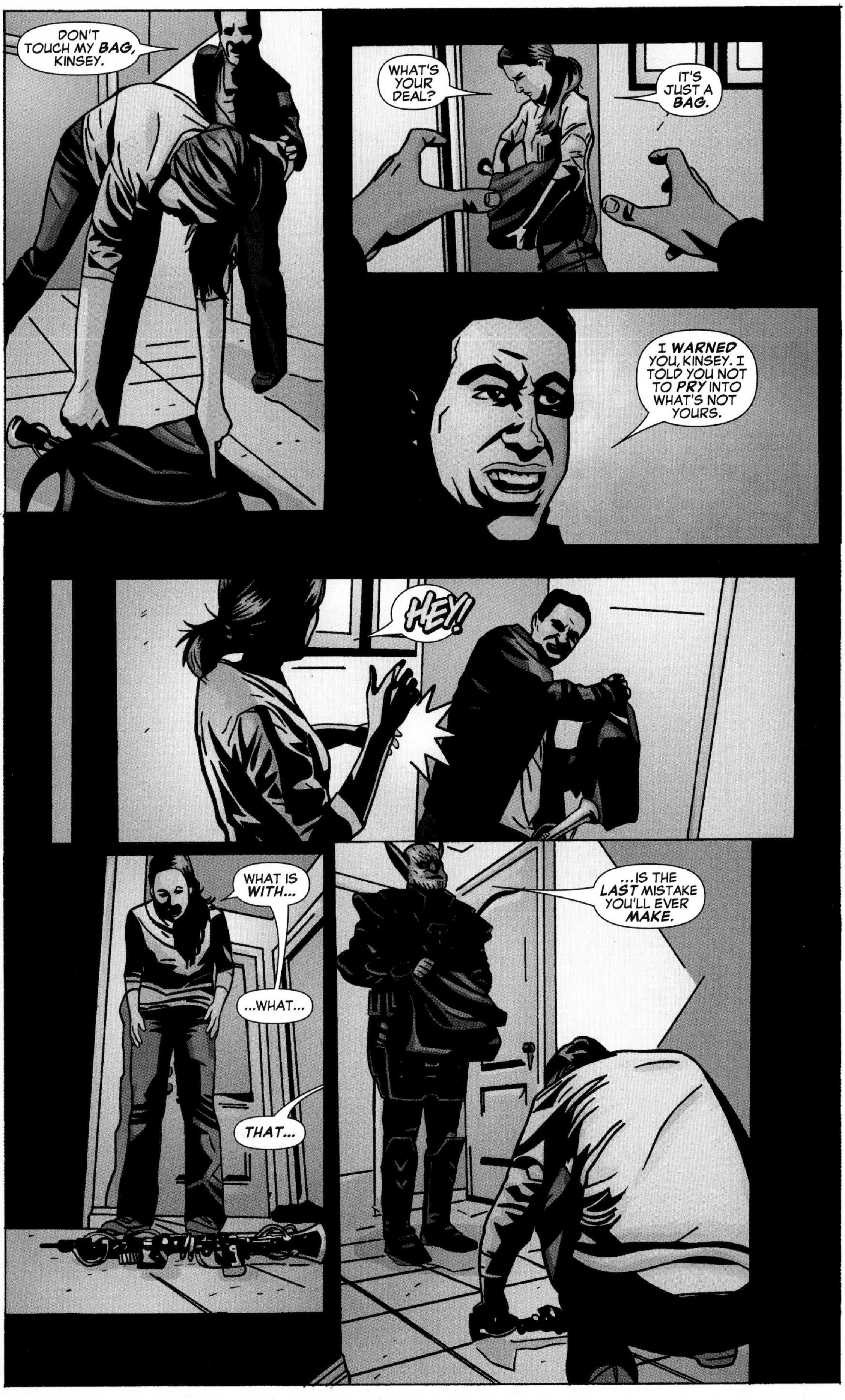
DON'T TOUCH MY BAG, KINSEY.
WHAT'S YOUR DEAL?
IT'S JUST A BAG.
I WARNED YOU, KINSEY. I TOLD YOU NOT TO PRY INTO WHAT'S NOT YOURS.
HEY!
WHAT IS WITH...
...WHAT...
THAT...
...IS THE LAST MISTAKE YOU'LL EVER MAKE.

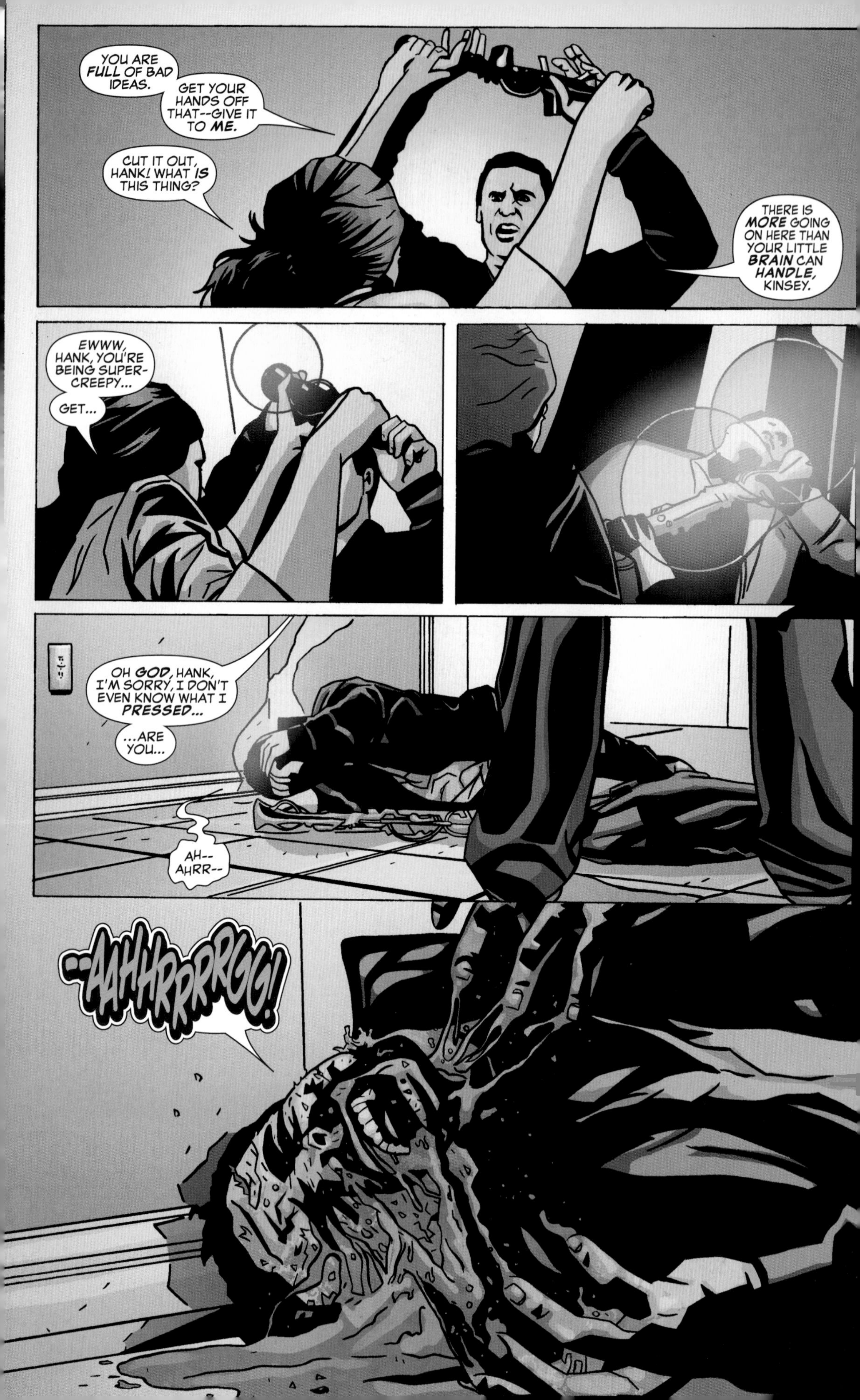
YOU ARE FULL OF BAD IDEAS.
GET YOUR HANDS OFF THAT--GIVE IT TO ME.
CUT IT OUT, HANK! WHAT IS THIS THING?
THERE IS MORE GOING ON HERE THAN YOUR LITTLE BRAIN CAN HANDLE, KINSEY.
EWWW, HANK, YOU'RE BEING SUPER-CREEPY...
GET...
OH GOD, HANK, I'M SORRY, I DON'T EVEN KNOW WHAT I PRESSED...
...ARE YOU...
AH-- AHRR--
--AAHHRRRRGG!

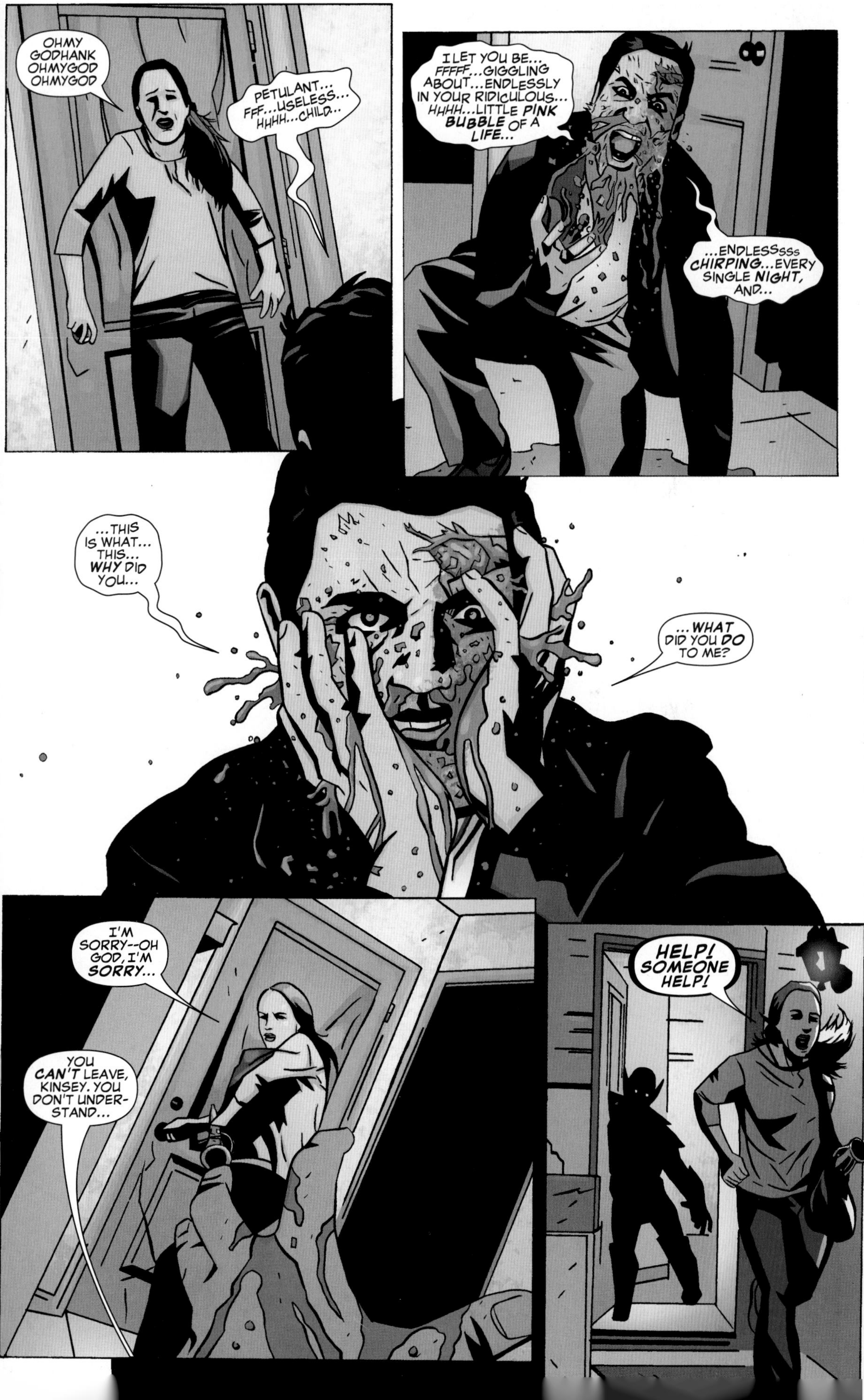
OHMY GODHANK OHMYGOD OHMYGOD
PETULANT... FFF...USELESS... HHHH...CHILD...
I LET YOU BE... FFFFF...GIGGLING ABOUT...ENDLESSLY IN YOUR RIDICULOUS... HHHH...LITTLE PINK BUBBLE OF A LIFE...
...ENDLESSsss CHIRPING...EVERY SINGLE NIGHT, AND...
...THIS IS WHAT... THIS... WHY DID YOU...
...WHAT DID YOU DO TO ME?
I'M SORRY--OH GOD, I'M SORRY...
YOU CAN'T LEAVE, KINSEY. YOU DON'T UNDER-STAND...
HELP! SOMEONE HELP!

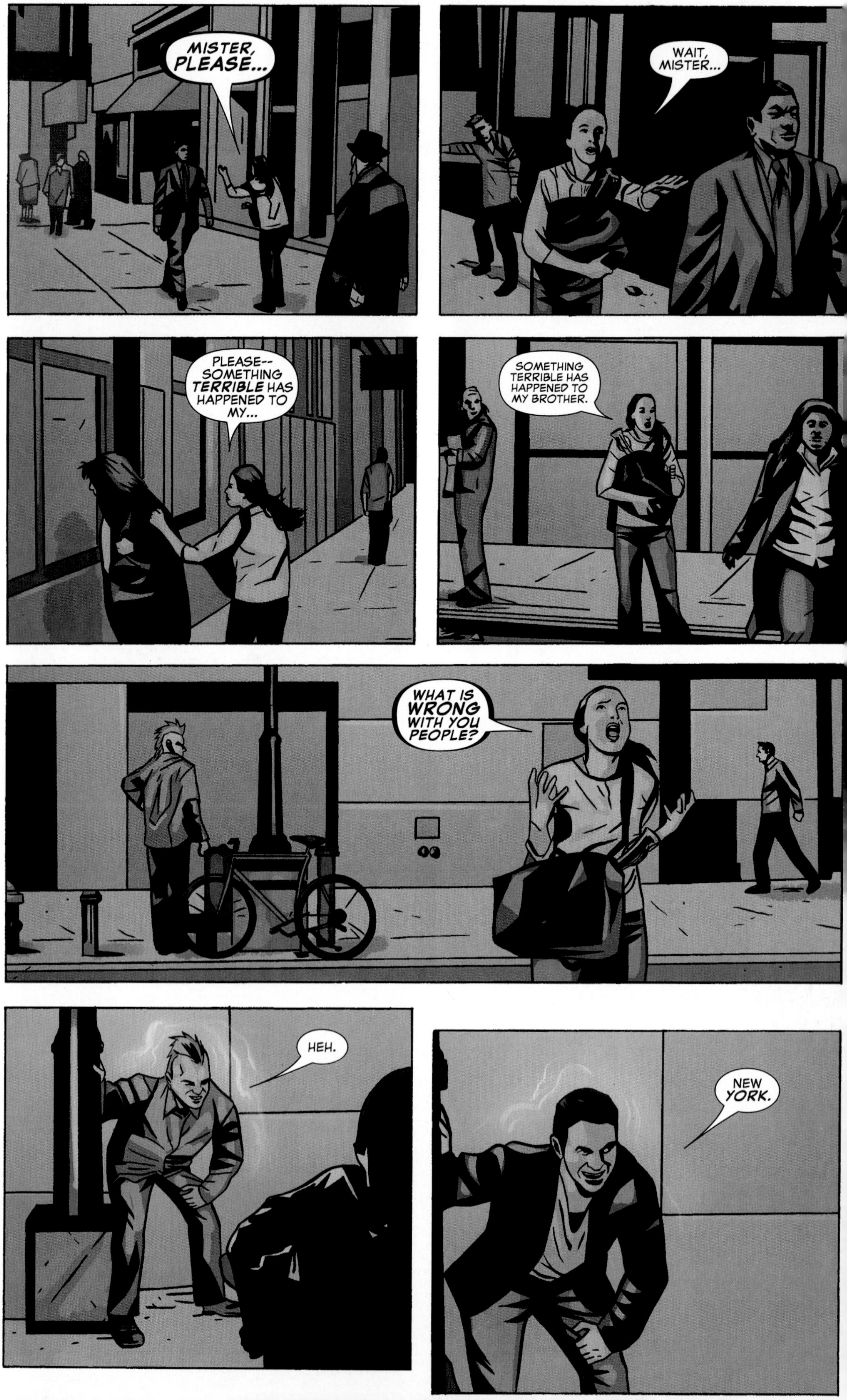
MISTER, PLEASE...
WAIT, MISTER...
PLEASE-- SOMETHING TERRIBLE HAS HAPPENED TO MY...
SOMETHING TERRIBLE HAS HAPPENED TO MY BROTHER.
WHAT IS WRONG WITH YOU PEOPLE?
HEH.
NEW YORK.

KINSEY, CALM **DOWN**...

I DON'T KNOW WHAT TO **DO**, MRS. STARCK--I FEEL LIKE MY **HEART'S** ABOUT TO **BURST**.

JUST COME **INSIDE**, OKAY?

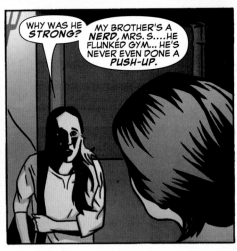

WHY WAS HE **STRONG**?

MY BROTHER'S A **NERD**, MRS. S....HE FLUNKED GYM... HE'S NEVER EVEN DONE A **PUSH-UP**.

HANK WAS **ALWAYS** A DORK, BUT JUST NOW, HE--HE WAS **GREEN**!

IS HE **SICK**? IS HE A **WERE-FROG** OR SOMETHING?!

MACKENZIE... COME **INSIDE**. THE **NEIGHBORS** ARE STARING.

COME AND SIT **DOWN**, KINSEY.

HE WAS HORRIBLE AND **BLEEDING**...I DIDN'T MEAN... OH, AND **ALI**!

WHAT HAS HE DONE TO **ALI**?

DONE TO **ME**?

GROSS.

NOT **YOU**, TOO--WHAT HAS HANK **DONE** TO YOU?!

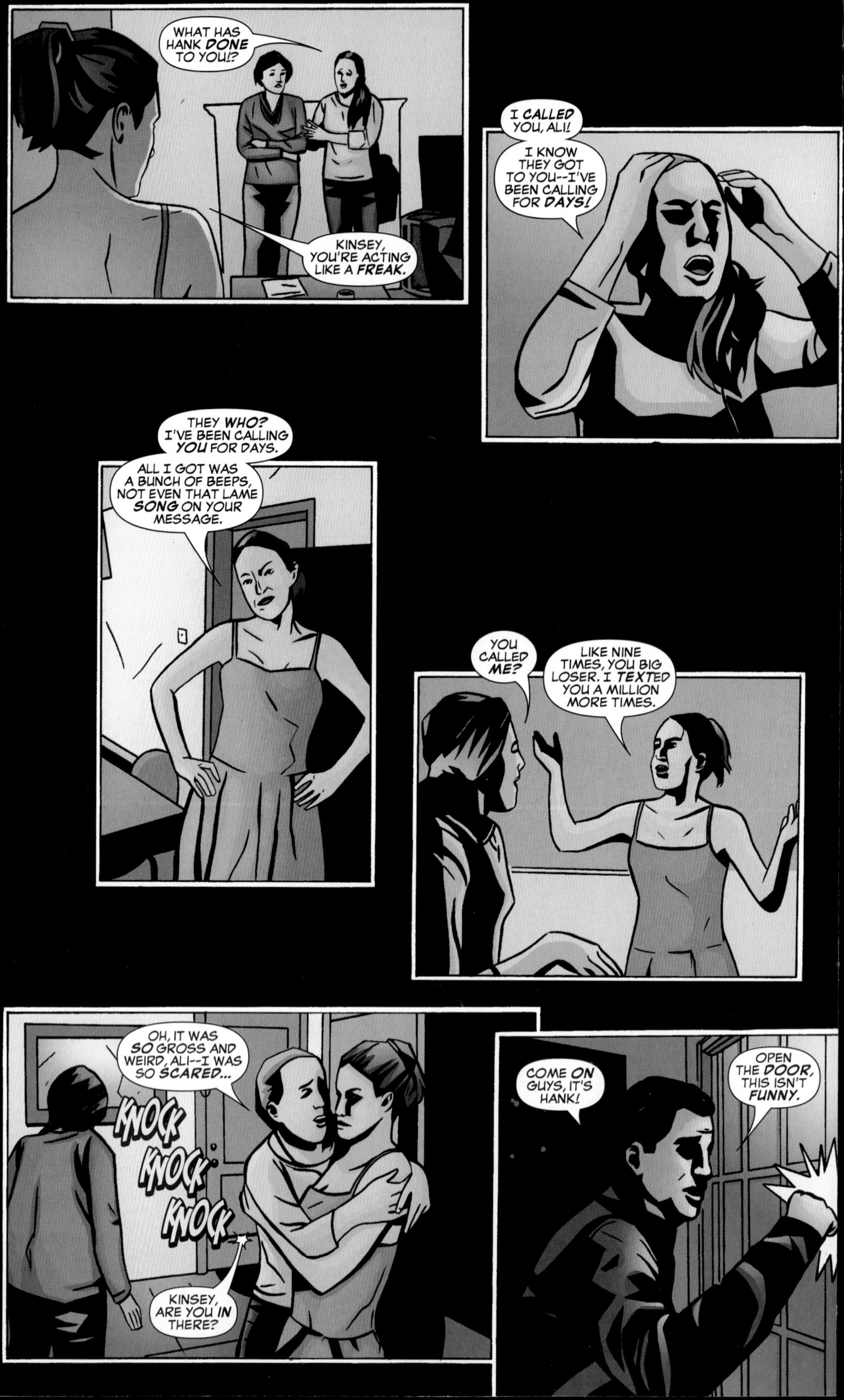

WHAT HAS HANK DONE TO YOU!?
KINSEY, YOU'RE ACTING LIKE A FREAK.
I CALLED YOU, ALI!
I KNOW THEY GOT TO YOU--I'VE BEEN CALLING FOR DAYS!
THEY WHO? I'VE BEEN CALLING YOU FOR DAYS.
ALL I GOT WAS A BUNCH OF BEEPS, NOT EVEN THAT LAME SONG ON YOUR MESSAGE.
YOU CALLED ME?
LIKE NINE TIMES, YOU BIG LOSER. I TEXTED YOU A MILLION MORE TIMES.
OH, IT WAS SO GROSS AND WEIRD, ALI--I WAS SO SCARED...
KNOCK
KNOCK
KNOCK
KINSEY, ARE YOU IN THERE?
COME ON GUYS, IT'S HANK!
OPEN THE DOOR, THIS ISN'T FUNNY.

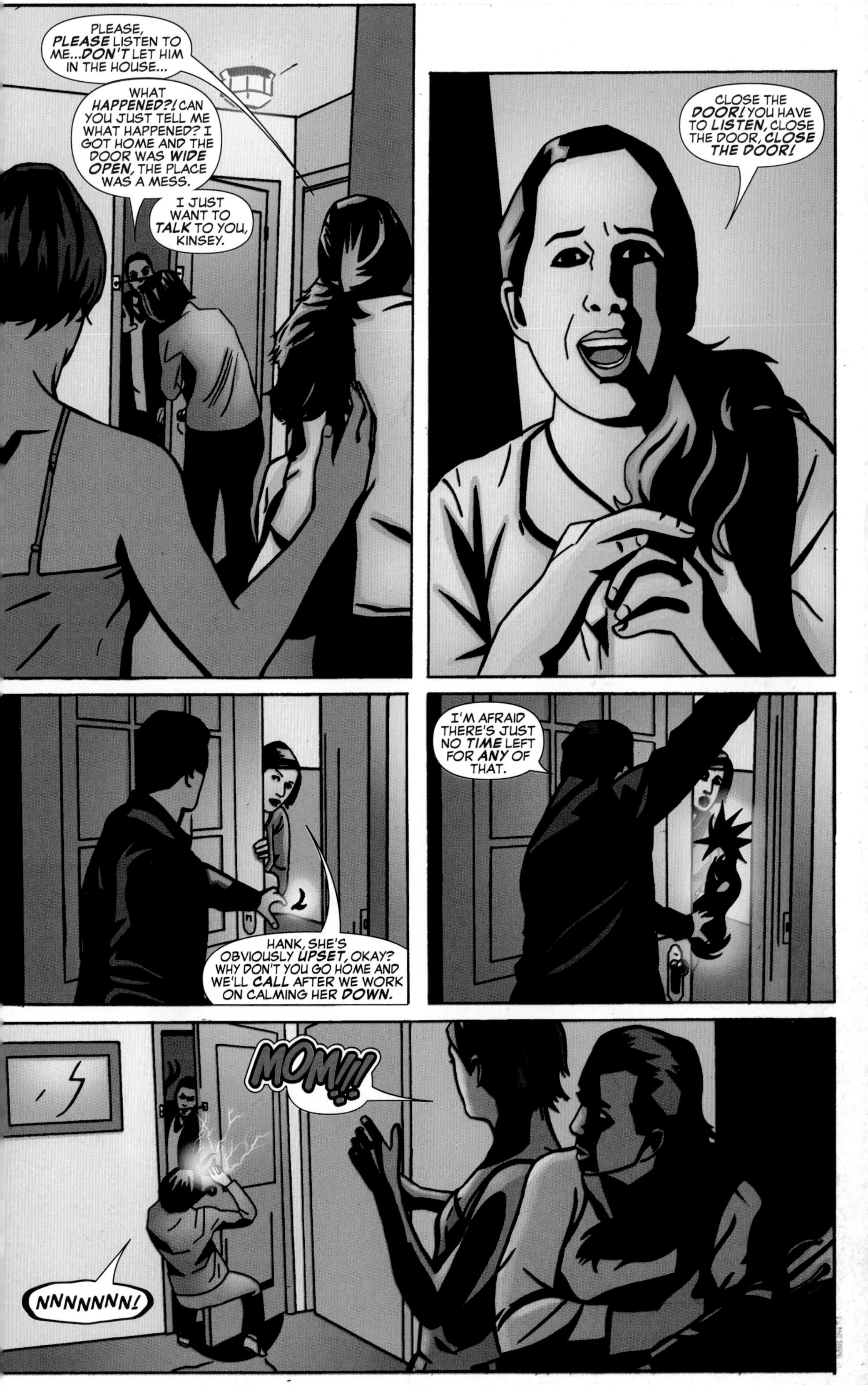
PLEASE, PLEASE LISTEN TO ME...DON'T LET HIM IN THE HOUSE...
WHAT HAPPENED?! CAN YOU JUST TELL ME WHAT HAPPENED? I GOT HOME AND THE DOOR WAS WIDE OPEN, THE PLACE WAS A MESS.
I JUST WANT TO TALK TO YOU, KINSEY.
CLOSE THE DOOR! YOU HAVE TO LISTEN, CLOSE THE DOOR, CLOSE THE DOOR!
HANK, SHE'S OBVIOUSLY UPSET, OKAY? WHY DON'T YOU GO HOME AND WE'LL CALL AFTER WE WORK ON CALMING HER DOWN.
I'M AFRAID THERE'S JUST NO TIME LEFT FOR ANY OF THAT.
MOM!!!
NNNNNNN!

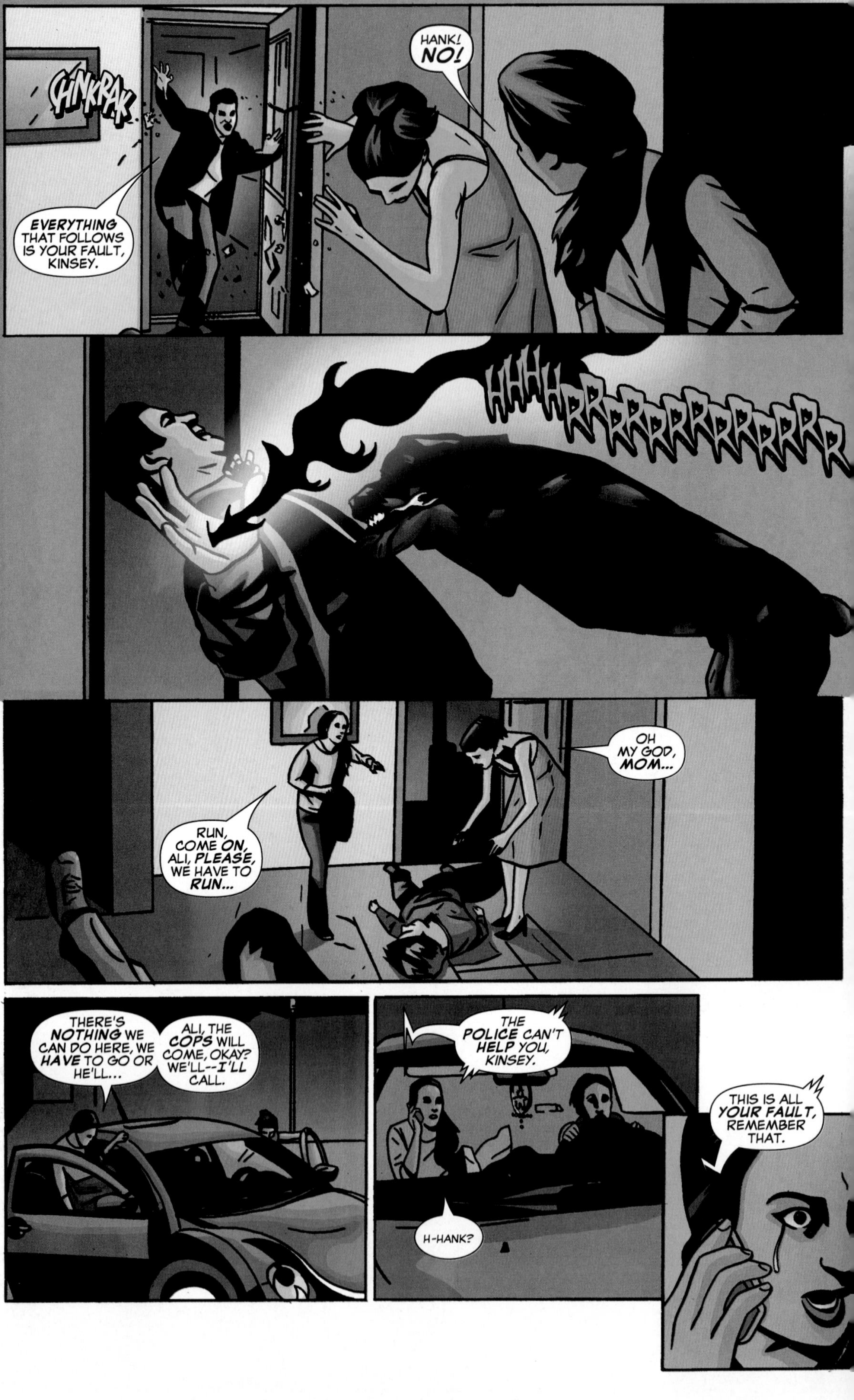
CHINKRAK
EVERYTHING THAT FOLLOWS IS YOUR FAULT, KINSEY.
HANK! NO!
HHHHRRRRRRRRRRRRRR
OH MY GOD, MOM...
RUN, COME ON, ALI, PLEASE, WE HAVE TO RUN...
THERE'S NOTHING WE CAN DO HERE, WE HAVE TO GO OR HE'LL...
ALI, THE COPS WILL COME, OKAY? WE'LL--I'LL CALL.
THE POLICE CAN'T HELP YOU, KINSEY.
H-HANK?
THIS IS ALL YOUR FAULT, REMEMBER THAT.

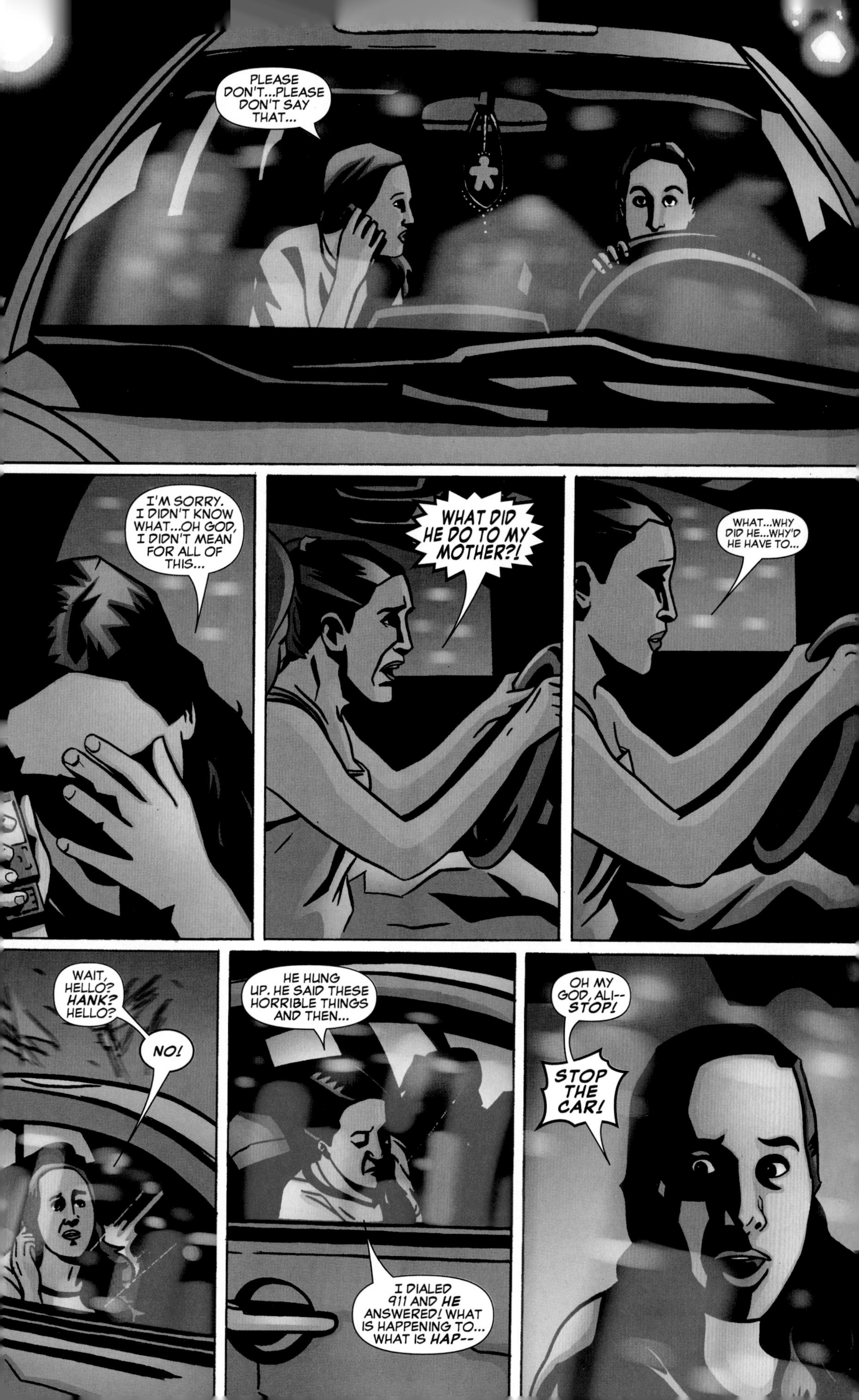
PLEASE DON'T...PLEASE DON'T SAY THAT...
I'M SORRY. I DIDN'T KNOW WHAT...OH GOD, I DIDN'T MEAN FOR ALL OF THIS...
WHAT DID HE DO TO MY MOTHER?!
WHAT...WHY DID HE...WHY'D HE HAVE TO...
WAIT, HELLO? HANK? HELLO?
NO!
HE HUNG UP. HE SAID THESE HORRIBLE THINGS AND THEN...
I DIALED 911 AND HE ANSWERED! WHAT IS HAPPENING TO... WHAT IS HAP--
OH MY GOD, ALI-- STOP!
STOP THE CAR!

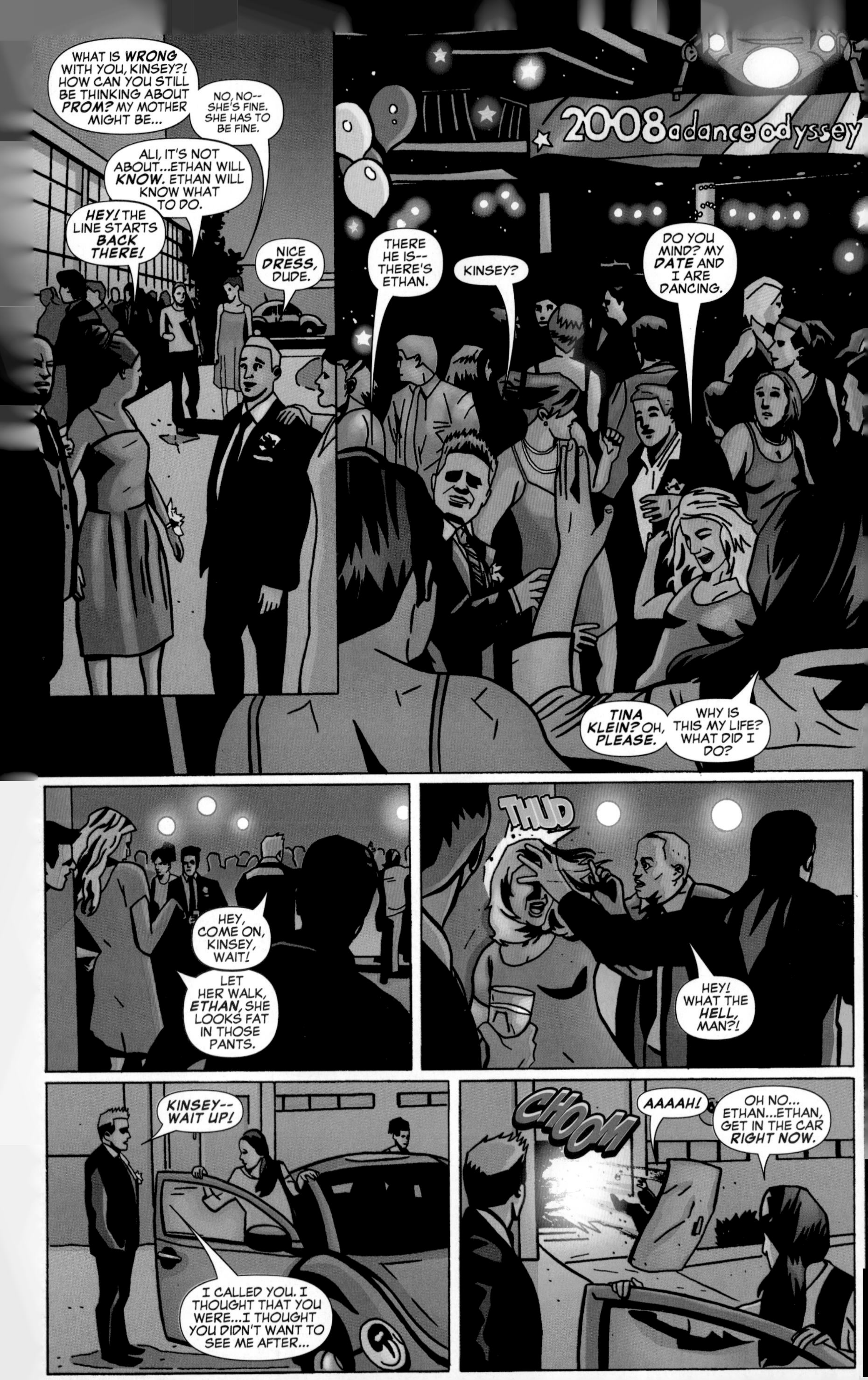

WHAT IS **WRONG** WITH YOU, KINSEY?! HOW CAN YOU STILL BE THINKING ABOUT **PROM?** MY MOTHER MIGHT BE...
NO, NO-- SHE'S FINE. SHE HAS TO BE FINE.
ALI, IT'S NOT ABOUT...ETHAN WILL **KNOW.** ETHAN WILL KNOW WHAT TO DO.
HEY! THE LINE STARTS **BACK THERE!**
NICE **DRESS,** DUDE.
2008 a dance odyssey
THERE HE IS-- THERE'S ETHAN.
KINSEY?
DO YOU MIND? MY **DATE** AND I ARE DANCING.
TINA KLEIN? OH, **PLEASE.**
WHY IS THIS MY LIFE? WHAT DID I DO?
HEY, COME ON, KINSEY, WAIT!
LET HER WALK, **ETHAN,** SHE LOOKS FAT IN THOSE PANTS.
THUD
HEY! WHAT THE **HELL,** MAN?!
KINSEY-- WAIT UP!
I CALLED YOU. I THOUGHT THAT YOU WERE...I THOUGHT YOU DIDN'T WANT TO SEE ME AFTER...
CHOOM
AAAAH!
OH NO... ETHAN...ETHAN, GET IN THE CAR **RIGHT NOW.**

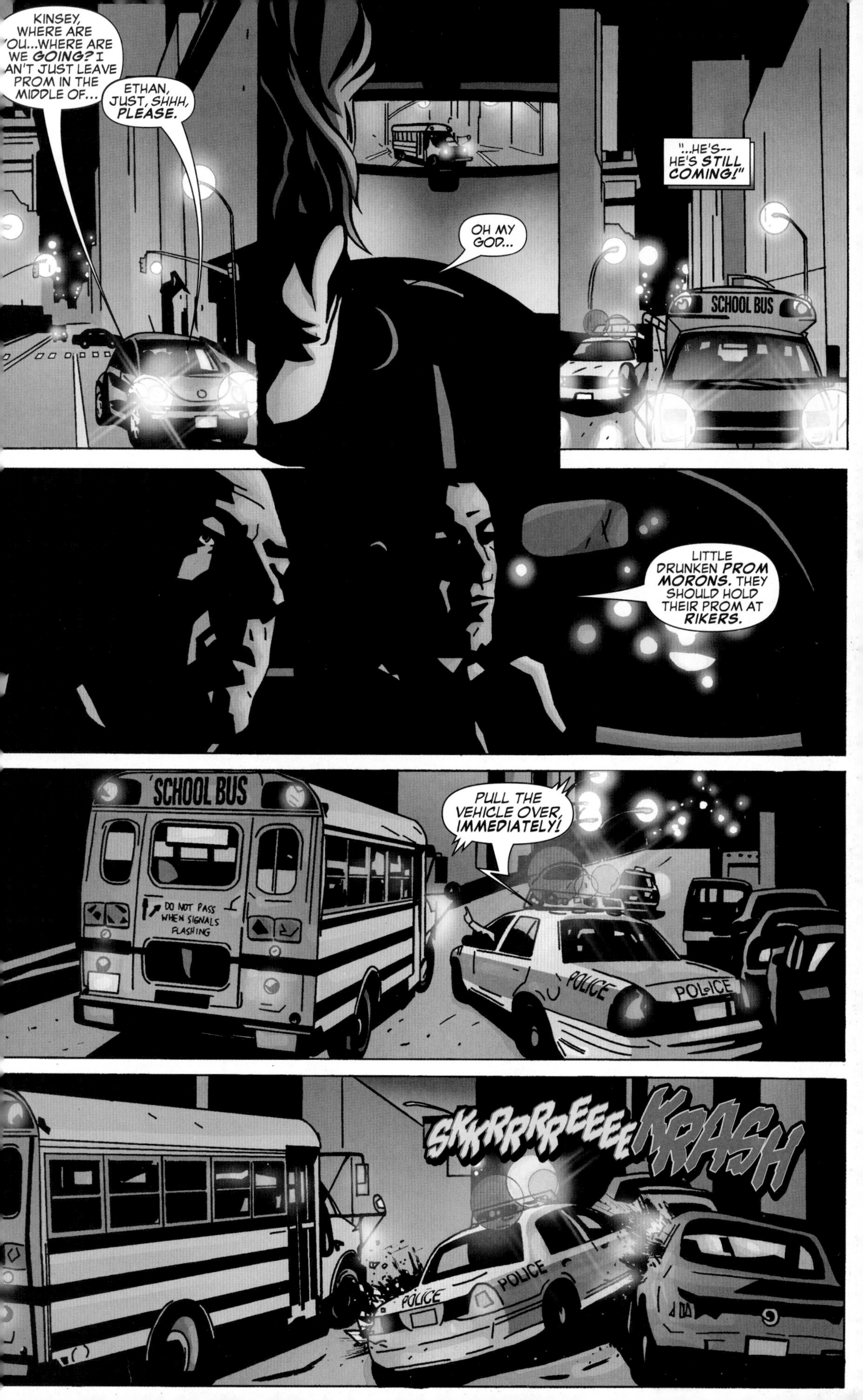
KINSEY, WHERE ARE 'OU...WHERE ARE WE GOING? I AN'T JUST LEAVE PROM IN THE MIDDLE OF...
ETHAN, JUST, SHHH, PLEASE.
OH MY GOD...
"...HE'S-- HE'S STILL COMING!"
SCHOOL BUS
LITTLE DRUNKEN PROM MORONS. THEY SHOULD HOLD THEIR PROM AT RIKERS.
SCHOOL BUS
DO NOT PASS WHEN SIGNALS FLASHING
PULL THE VEHICLE OVER, IMMEDIATELY!
POLICE
POLICE
SKKRRRREEEEKRASH
POLICE
POLICE

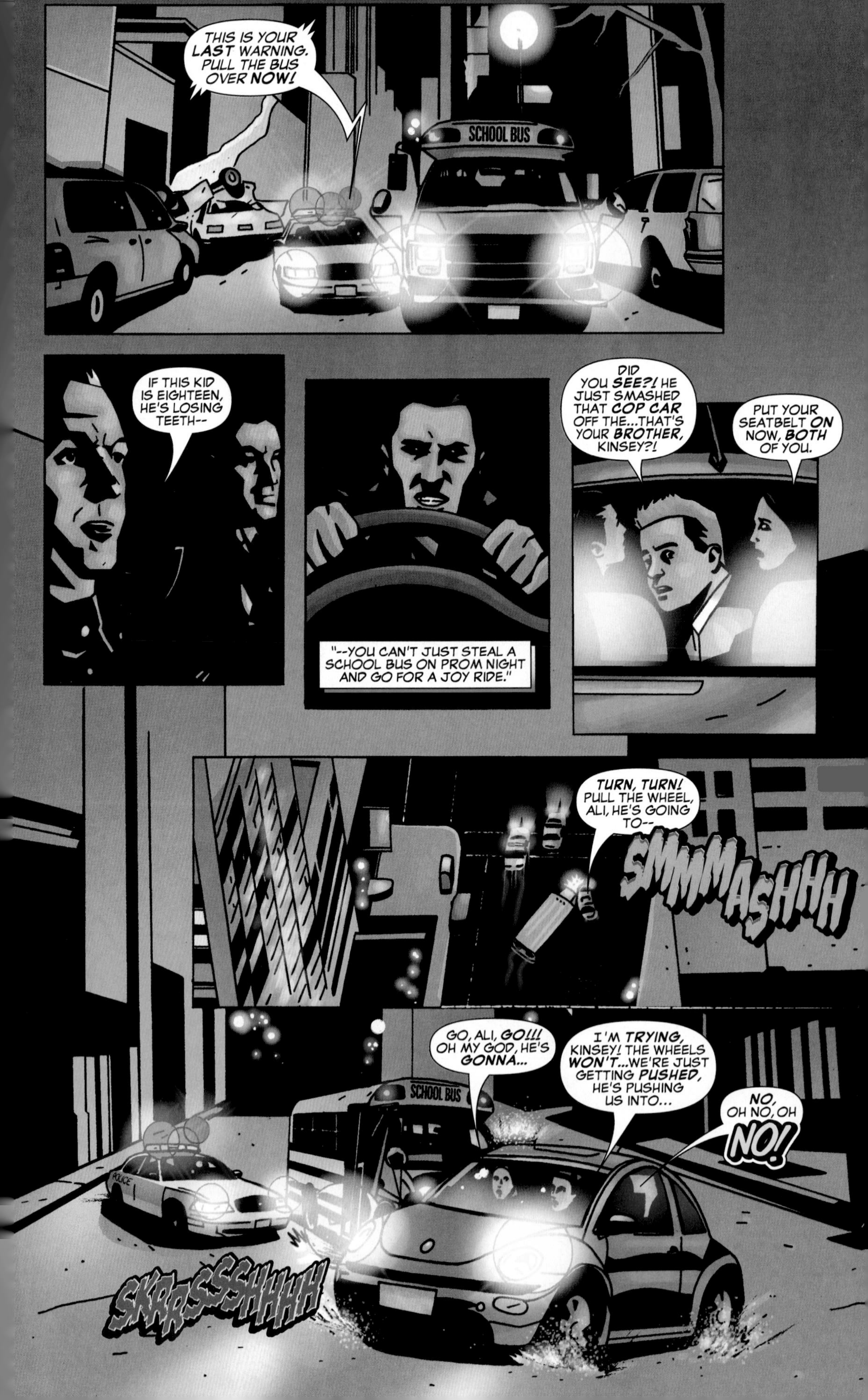
THIS IS YOUR LAST WARNING. PULL THE BUS OVER NOW!
SCHOOL BUS
IF THIS KID IS EIGHTEEN, HE'S LOSING TEETH--
"--YOU CAN'T JUST STEAL A SCHOOL BUS ON PROM NIGHT AND GO FOR A JOY RIDE."
DID YOU SEE?! HE JUST SMASHED THAT COP CAR OFF THE...THAT'S YOUR BROTHER, KINSEY?!
PUT YOUR SEATBELT ON NOW, BOTH OF YOU.
TURN, TURN! PULL THE WHEEL, ALI, HE'S GOING TO--
SMMMASHHH
GO, ALI, GO!!! OH MY GOD, HE'S GONNA...
I'M TRYING, KINSEY! THE WHEELS WON'T...WE'RE JUST GETTING PUSHED, HE'S PUSHING US INTO...
NO, OH NO, OH NO!
SCHOOL BUS
POLICE
SKRRSSSHHHH

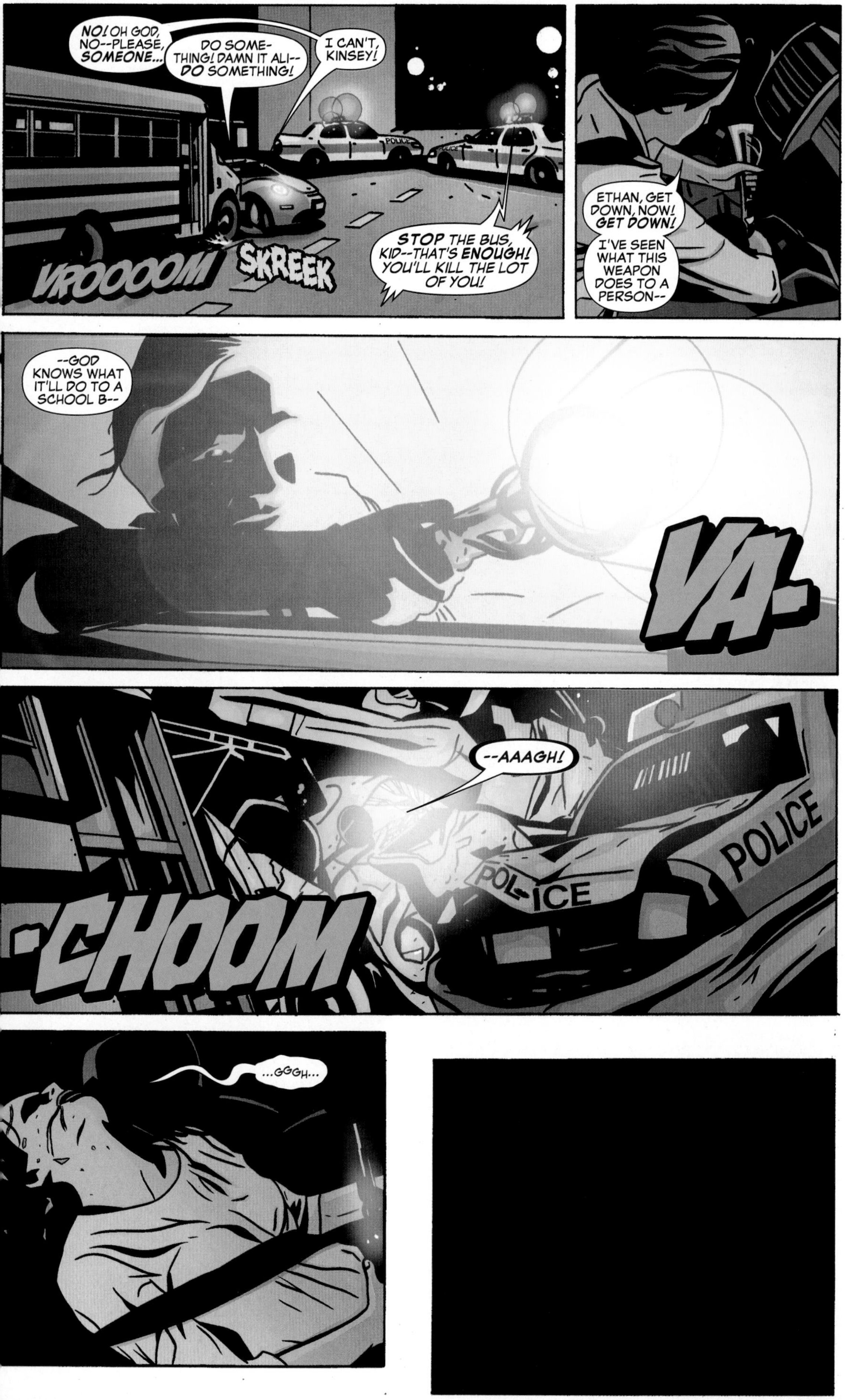
NO! OH GOD, NO--PLEASE, SOMEONE...
DO SOME-THING! DAMN IT ALI-- DO SOMETHING!
I CAN'T, KINSEY!
POLICE
VROOOOM
SKREEK
STOP THE BUS, KID--THAT'S ENOUGH! YOU'LL KILL THE LOT OF YOU!
ETHAN, GET DOWN, NOW! GET DOWN!
I'VE SEEN WHAT THIS WEAPON DOES TO A PERSON--
--GOD KNOWS WHAT IT'LL DO TO A SCHOOL B--
VA-
--AAAGH!
POL-ICE
POLICE
-CHOOM
...GGGH...

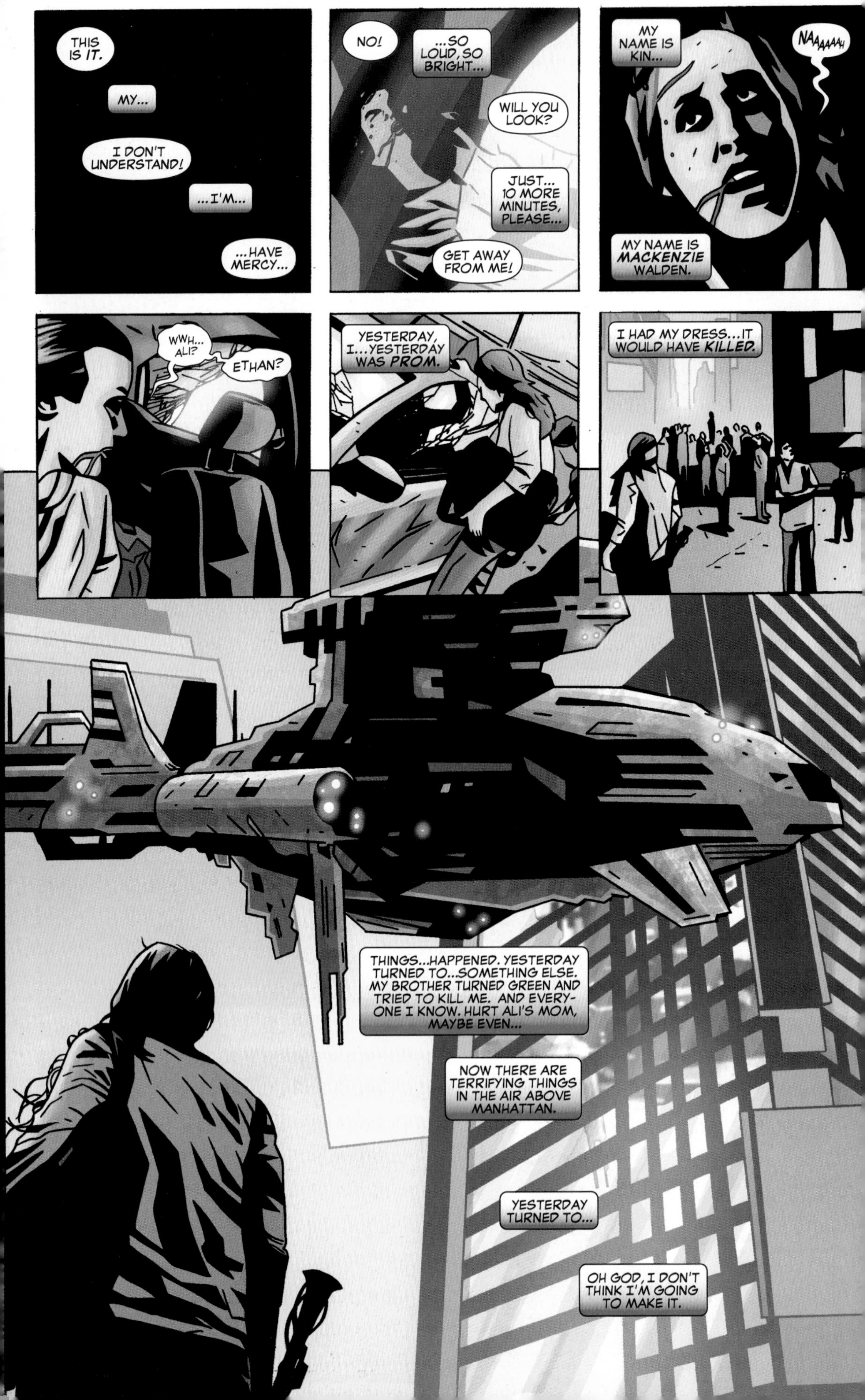
THIS IS IT.
MY...
I DON'T UNDERSTAND!
...I'M...
...HAVE MERCY...
NO!
...SO LOUD, SO BRIGHT...
WILL YOU LOOK?
JUST... 10 MORE MINUTES, PLEASE...
GET AWAY FROM ME!
MY NAME IS KIN...
NAAAAAAH
MY NAME IS MACKENZIE WALDEN.
WWH... ALI?
ETHAN?
YESTERDAY, I...YESTERDAY WAS PROM.
I HAD MY DRESS...IT WOULD HAVE KILLED.
THINGS...HAPPENED. YESTERDAY TURNED TO...SOMETHING ELSE. MY BROTHER TURNED GREEN AND TRIED TO KILL ME. AND EVERY-ONE I KNOW. HURT ALI'S MOM, MAYBE EVEN...
NOW THERE ARE TERRIFYING THINGS IN THE AIR ABOVE MANHATTAN.
YESTERDAY TURNED TO...
OH GOD, I DON'T THINK I'M GOING TO MAKE IT.

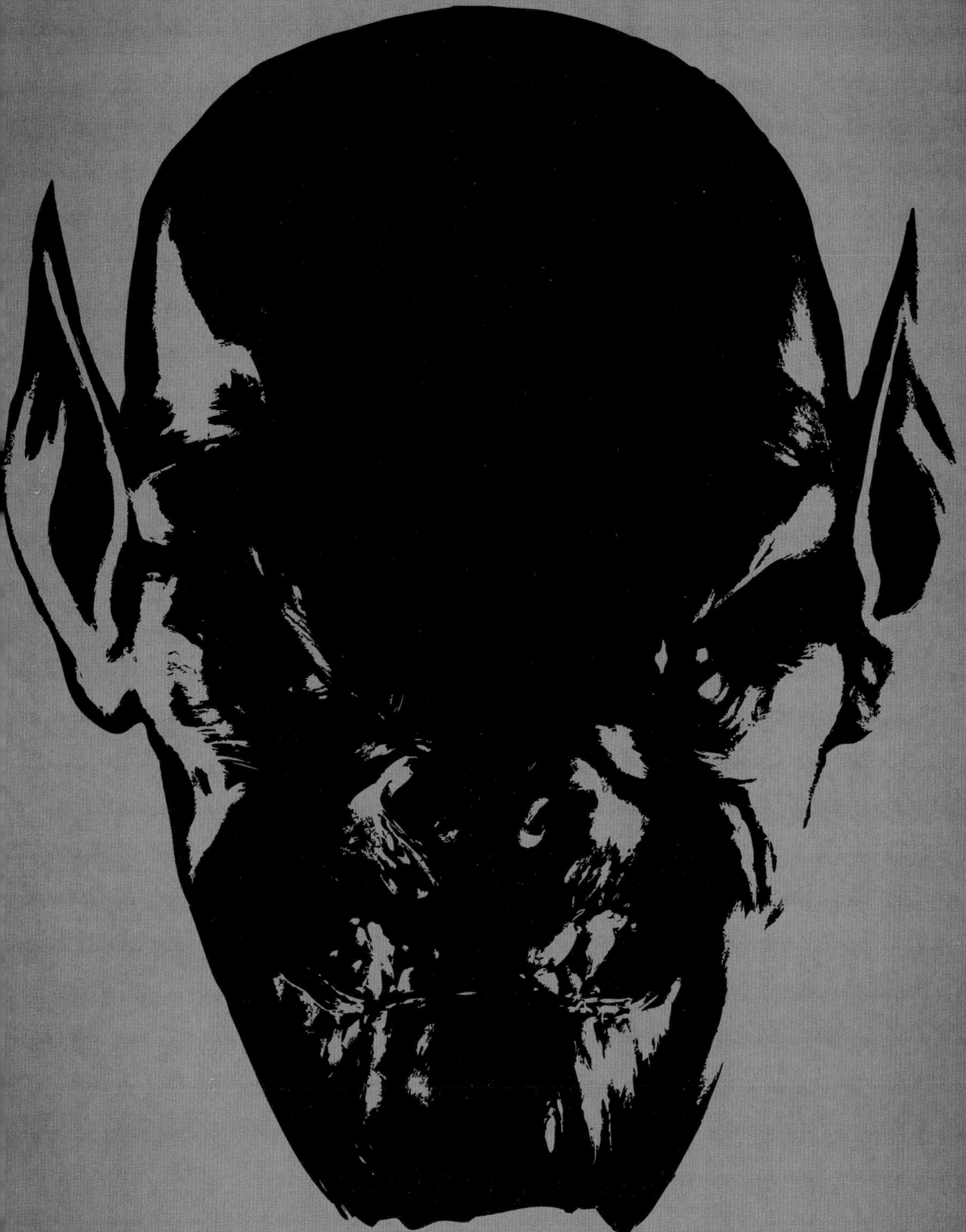

CHAPTER 2

...NO FORMAL CONFIRMATION AS THOUSANDS FLOOD THE BRIDGES AND TUNNELS--

--FLEEING WHAT APPEARS TO BE SOME SORT OF UNIDENTIFIABLE AIRCRAFT--OR CRAFTS--HOVERING IN THE AIR ABOVE MIDTOWN MANHATTAN.

TRAFFIC IS LOCKED AT A STAND-STILL THROUGHOUT THE BOROUGHS AND COMMUTER ROUTES IN CONNECTICUT AND NORTHERN NEW JERSEY...

OKAY...OKAY, GUYS! COME ON OUT, OKAY...?

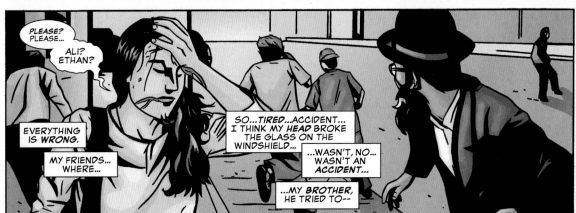

PLEASE? PLEASE... ALI? ETHAN?

EVERYTHING IS WRONG.

MY FRIENDS... WHERE...

SO...TIRED...ACCIDENT... I THINK MY HEAD BROKE THE GLASS ON THE WINDSHIELD...

...WASN'T, NO... WASN'T AN ACCIDENT...

...MY BROTHER, HE TRIED TO--

SOMEONE, ANYONE--HELP ME...

--HE TRIED TO--

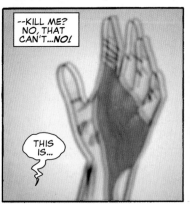

--KILL ME? NO, THAT CAN'T...NO!

THIS IS...

...THIS IS ALL WRONG.

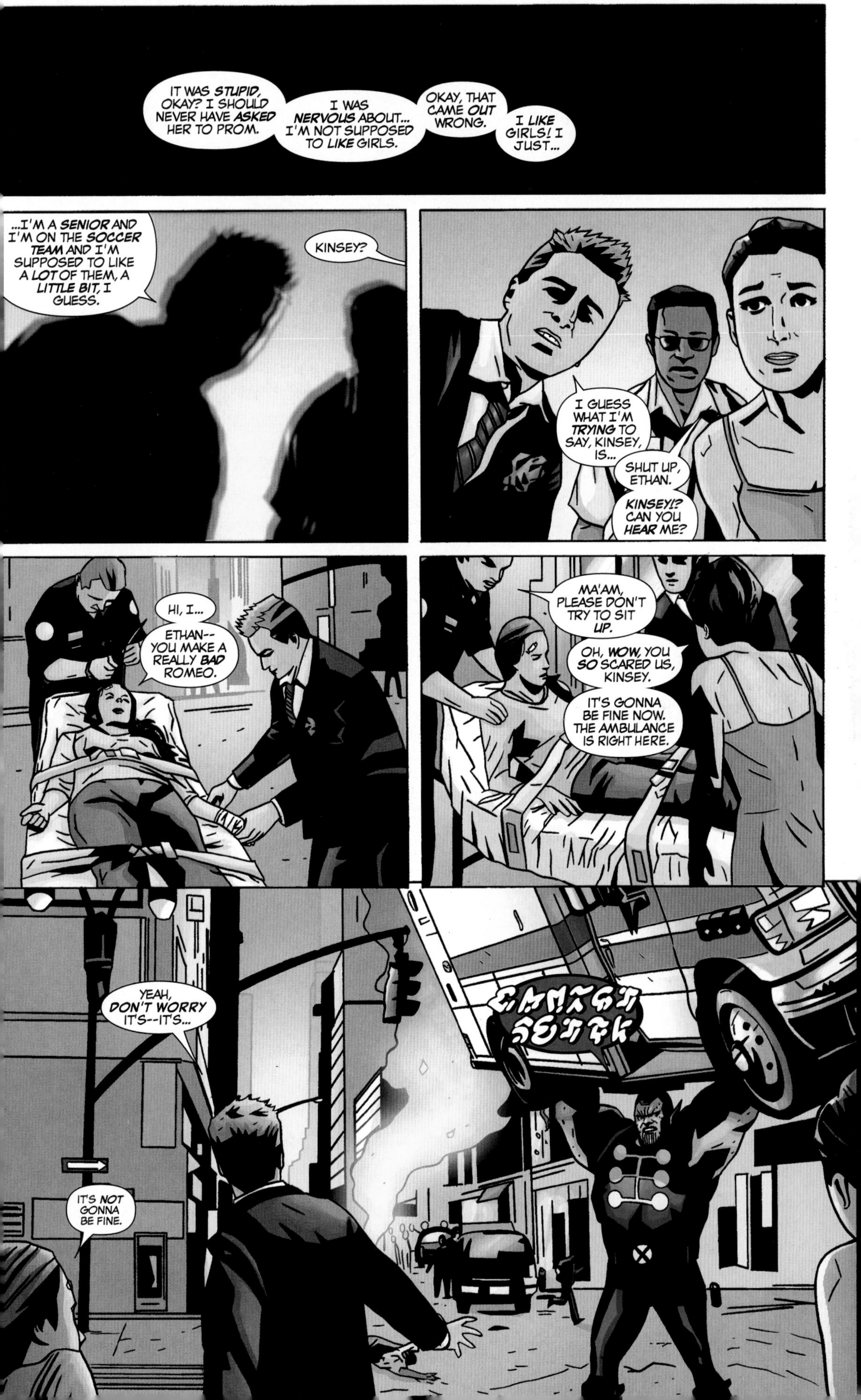
IT WAS STUPID, OKAY? I SHOULD NEVER HAVE ASKED HER TO PROM.
I WAS NERVOUS ABOUT... I'M NOT SUPPOSED TO LIKE GIRLS.
OKAY, THAT CAME OUT WRONG.
I LIKE GIRLS! I JUST...
...I'M A SENIOR AND I'M ON THE SOCCER TEAM AND I'M SUPPOSED TO LIKE A LOT OF THEM, A LITTLE BIT, I GUESS.
KINSEY?
I GUESS WHAT I'M TRYING TO SAY, KINSEY, IS...
SHUT UP, ETHAN.
KINSEY!? CAN YOU HEAR ME?
HI, I...
ETHAN-- YOU MAKE A REALLY BAD ROMEO.
MA'AM, PLEASE DON'T TRY TO SIT UP.
OH, WOW, YOU SO SCARED US, KINSEY.
IT'S GONNA BE FINE NOW. THE AMBULANCE IS RIGHT HERE.
YEAH, DON'T WORRY IT'S--IT'S...
IT'S NOT GONNA BE FINE.

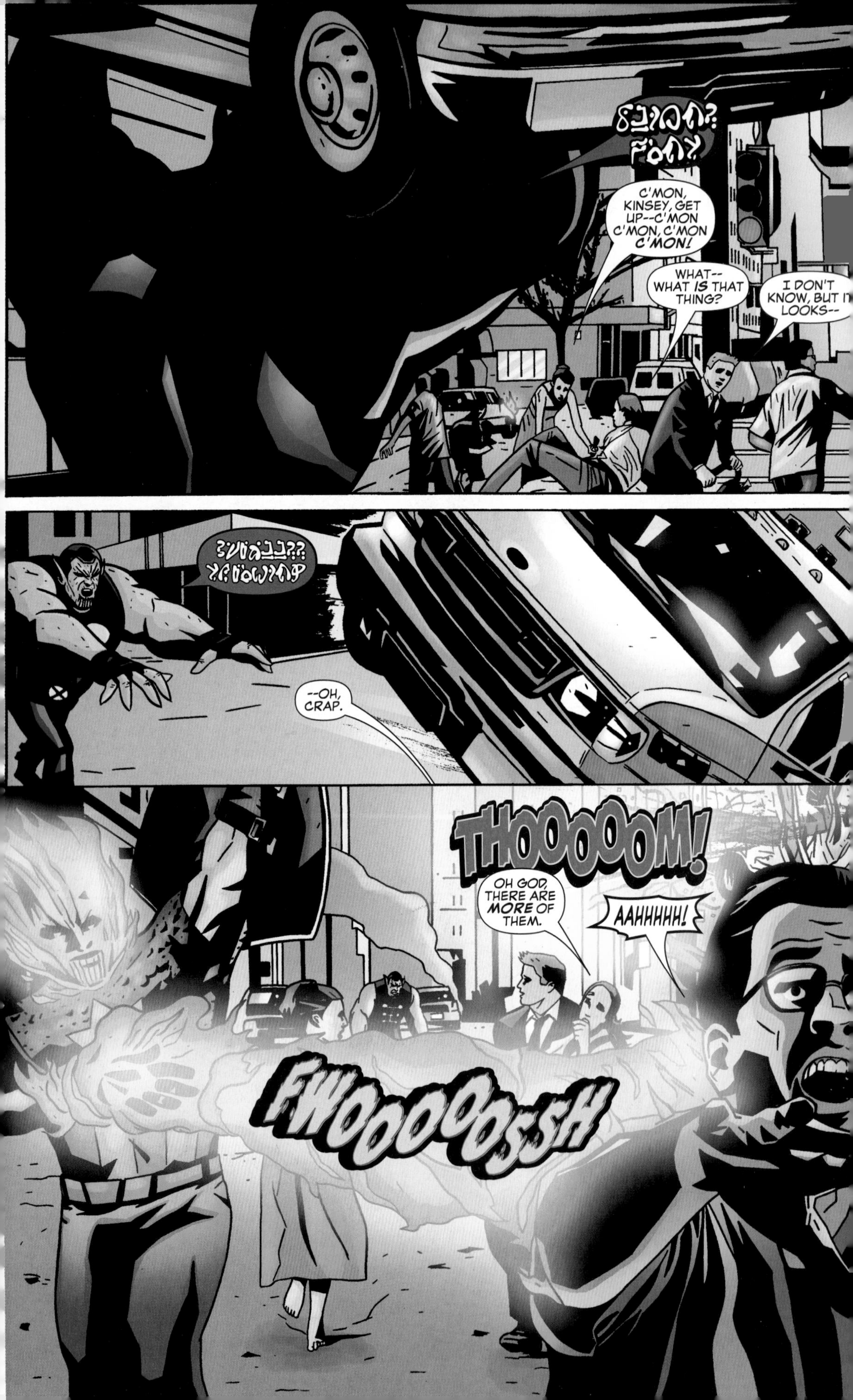
C'MON, KINSEY, GET UP--C'MON C'MON, C'MON C'MON!
WHAT-- WHAT IS THAT THING?
I DON'T KNOW, BUT IT LOOKS--
--OH, CRAP.
THOOOOOM!
OH GOD, THERE ARE MORE OF THEM.
AAHHHHH!
FWOOOOOSSH

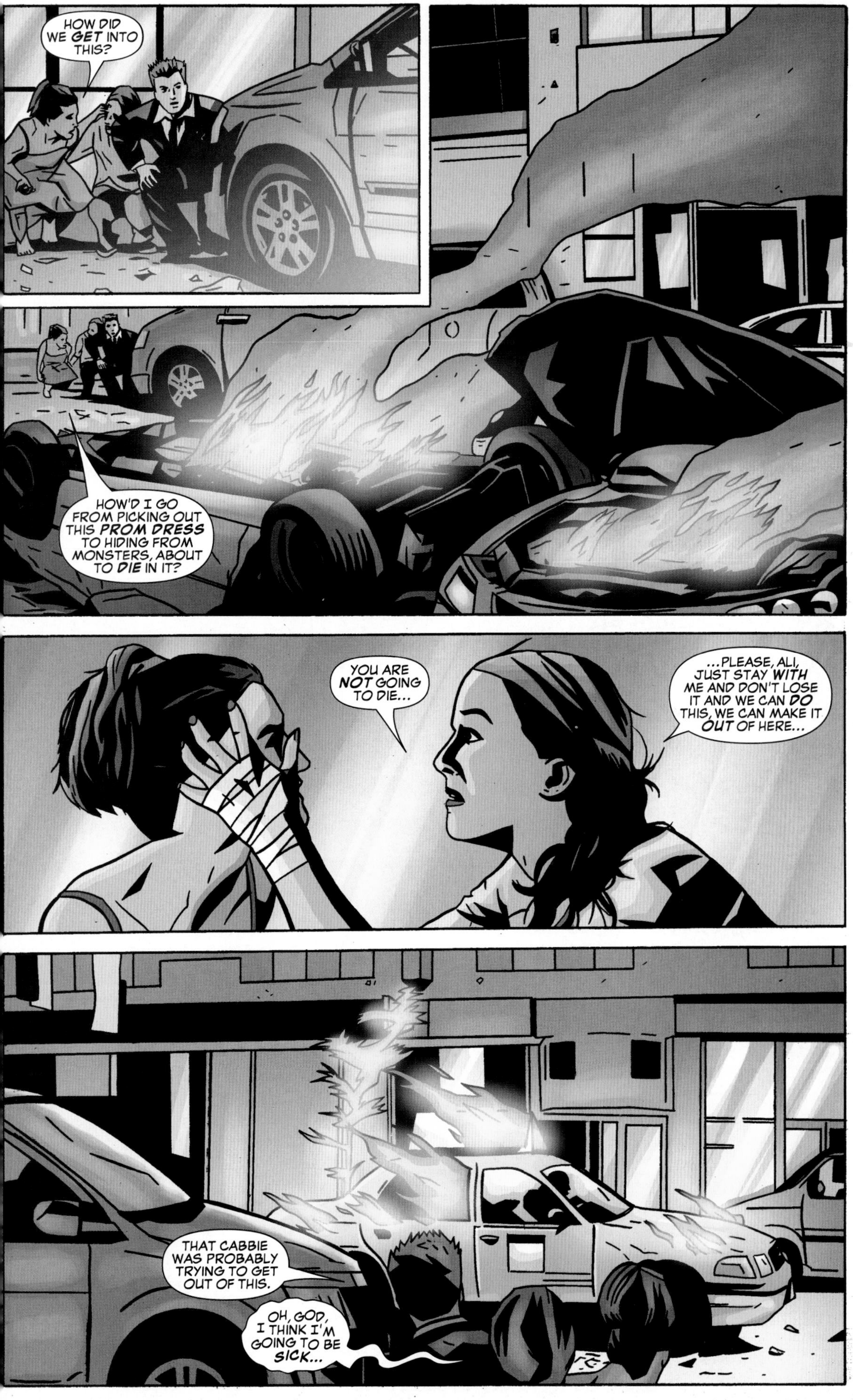

HOW DID WE GET INTO THIS?
HOW'D I GO FROM PICKING OUT THIS PROM DRESS TO HIDING FROM MONSTERS, ABOUT TO DIE IN IT?
YOU ARE NOT GOING TO DIE...
...PLEASE, ALI, JUST STAY WITH ME AND DON'T LOSE IT AND WE CAN DO THIS, WE CAN MAKE IT OUT OF HERE...
THAT CABBIE WAS PROBABLY TRYING TO GET OUT OF THIS.
OH, GOD, I THINK I'M GOING TO BE SICK...

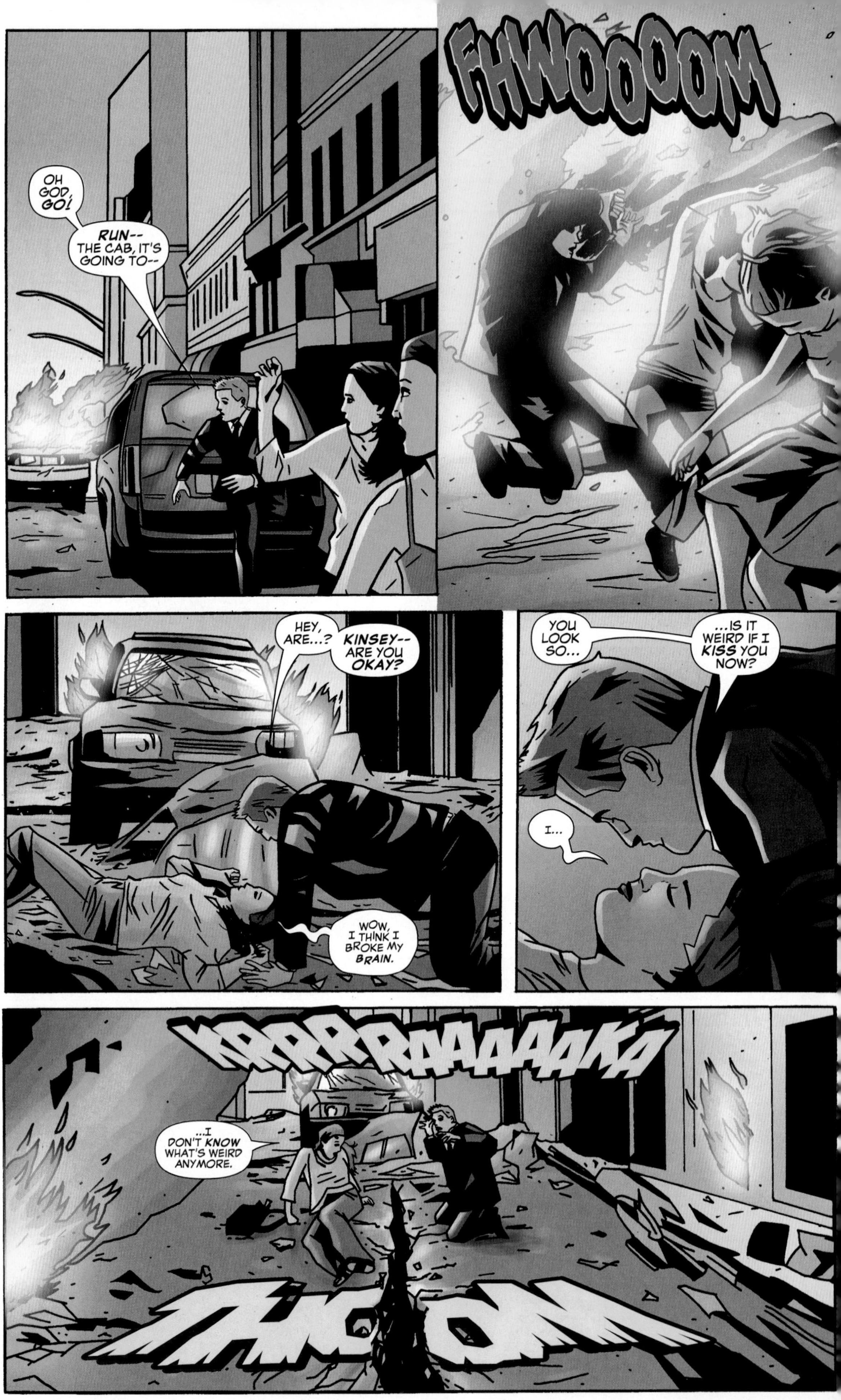
OH GOD, GO!
RUN-- THE CAB, IT'S GOING TO--
FHWOOOOM
HEY, ARE...?
KINSEY-- ARE YOU OKAY?
WOW, I THINK I BROKE MY BRAIN.
YOU LOOK SO...
...IS IT WEIRD IF I KISS YOU NOW?
I...
KRRRRAAAAAKA
...I DON'T KNOW WHAT'S WEIRD ANYMORE.
THOOM

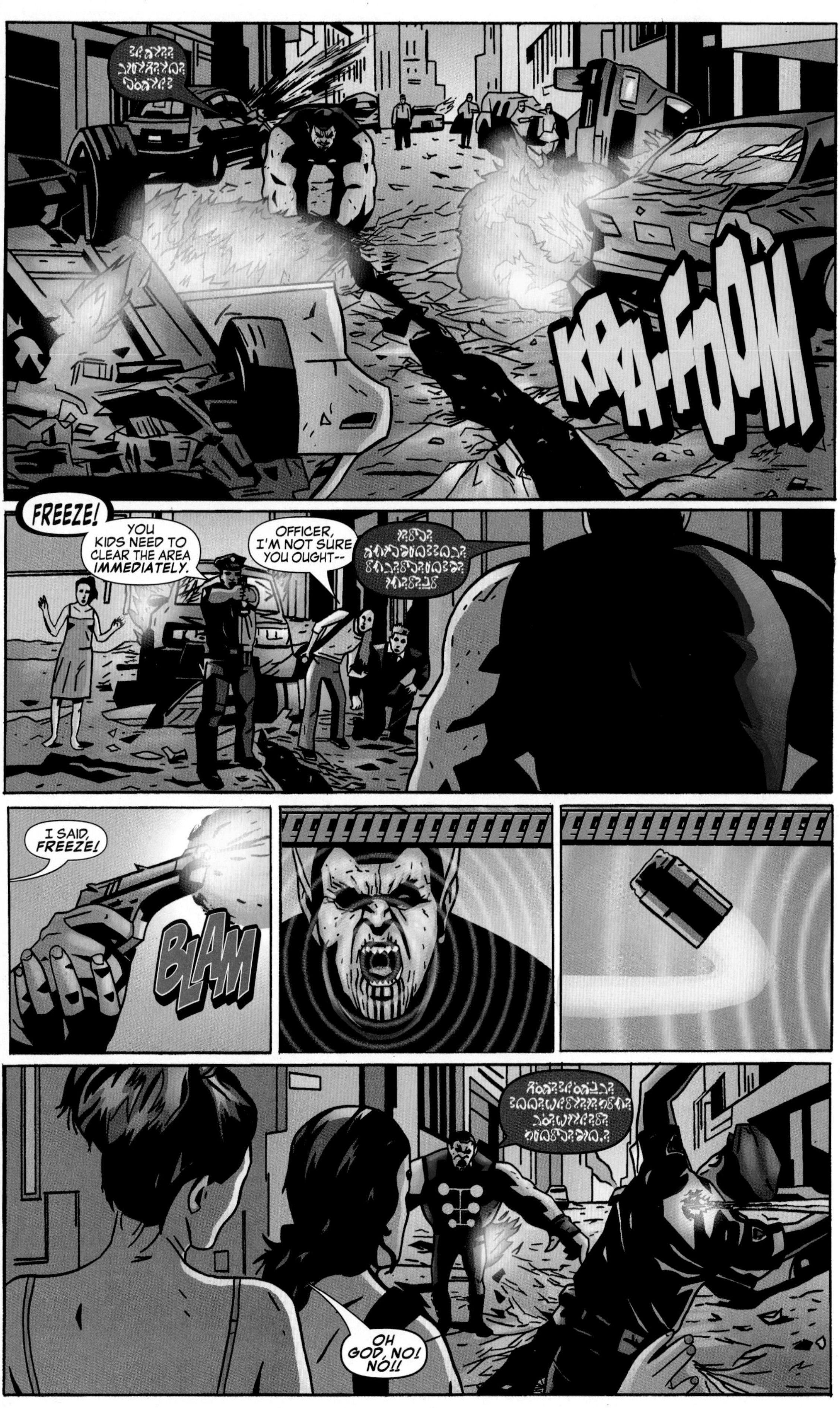
KRA-FOOM
FREEZE!
YOU KIDS NEED TO CLEAR THE AREA IMMEDIATELY.
OFFICER, I'M NOT SURE YOU OUGHT--
I SAID, FREEZE!
BLAM
EEEEEEEEEEEEEEEE
EEEEEEEEEEEEEEEE
OH GOD, NO! NO!!

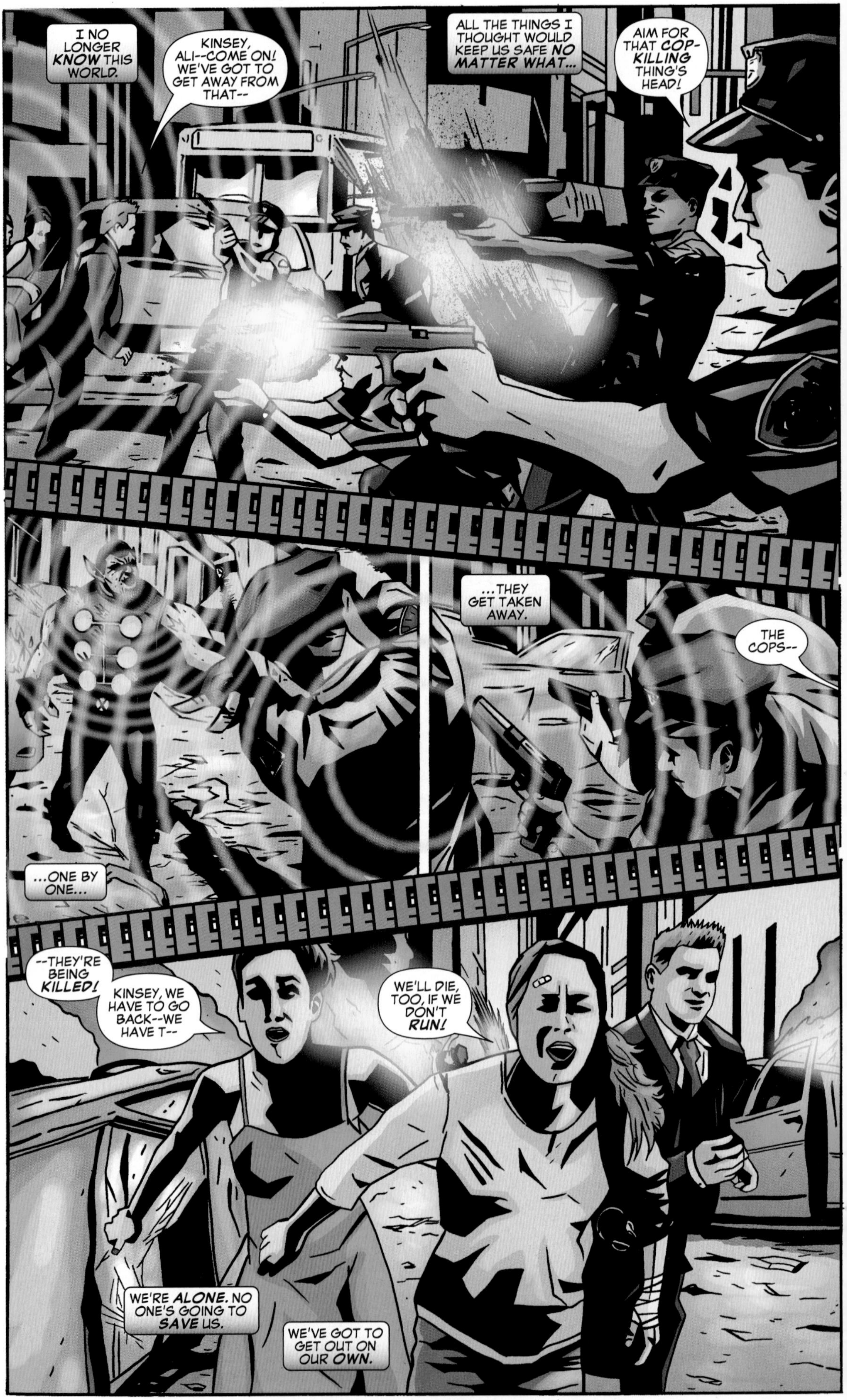
I NO LONGER KNOW THIS WORLD.
KINSEY, ALI--COME ON! WE'VE GOT TO GET AWAY FROM THAT--
ALL THE THINGS I THOUGHT WOULD KEEP US SAFE NO MATTER WHAT...
AIM FOR THAT COP-KILLING THING'S HEAD!
EEEEEEEEEEEEEEEEEEEEEEEEEEEEEEEEEEEEEE
...THEY GET TAKEN AWAY.
THE COPS--
...ONE BY ONE...
EEEEEEEEEEEEEEEEEEEEEEEEEEEEEEEEEEEEEE
--THEY'RE BEING KILLED!
KINSEY, WE HAVE TO GO BACK--WE HAVE T--
WE'LL DIE, TOO, IF WE DON'T RUN!
WE'RE ALONE. NO ONE'S GOING TO SAVE US.
WE'VE GOT TO GET OUT ON OUR OWN.

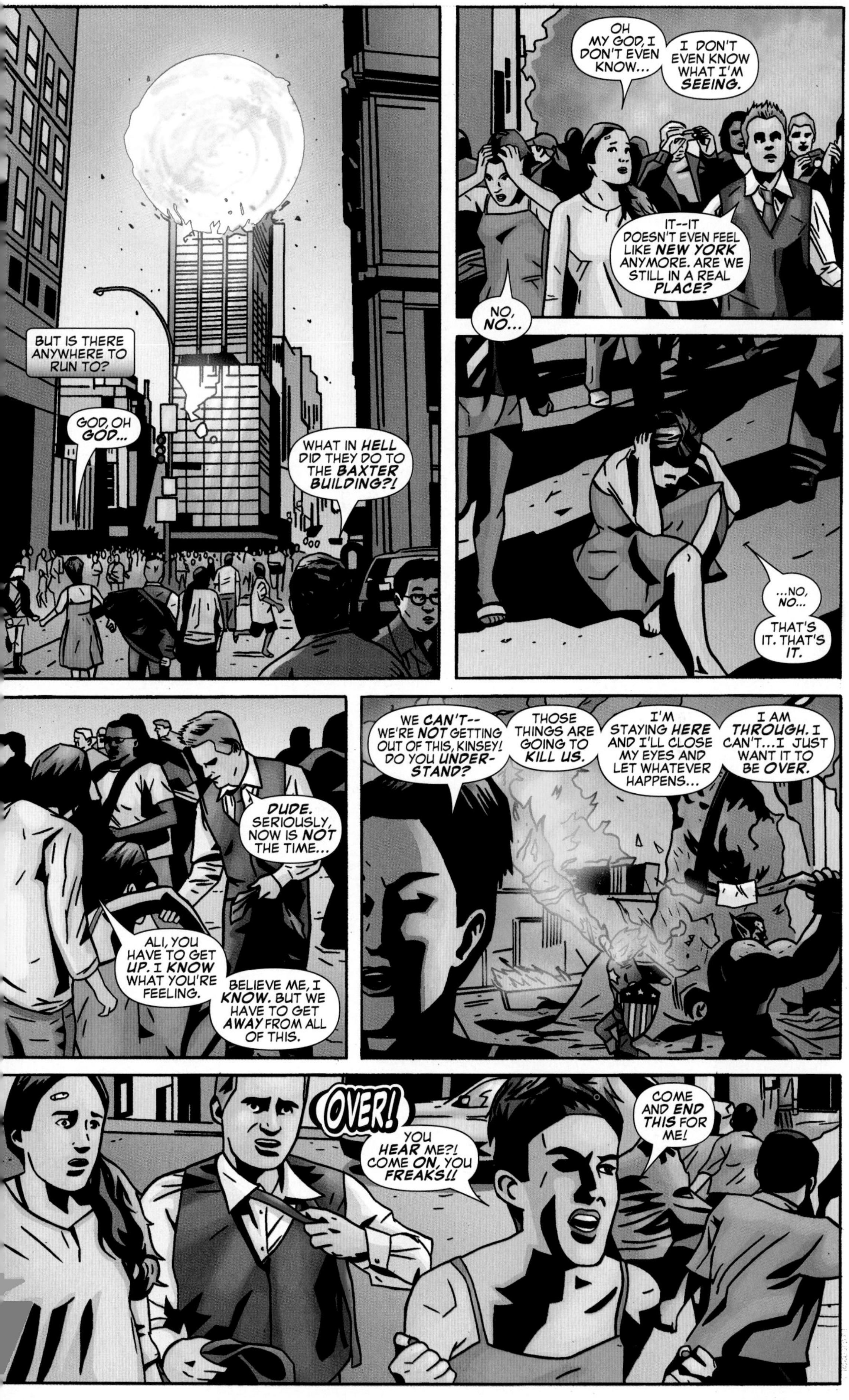
BUT IS THERE ANYWHERE TO RUN TO?
GOD, OH GOD...
WHAT IN HELL DID THEY DO TO THE BAXTER BUILDING?!
OH MY GOD, I DON'T EVEN KNOW...
I DON'T EVEN KNOW WHAT I'M SEEING.
IT--IT DOESN'T EVEN FEEL LIKE NEW YORK ANYMORE. ARE WE STILL IN A REAL PLACE?
NO, NO...
...NO, NO...
THAT'S IT. THAT'S IT.
DUDE. SERIOUSLY, NOW IS NOT THE TIME...
ALI, YOU HAVE TO GET UP. I KNOW WHAT YOU'RE FEELING.
BELIEVE ME, I KNOW. BUT WE HAVE TO GET AWAY FROM ALL OF THIS.
WE CAN'T-- WE'RE NOT GETTING OUT OF THIS, KINSEY! DO YOU UNDERSTAND?
THOSE THINGS ARE GOING TO KILL US.
I'M STAYING HERE AND I'LL CLOSE MY EYES AND LET WHATEVER HAPPENS...
I AM THROUGH. I CAN'T...I JUST WANT IT TO BE OVER.
OVER!
YOU HEAR ME?! COME ON, YOU FREAKS!!
COME AND END THIS FOR ME!

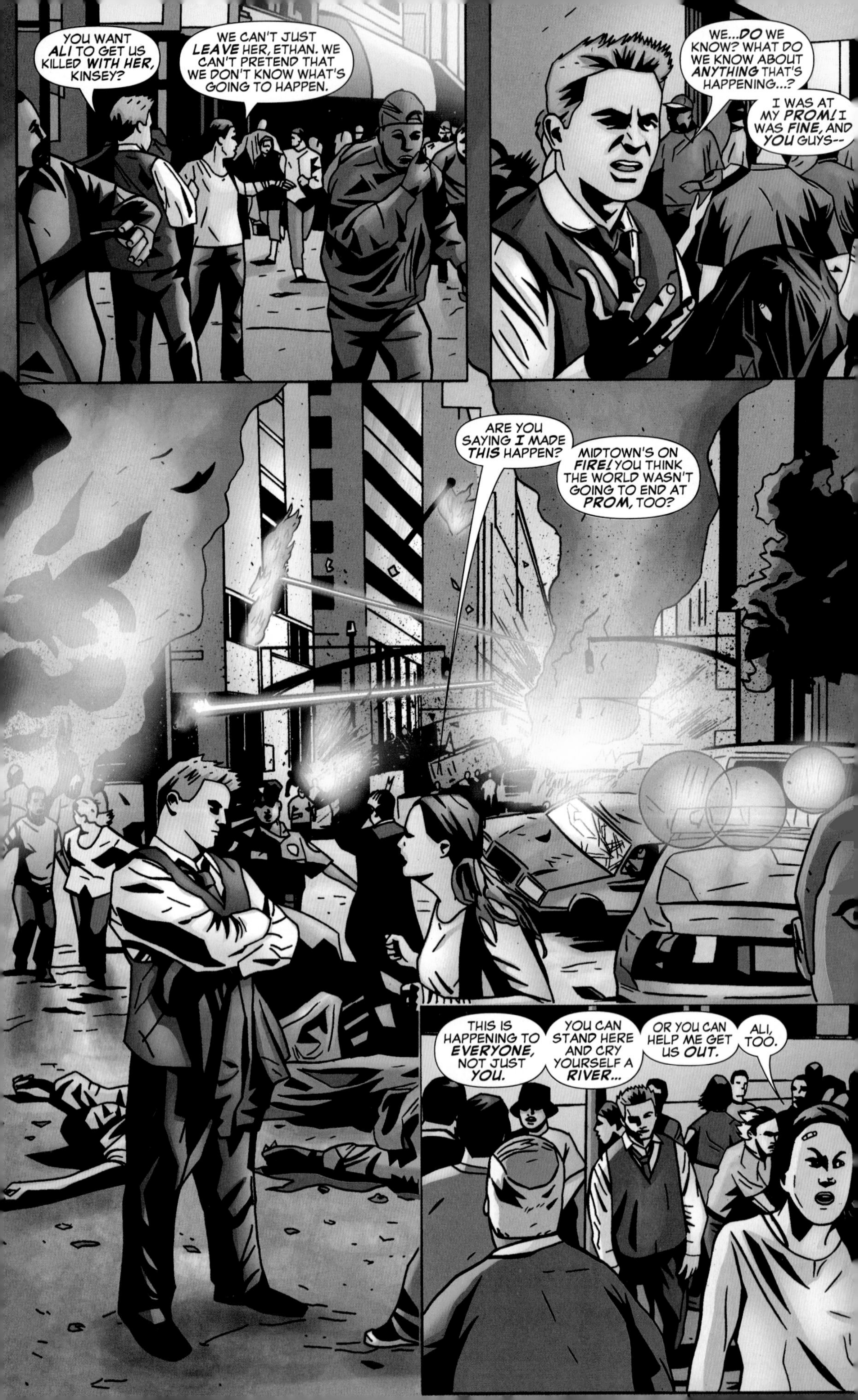
YOU WANT ALI TO GET US KILLED WITH HER, KINSEY?
WE CAN'T JUST LEAVE HER, ETHAN. WE CAN'T PRETEND THAT WE DON'T KNOW WHAT'S GOING TO HAPPEN.
WE...DO WE KNOW? WHAT DO WE KNOW ABOUT ANYTHING THAT'S HAPPENING...?
I WAS AT MY PROM! I WAS FINE, AND YOU GUYS--
ARE YOU SAYING I MADE THIS HAPPEN?
MIDTOWN'S ON FIRE! YOU THINK THE WORLD WASN'T GOING TO END AT PROM, TOO?
THIS IS HAPPENING TO EVERYONE, NOT JUST YOU.
YOU CAN STAND HERE AND CRY YOURSELF A RIVER...
OR YOU CAN HELP ME GET US OUT.
ALI, TOO.

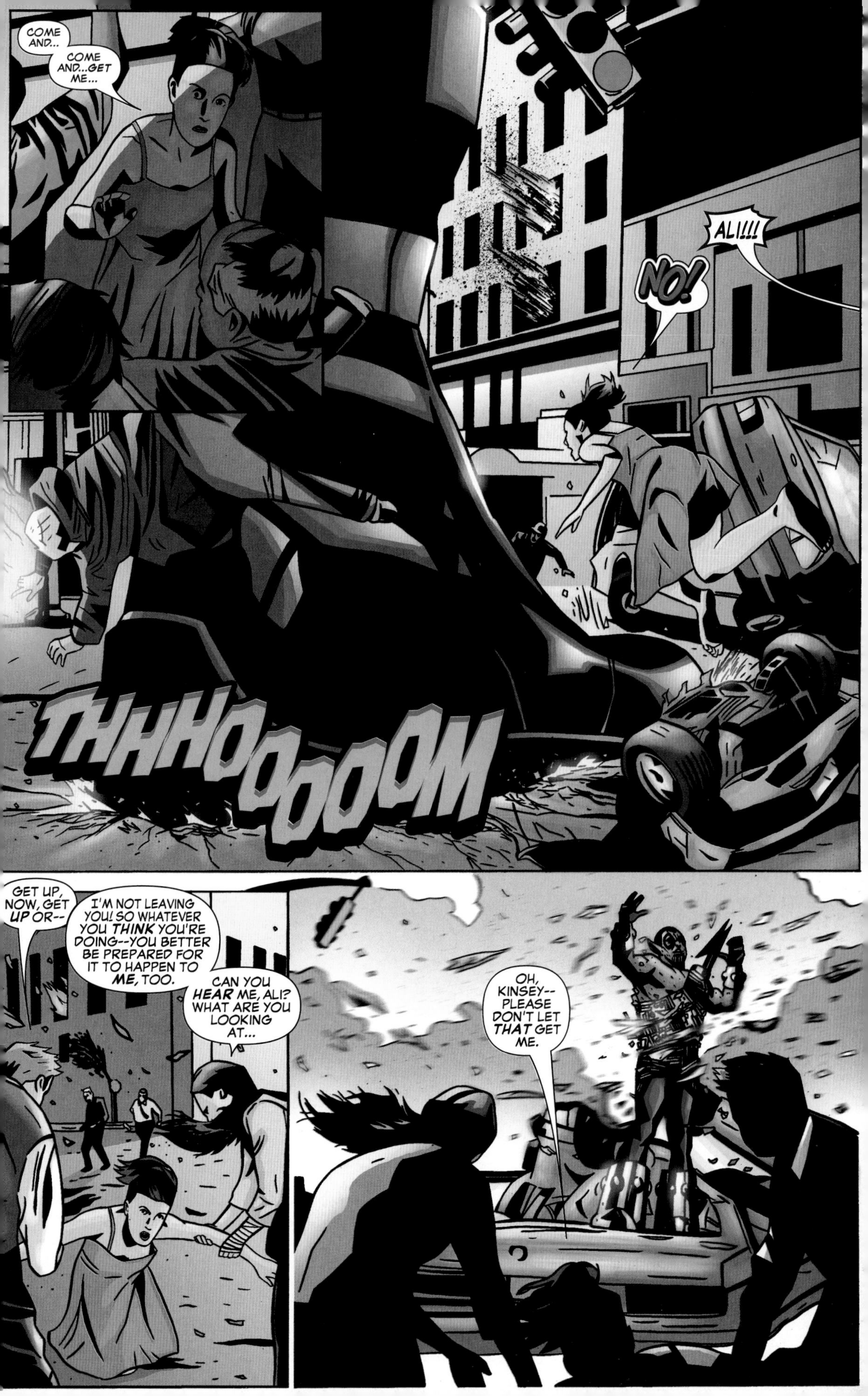
COME AND...
COME AND...GET ME...
ALI!!!
NO!
THHHOOOOOOM
GET UP, NOW, GET UP OR--
I'M NOT LEAVING YOU! SO WHATEVER YOU THINK YOU'RE DOING--YOU BETTER BE PREPARED FOR IT TO HAPPEN TO ME, TOO.
CAN YOU HEAR ME, ALI? WHAT ARE YOU LOOKING AT...
OH, KINSEY-- PLEASE DON'T LET THAT GET ME.

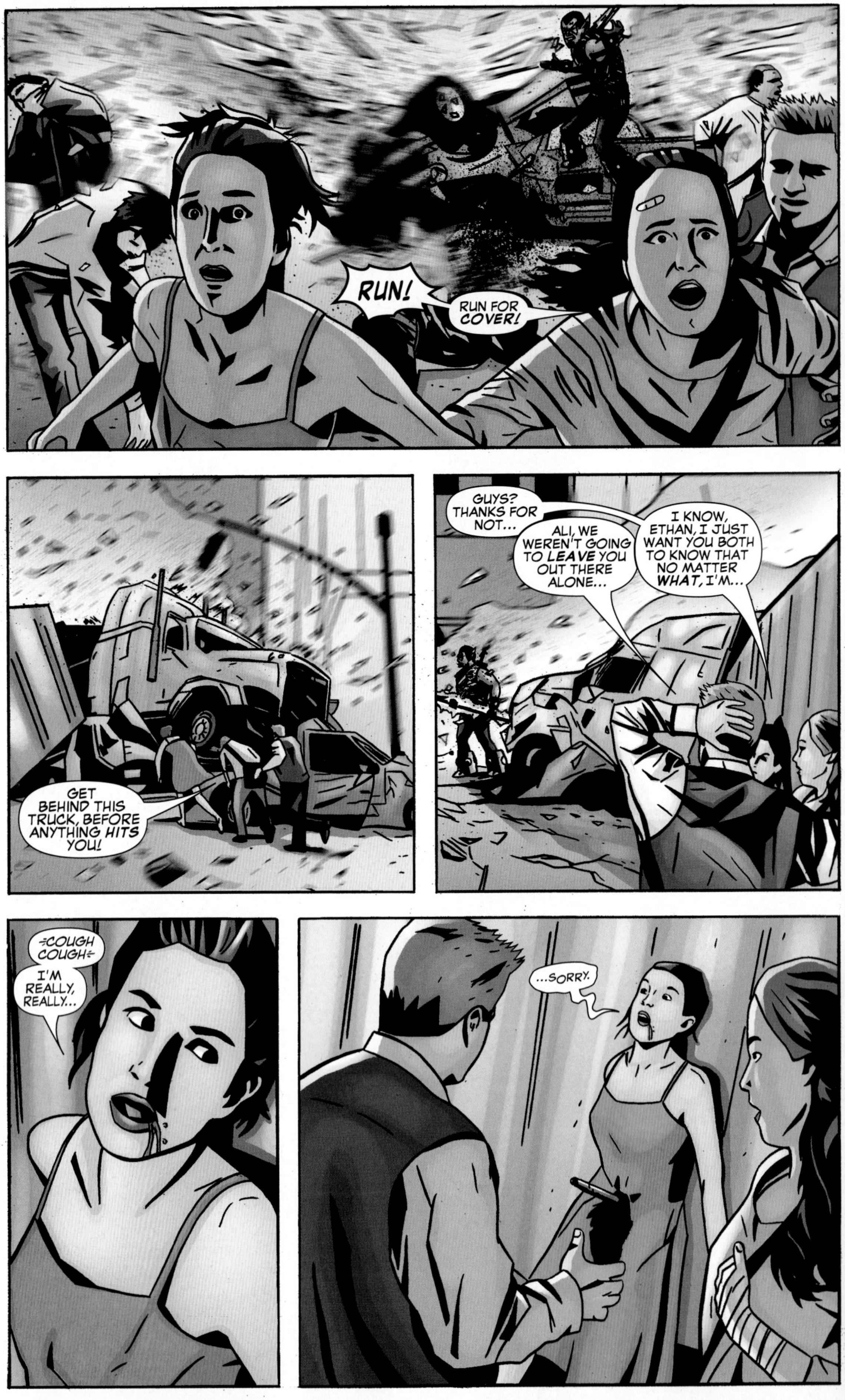
RUN!
RUN FOR COVER!
GET BEHIND THIS TRUCK, BEFORE ANYTHING HITS YOU!
GUYS? THANKS FOR NOT...
ALI, WE WEREN'T GOING TO LEAVE YOU OUT THERE ALONE...
I KNOW, ETHAN, I JUST WANT YOU BOTH TO KNOW THAT NO MATTER WHAT, I'M...
COUGH COUGH
I'M REALLY, REALLY...
...SORRY.

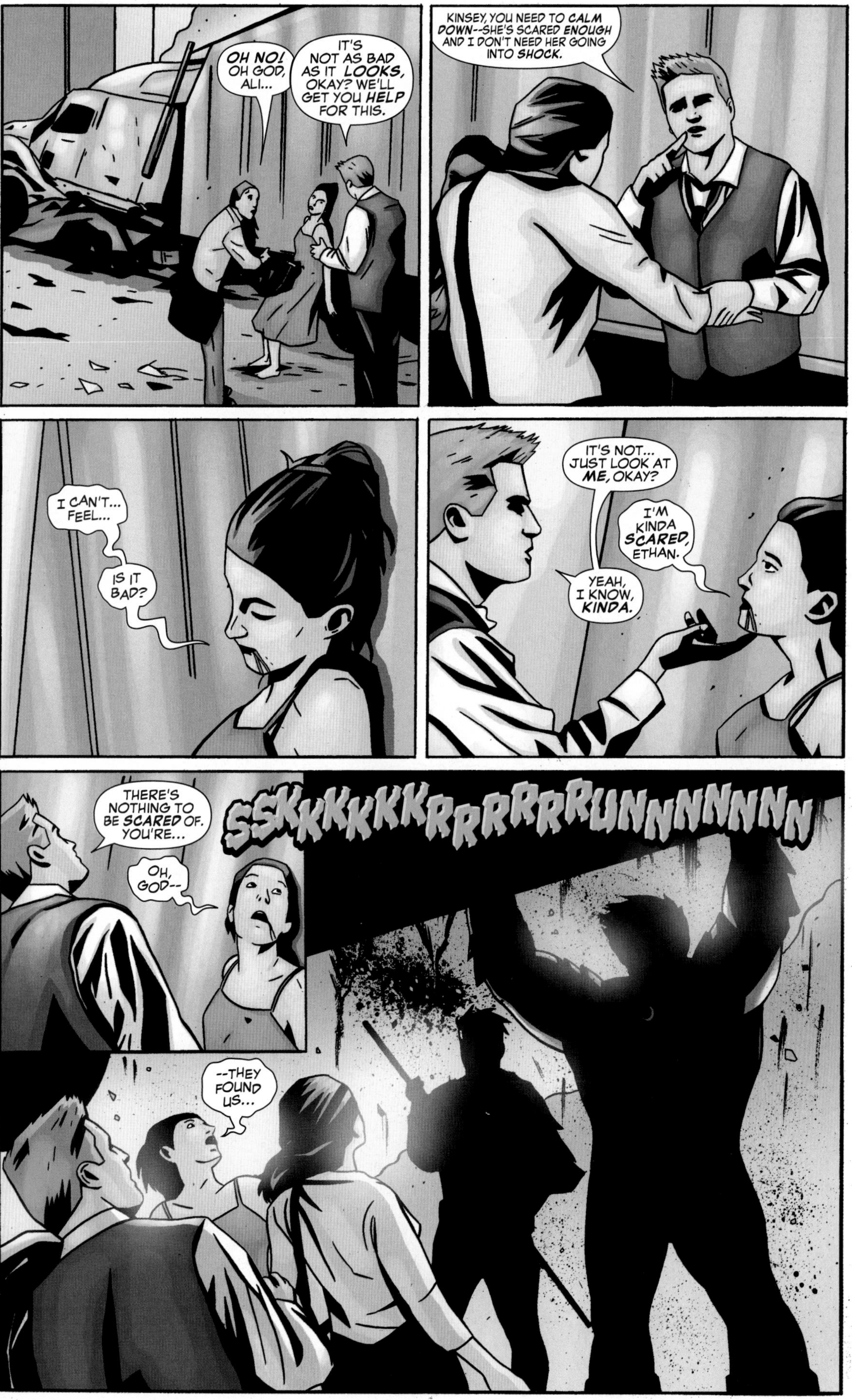
OH NO! OH GOD, ALI...
IT'S NOT AS BAD AS IT LOOKS, OKAY? WE'LL GET YOU HELP FOR THIS.
KINSEY, YOU NEED TO CALM DOWN--SHE'S SCARED ENOUGH AND I DON'T NEED HER GOING INTO SHOCK.
I CAN'T... FEEL...
IS IT BAD?
IT'S NOT... JUST LOOK AT ME, OKAY?
I'M KINDA SCARED, ETHAN.
YEAH, I KNOW, KINDA.
THERE'S NOTHING TO BE SCARED OF. YOU'RE...
OH, GOD--
SSKKKKKKRRRRRRUNNNNNNNN
--THEY FOUND US...

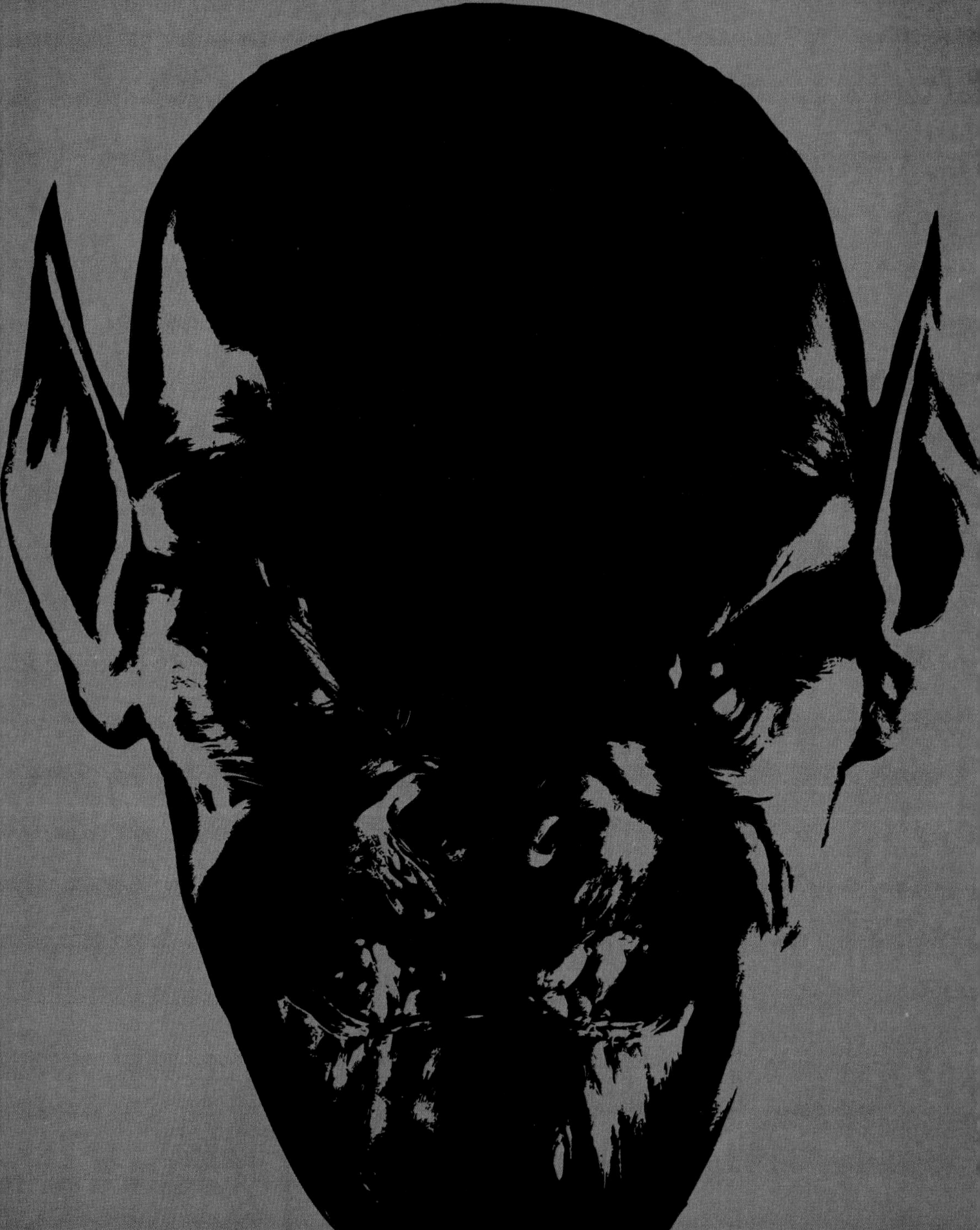

CHAPTER 3

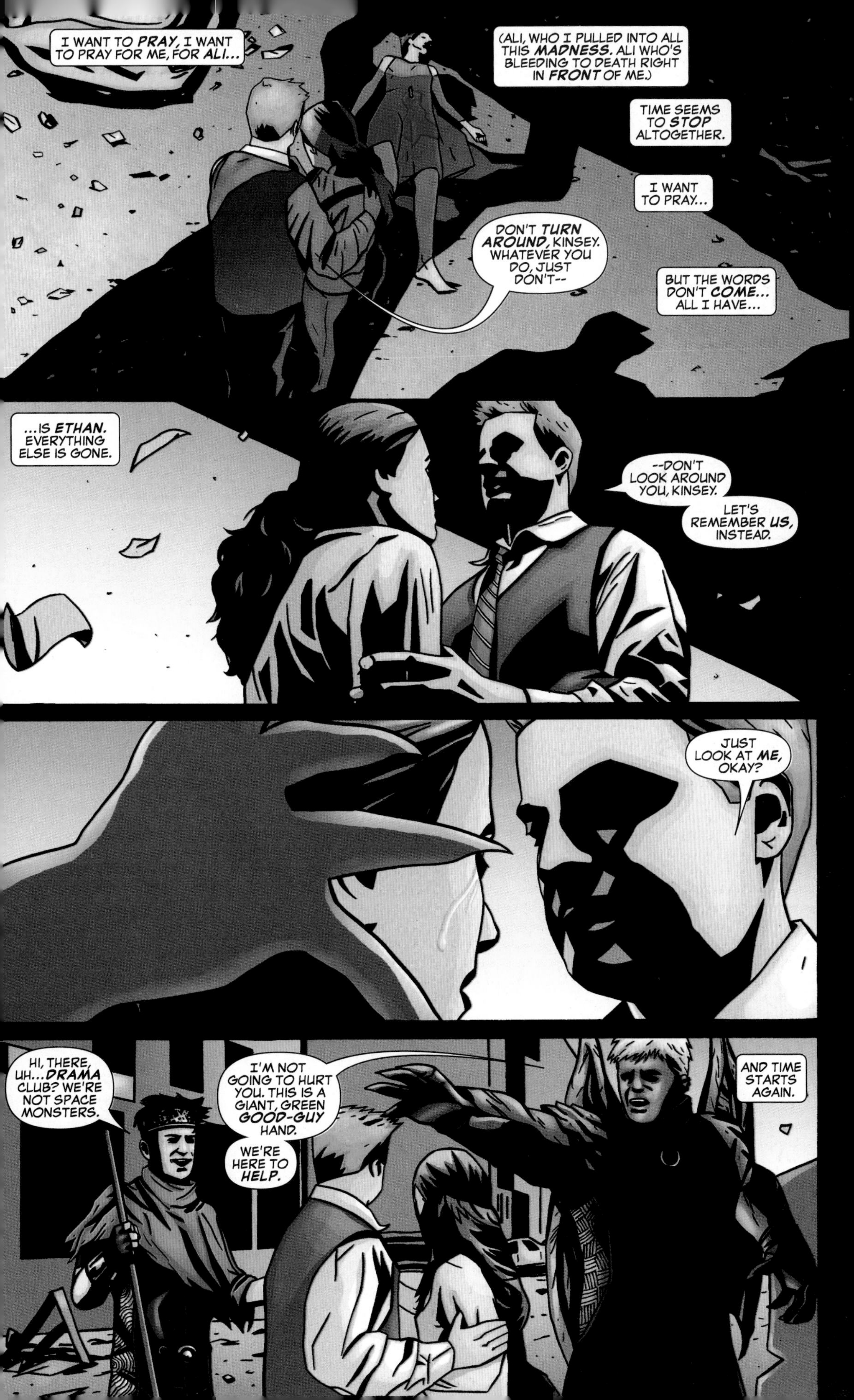
I WANT TO PRAY, I WANT TO PRAY FOR ME, FOR ALI...
(ALI, WHO I PULLED INTO ALL THIS MADNESS. ALI WHO'S BLEEDING TO DEATH RIGHT IN FRONT OF ME.)
TIME SEEMS TO STOP ALTOGETHER.
I WANT TO PRAY...
DON'T TURN AROUND, KINSEY. WHATEVER YOU DO, JUST DON'T--
BUT THE WORDS DON'T COME... ALL I HAVE...
...IS ETHAN. EVERYTHING ELSE IS GONE.
--DON'T LOOK AROUND YOU, KINSEY.
LET'S REMEMBER US, INSTEAD.
JUST LOOK AT ME, OKAY?
HI, THERE, UH... DRAMA CLUB? WE'RE NOT SPACE MONSTERS.
I'M NOT GOING TO HURT YOU. THIS IS A GIANT, GREEN GOOD-GUY HAND.
WE'RE HERE TO HELP.
AND TIME STARTS AGAIN.

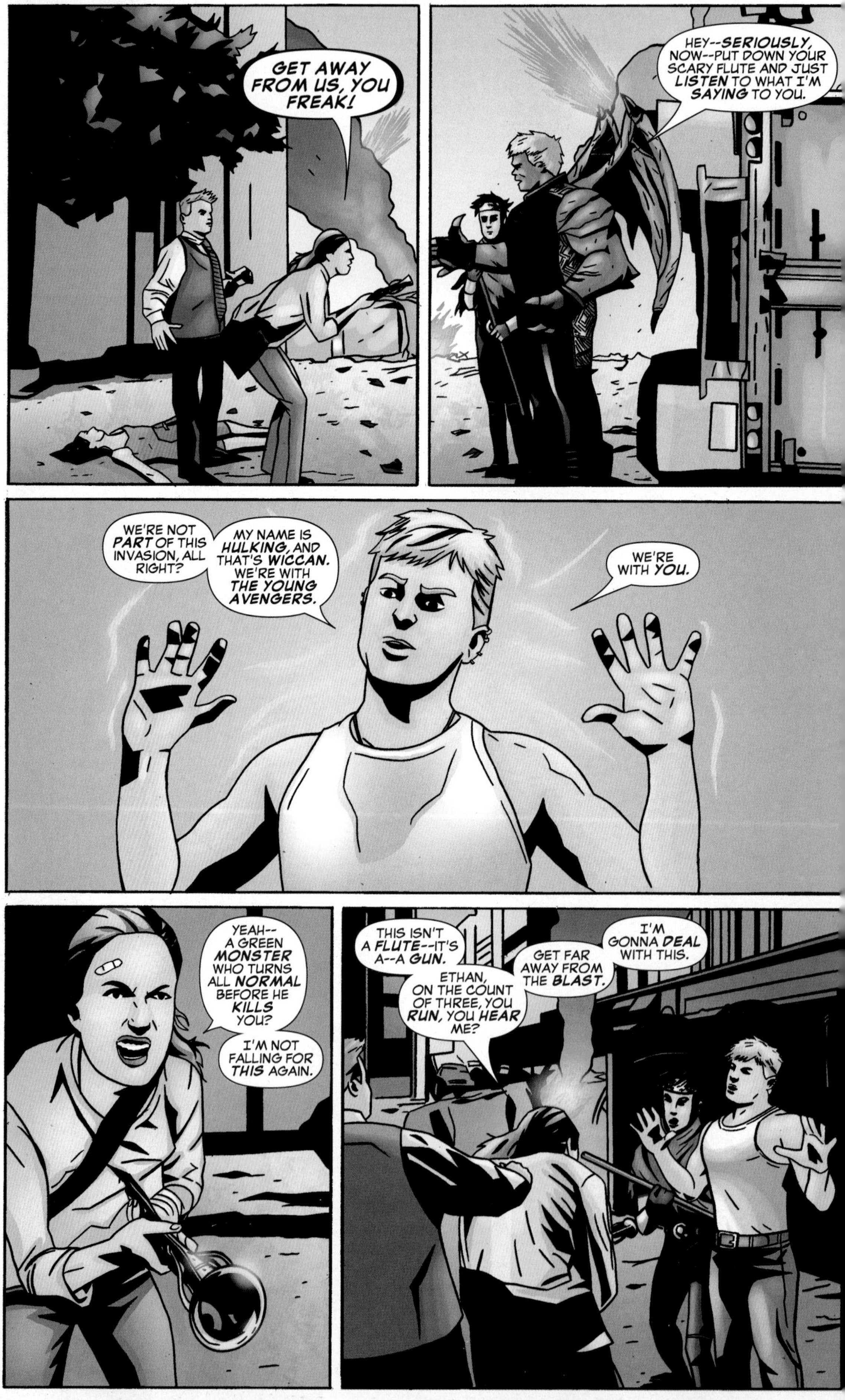
GET AWAY FROM US, YOU FREAK!
HEY--SERIOUSLY, NOW--PUT DOWN YOUR SCARY FLUTE AND JUST LISTEN TO WHAT I'M SAYING TO YOU.
WE'RE NOT PART OF THIS INVASION, ALL RIGHT?
MY NAME IS HULKING, AND THAT'S WICCAN. WE'RE WITH THE YOUNG AVENGERS.
WE'RE WITH YOU.
YEAH-- A GREEN MONSTER WHO TURNS ALL NORMAL BEFORE HE KILLS YOU?
I'M NOT FALLING FOR THIS AGAIN.
THIS ISN'T A FLUTE--IT'S A--A GUN.
ETHAN, ON THE COUNT OF THREE, YOU RUN, YOU HEAR ME?
GET FAR AWAY FROM THE BLAST.
I'M GONNA DEAL WITH THIS.

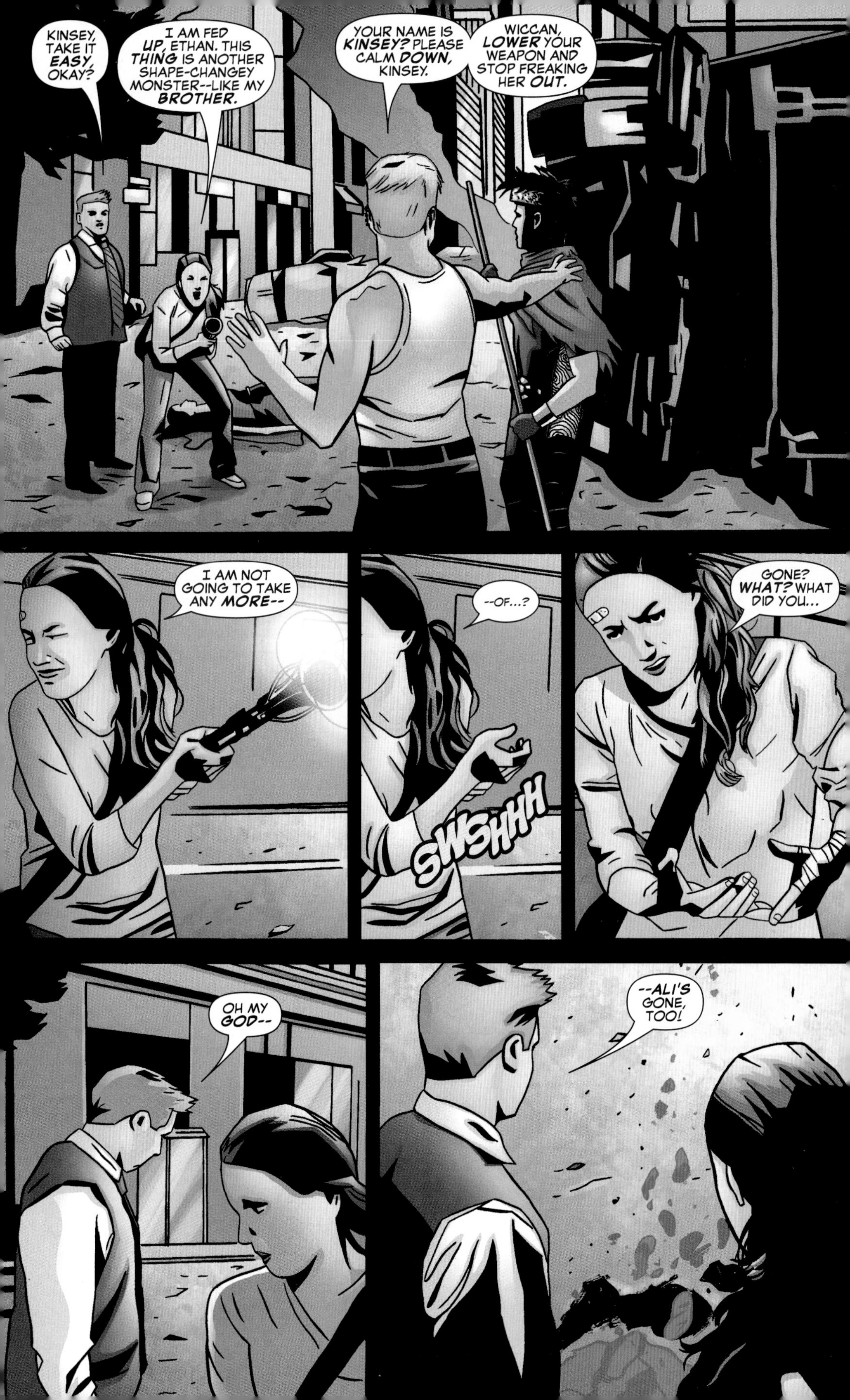
KINSEY, TAKE IT EASY, OKAY?
I AM FED UP, ETHAN. THIS THING IS ANOTHER SHAPE-CHANGEY MONSTER--LIKE MY BROTHER.
YOUR NAME IS KINSEY? PLEASE CALM DOWN, KINSEY.
WICCAN, LOWER YOUR WEAPON AND STOP FREAKING HER OUT.
I AM NOT GOING TO TAKE ANY MORE--
--OF...?
SWSHHH
GONE? WHAT? WHAT DID YOU...
OH MY GOD--
--ALI'S GONE, TOO!

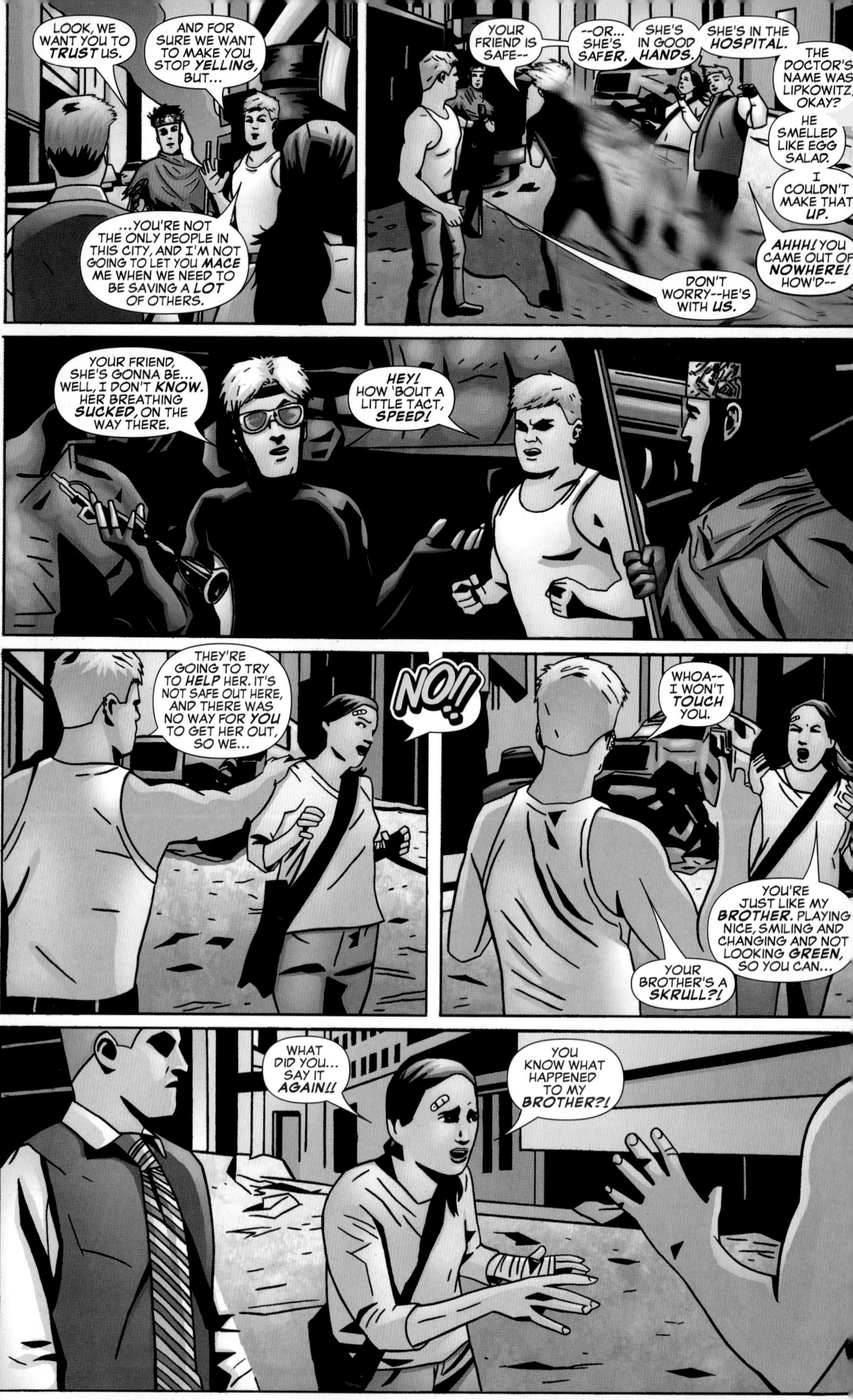
LOOK, WE WANT YOU TO TRUST US.
AND FOR SURE WE WANT TO MAKE YOU STOP YELLING, BUT...
...YOU'RE NOT THE ONLY PEOPLE IN THIS CITY, AND I'M NOT GOING TO LET YOU MACE ME WHEN WE NEED TO BE SAVING A LOT OF OTHERS.
YOUR FRIEND IS SAFE--
--OR... SHE'S SAFER.
SHE'S IN GOOD HANDS.
SHE'S IN THE HOSPITAL.
THE DOCTOR'S NAME WAS LIPKOWITZ, OKAY?
HE SMELLED LIKE EGG SALAD.
I COULDN'T MAKE THAT UP.
AHHH! YOU CAME OUT OF NOWHERE! HOW'D--
DON'T WORRY--HE'S WITH US.
YOUR FRIEND, SHE'S GONNA BE... WELL, I DON'T KNOW. HER BREATHING SUCKED, ON THE WAY THERE.
HEY! HOW 'BOUT A LITTLE TACT, SPEED!
THEY'RE GOING TO TRY TO HELP HER. IT'S NOT SAFE OUT HERE, AND THERE WAS NO WAY FOR YOU TO GET HER OUT, SO WE...
NO!!
WHOA-- I WON'T TOUCH YOU.
YOU'RE JUST LIKE MY BROTHER. PLAYING NICE, SMILING AND CHANGING AND NOT LOOKING GREEN, SO YOU CAN...
YOUR BROTHER'S A SKRULL?!
WHAT DID YOU... SAY IT AGAIN!!
YOU KNOW WHAT HAPPENED TO MY BROTHER?!

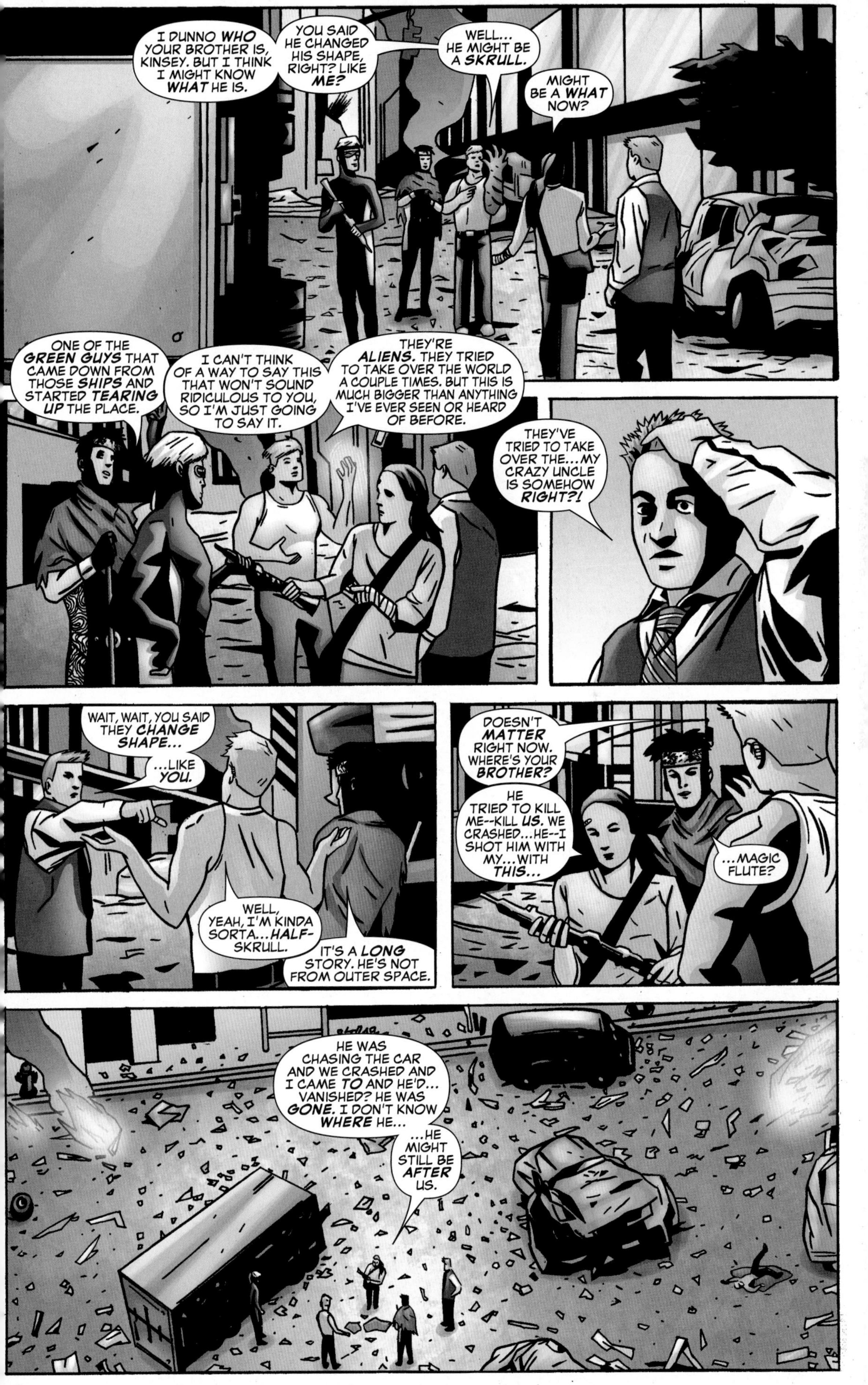
I DUNNO WHO YOUR BROTHER IS, KINSEY. BUT I THINK I MIGHT KNOW WHAT HE IS.
YOU SAID HE CHANGED HIS SHAPE, RIGHT? LIKE ME?
WELL... HE MIGHT BE A SKRULL.
MIGHT BE A WHAT NOW?
ONE OF THE GREEN GUYS THAT CAME DOWN FROM THOSE SHIPS AND STARTED TEARING UP THE PLACE.
I CAN'T THINK OF A WAY TO SAY THIS THAT WON'T SOUND RIDICULOUS TO YOU, SO I'M JUST GOING TO SAY IT.
THEY'RE ALIENS. THEY TRIED TO TAKE OVER THE WORLD A COUPLE TIMES. BUT THIS IS MUCH BIGGER THAN ANYTHING I'VE EVER SEEN OR HEARD OF BEFORE.
THEY'VE TRIED TO TAKE OVER THE... MY CRAZY UNCLE IS SOMEHOW RIGHT?!
WAIT, WAIT, YOU SAID THEY CHANGE SHAPE...
...LIKE YOU.
WELL, YEAH, I'M KINDA SORTA... HALF-SKRULL.
IT'S A LONG STORY. HE'S NOT FROM OUTER SPACE.
DOESN'T MATTER RIGHT NOW. WHERE'S YOUR BROTHER?
HE TRIED TO KILL ME--KILL US. WE CRASHED... HE--I SHOT HIM WITH MY... WITH THIS...
...MAGIC FLUTE?
HE WAS CHASING THE CAR AND WE CRASHED AND I CAME TO AND HE'D... VANISHED? HE WAS GONE. I DON'T KNOW WHERE HE...
...HE MIGHT STILL BE AFTER US.

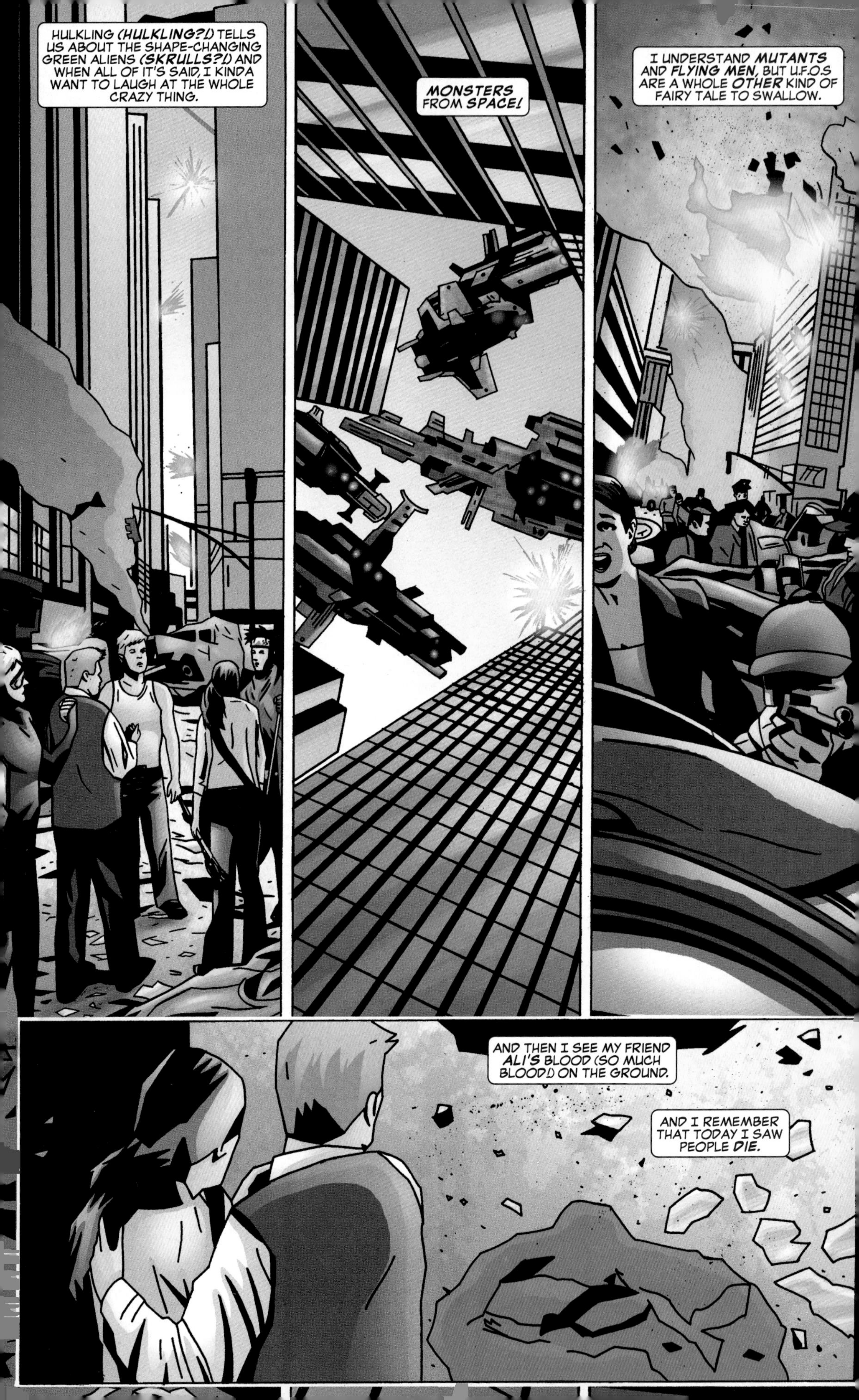
HULKLING (HULKLING?!) TELLS US ABOUT THE SHAPE-CHANGING GREEN ALIENS (SKRULLS?!) AND WHEN ALL OF IT'S SAID, I KINDA WANT TO LAUGH AT THE WHOLE CRAZY THING.
MONSTERS FROM SPACE!
I UNDERSTAND MUTANTS AND FLYING MEN, BUT U.F.O.S ARE A WHOLE OTHER KIND OF FAIRY TALE TO SWALLOW.
AND THEN I SEE MY FRIEND ALI'S BLOOD (SO MUCH BLOOD!) ON THE GROUND.
AND I REMEMBER THAT TODAY I SAW PEOPLE DIE.

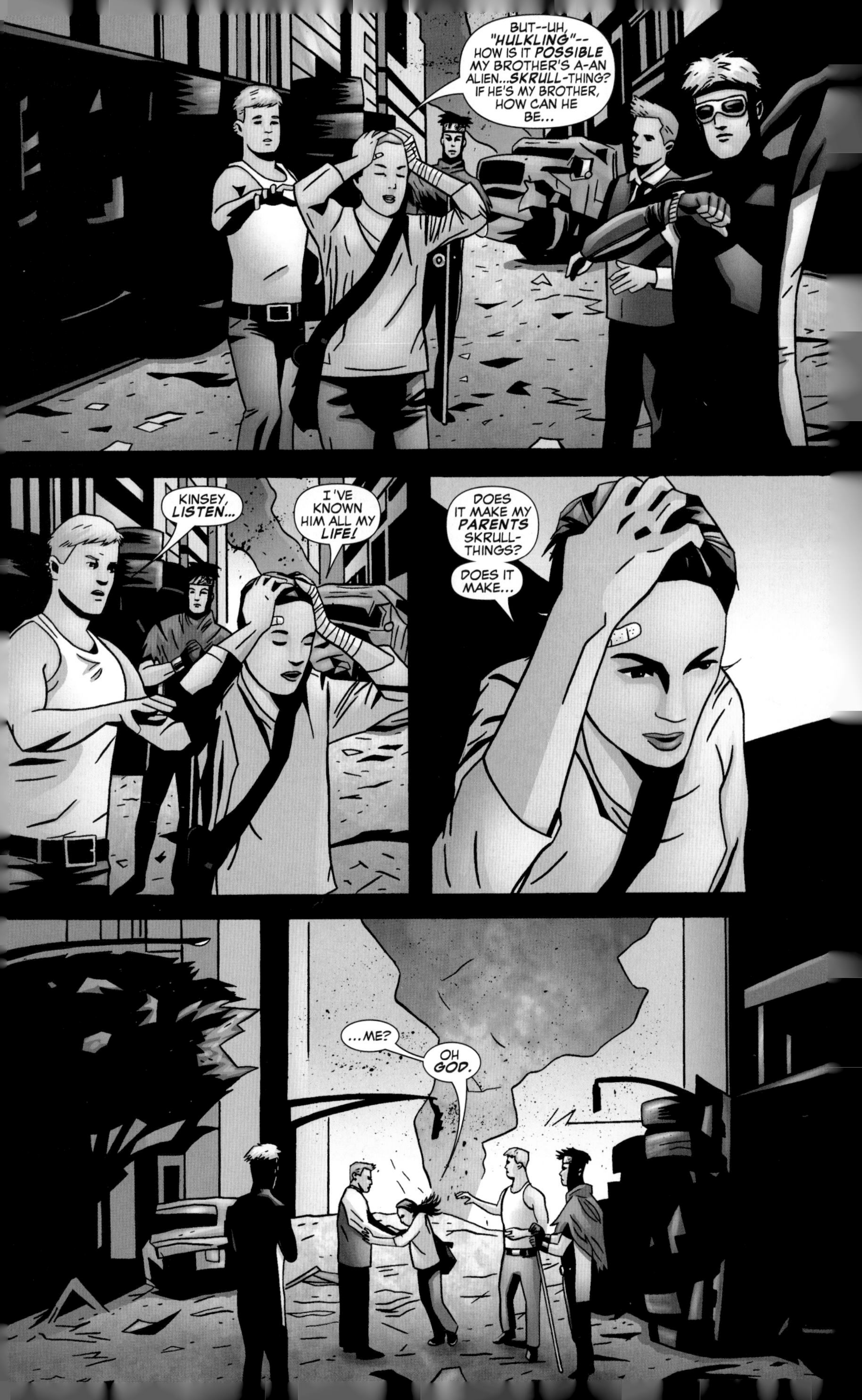
BUT--UH, "HULKLING"--HOW IS IT POSSIBLE MY BROTHER'S A-AN ALIEN...SKRULL-THING? IF HE'S MY BROTHER, HOW CAN HE BE...
KINSEY, LISTEN...
I'VE KNOWN HIM ALL MY LIFE!
DOES IT MAKE MY PARENTS SKRULL-THINGS?
DOES IT MAKE...
...ME?
OH GOD.

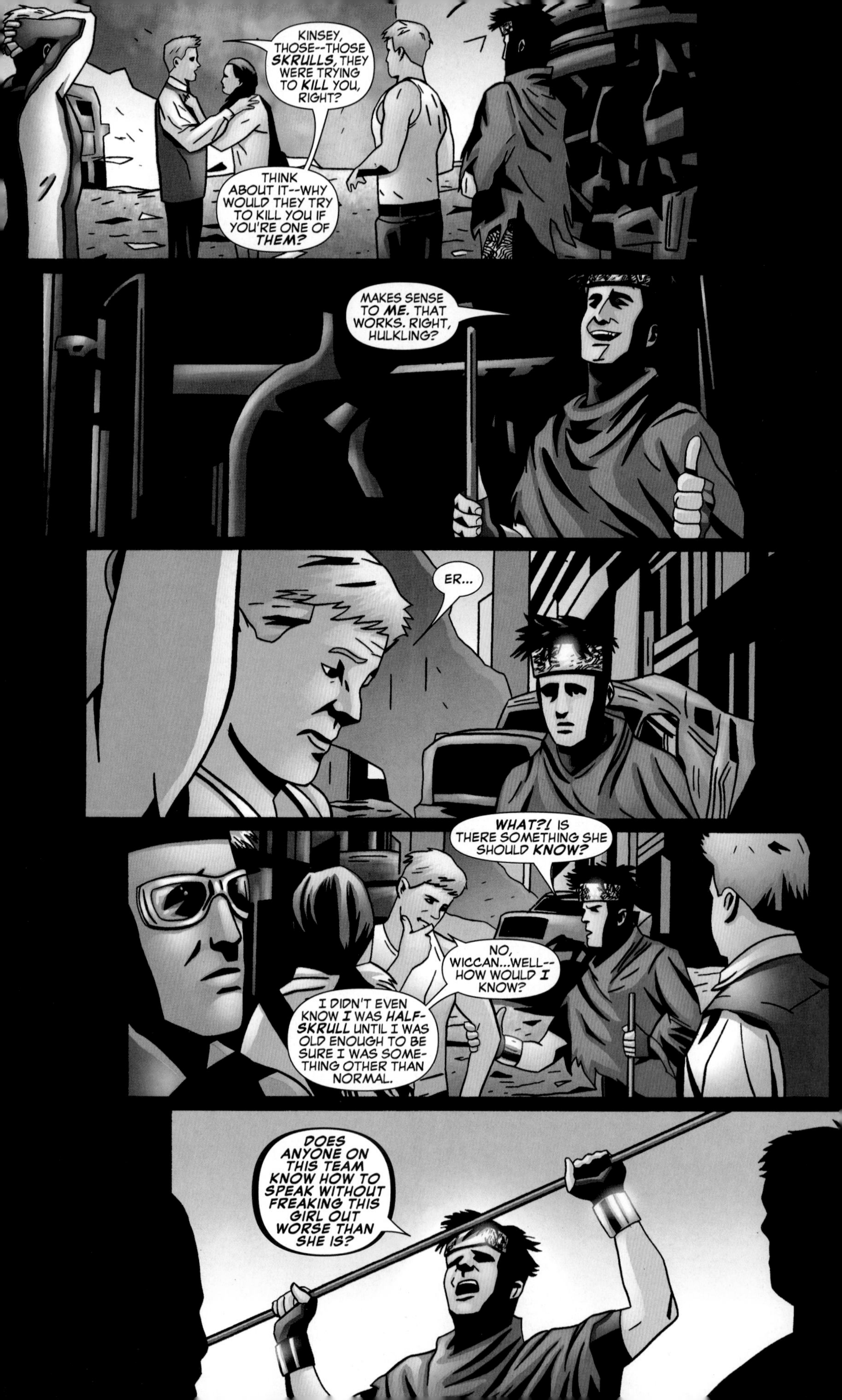
KINSEY, THOSE--THOSE SKRULLS, THEY WERE TRYING TO KILL YOU, RIGHT?
THINK ABOUT IT--WHY WOULD THEY TRY TO KILL YOU IF YOU'RE ONE OF THEM?
MAKES SENSE TO ME. THAT WORKS. RIGHT, HULKLING?
ER...
WHAT?! IS THERE SOMETHING SHE SHOULD KNOW?
NO, WICCAN...WELL-- HOW WOULD I KNOW?
I DIDN'T EVEN KNOW I WAS HALF-SKRULL UNTIL I WAS OLD ENOUGH TO BE SURE I WAS SOME-THING OTHER THAN NORMAL.
DOES ANYONE ON THIS TEAM KNOW HOW TO SPEAK WITHOUT FREAKING THIS GIRL OUT WORSE THAN SHE IS?

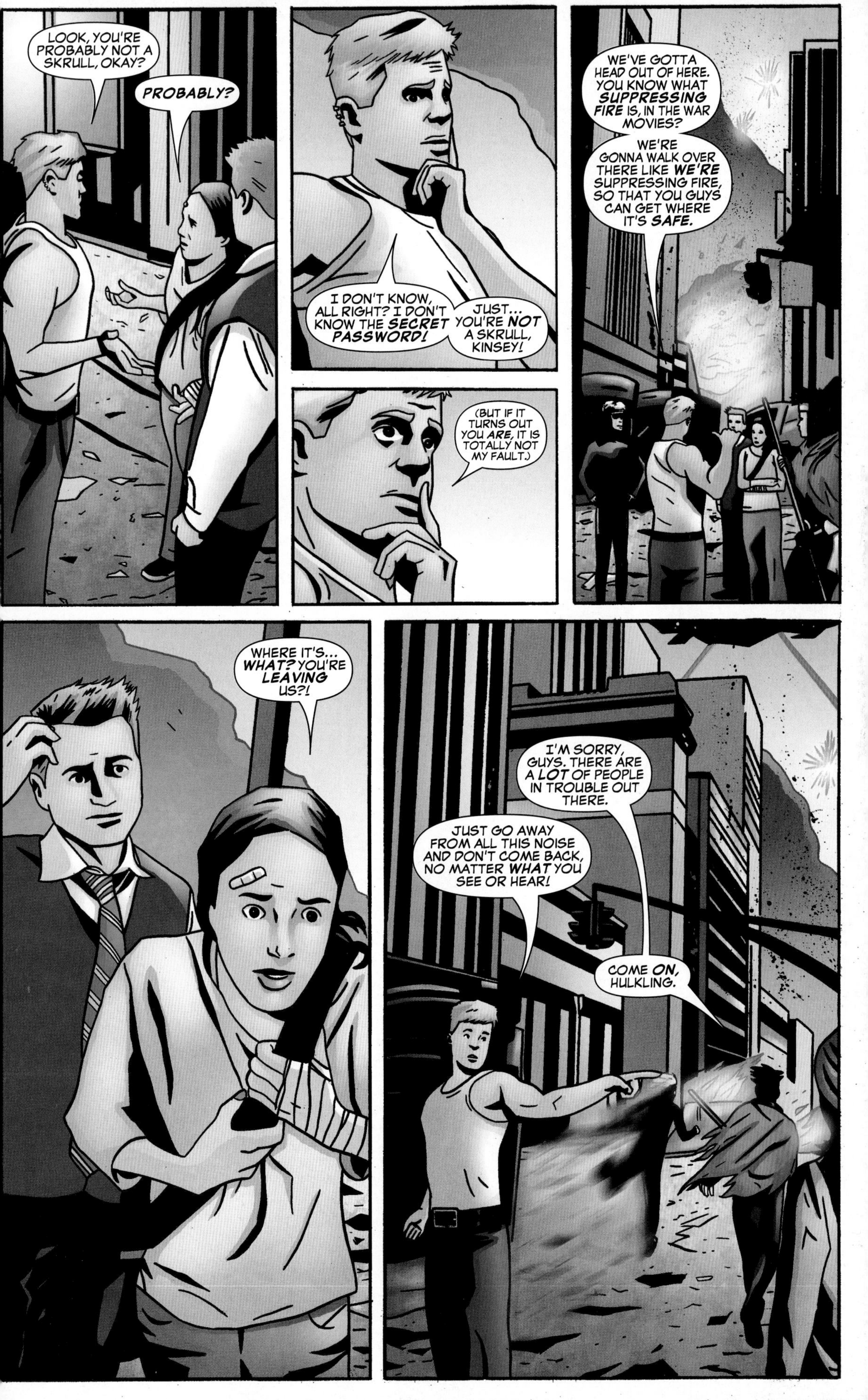
LOOK, YOU'RE PROBABLY NOT A SKRULL, OKAY?
PROBABLY?
I DON'T KNOW, ALL RIGHT? I DON'T KNOW THE SECRET PASSWORD!
JUST... YOU'RE NOT A SKRULL, KINSEY!
(BUT IF IT TURNS OUT YOU ARE, IT IS TOTALLY NOT MY FAULT.)
WE'VE GOTTA HEAD OUT OF HERE. YOU KNOW WHAT SUPPRESSING FIRE IS, IN THE WAR MOVIES?
WE'RE GONNA WALK OVER THERE LIKE WE'RE SUPPRESSING FIRE, SO THAT YOU GUYS CAN GET WHERE IT'S SAFE.
WHERE IT'S... WHAT? YOU'RE LEAVING US?!
I'M SORRY, GUYS. THERE ARE A LOT OF PEOPLE IN TROUBLE OUT THERE.
JUST GO AWAY FROM ALL THIS NOISE AND DON'T COME BACK, NO MATTER WHAT YOU SEE OR HEAR!
COME ON, HULKLING.

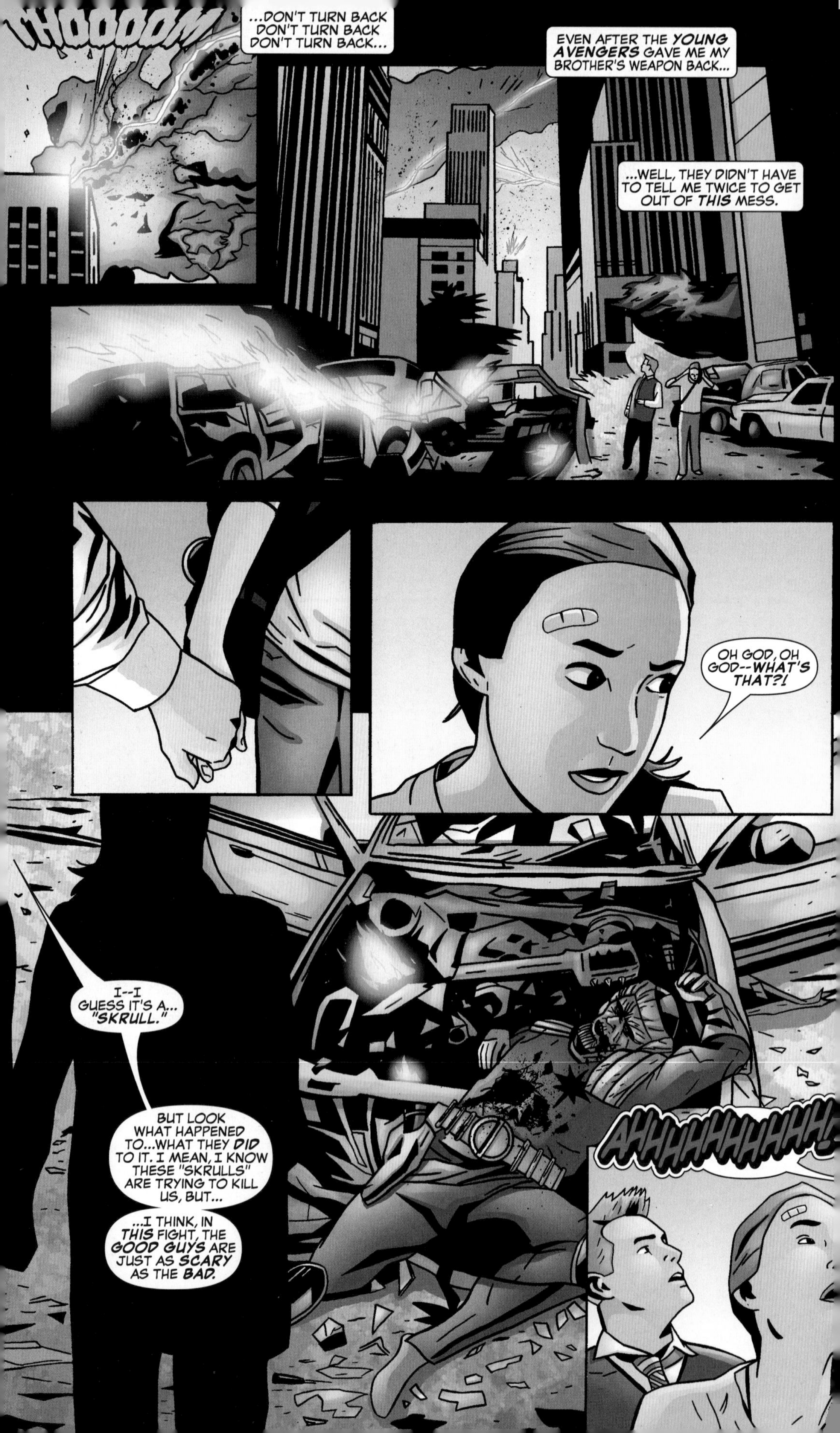
THOOOOM
...DON'T TURN BACK DON'T TURN BACK DON'T TURN BACK...
EVEN AFTER THE YOUNG AVENGERS GAVE ME MY BROTHER'S WEAPON BACK...
...WELL, THEY DIDN'T HAVE TO TELL ME TWICE TO GET OUT OF THIS MESS.
OH GOD, OH GOD--WHAT'S THAT?!
I--I GUESS IT'S A... "SKRULL."
BUT LOOK WHAT HAPPENED TO...WHAT THEY DID TO IT. I MEAN, I KNOW THESE "SKRULLS" ARE TRYING TO KILL US, BUT...
...I THINK, IN THIS FIGHT, THE GOOD GUYS ARE JUST AS SCARY AS THE BAD.
AHHHHHHHHHHH!

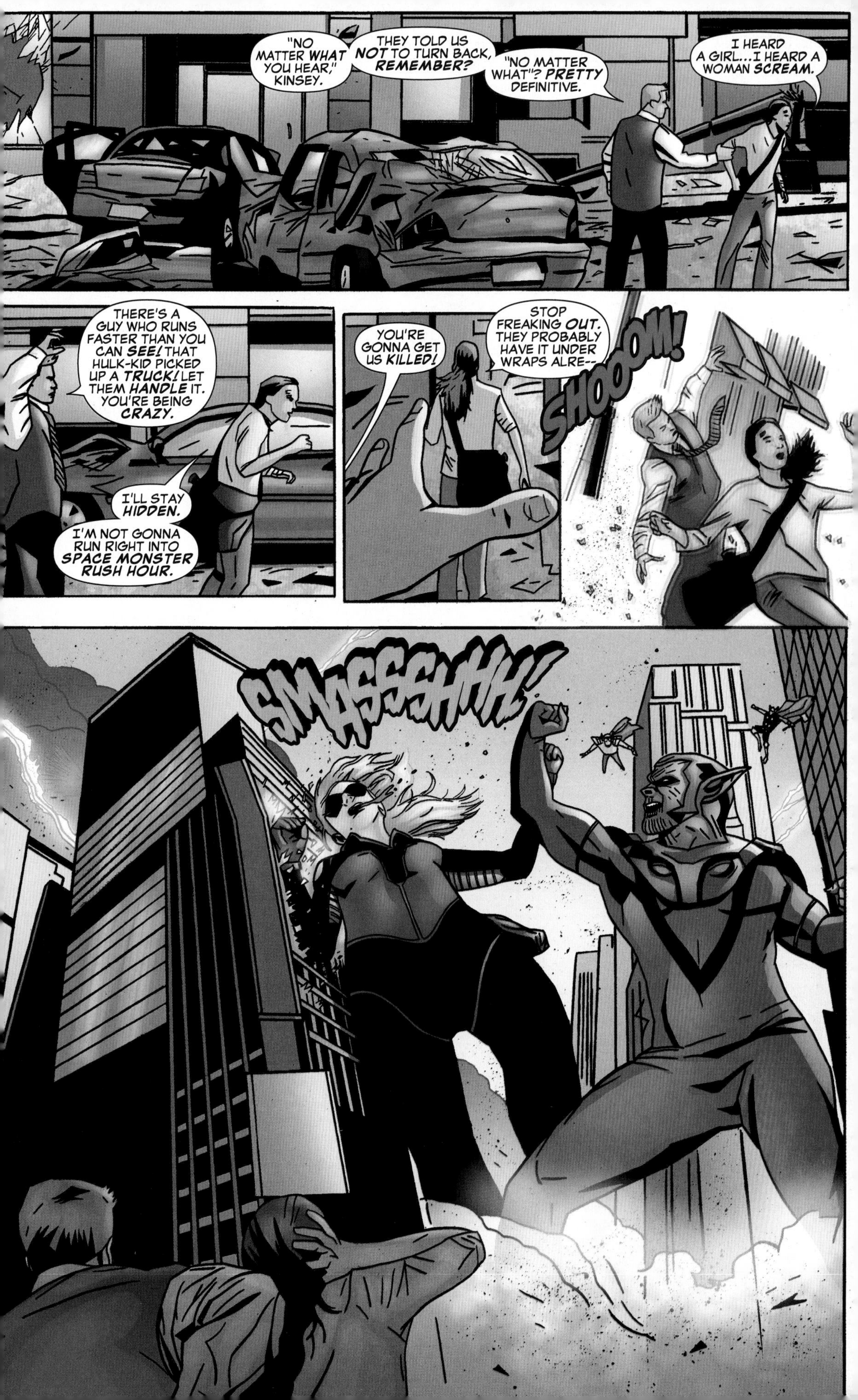

"NO MATTER WHAT YOU HEAR," KINSEY.
THEY TOLD US NOT TO TURN BACK, REMEMBER?
"NO MATTER WHAT"? PRETTY DEFINITIVE.
I HEARD A GIRL...I HEARD A WOMAN SCREAM.
THERE'S A GUY WHO RUNS FASTER THAN YOU CAN SEE! THAT HULK-KID PICKED UP A TRUCK! LET THEM HANDLE IT. YOU'RE BEING CRAZY.
I'LL STAY HIDDEN.
I'M NOT GONNA RUN RIGHT INTO SPACE MONSTER RUSH HOUR.
YOU'RE GONNA GET US KILLED!
STOP FREAKING OUT. THEY PROBABLY HAVE IT UNDER WRAPS ALRE--
SHOOOOM!
SMASSSHHH!

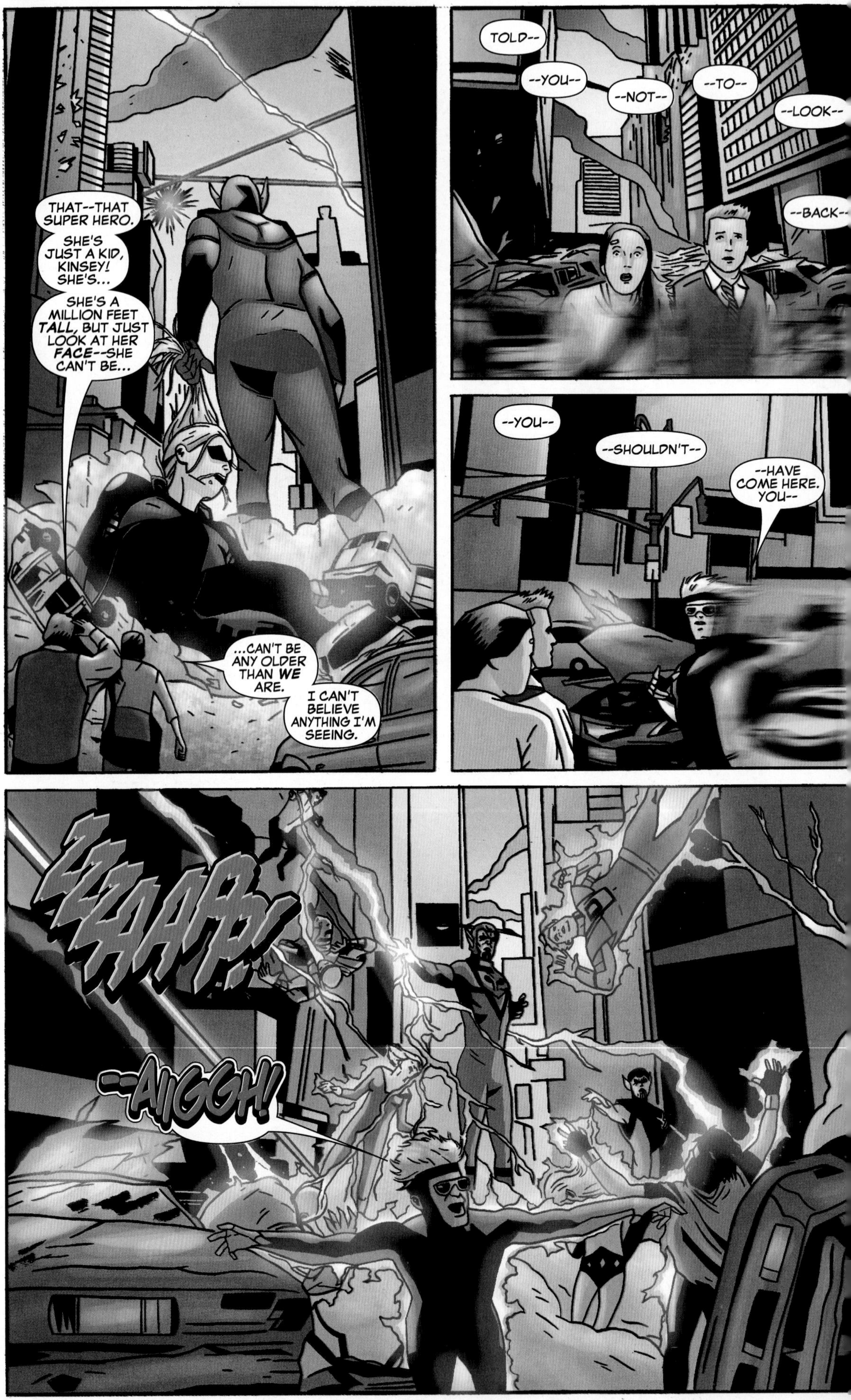
THAT--THAT SUPER HERO.
SHE'S JUST A KID, KINSEY! SHE'S...
SHE'S A MILLION FEET TALL, BUT JUST LOOK AT HER FACE--SHE CAN'T BE...
...CAN'T BE ANY OLDER THAN WE ARE.
I CAN'T BELIEVE ANYTHING I'M SEEING.
TOLD--
--YOU--
--NOT--
--TO--
--LOOK--
--BACK--
--YOU--
--SHOULDN'T--
--HAVE COME HERE. YOU--
ZZZAPP!
--AIIGGH!

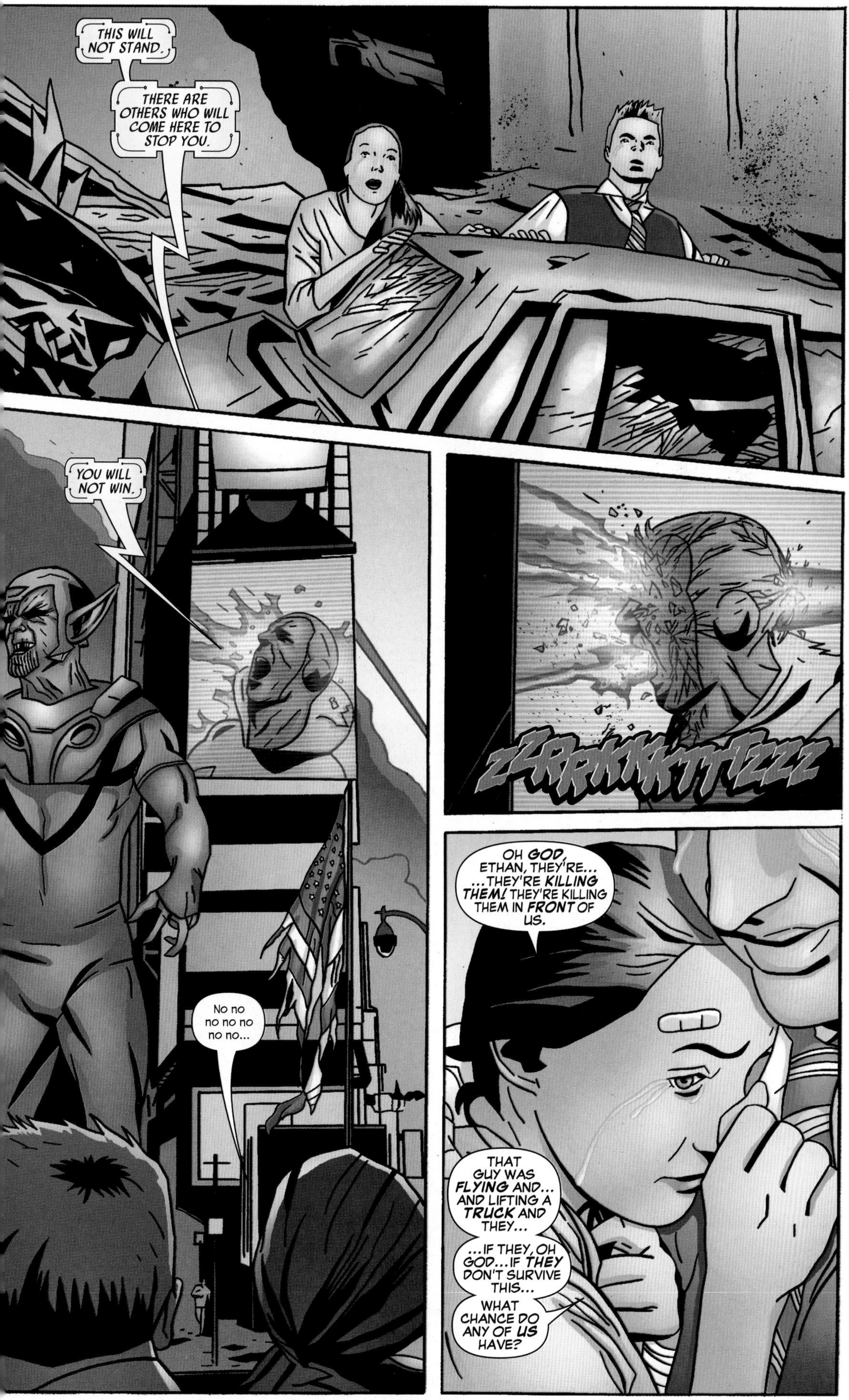
THIS WILL NOT STAND.
THERE ARE OTHERS WHO WILL COME HERE TO STOP YOU.
YOU WILL NOT WIN.
ZZRRKKKKTTTZZZ
No no no no no no no...
OH GOD, ETHAN, THEY'RE... ...THEY'RE KILLING THEM! THEY'RE KILLING THEM IN FRONT OF US.
THAT GUY WAS FLYING AND... AND LIFTING A TRUCK AND THEY...
...IF THEY, OH GOD...IF THEY DON'T SURVIVE THIS...
WHAT CHANCE DO ANY OF US HAVE?

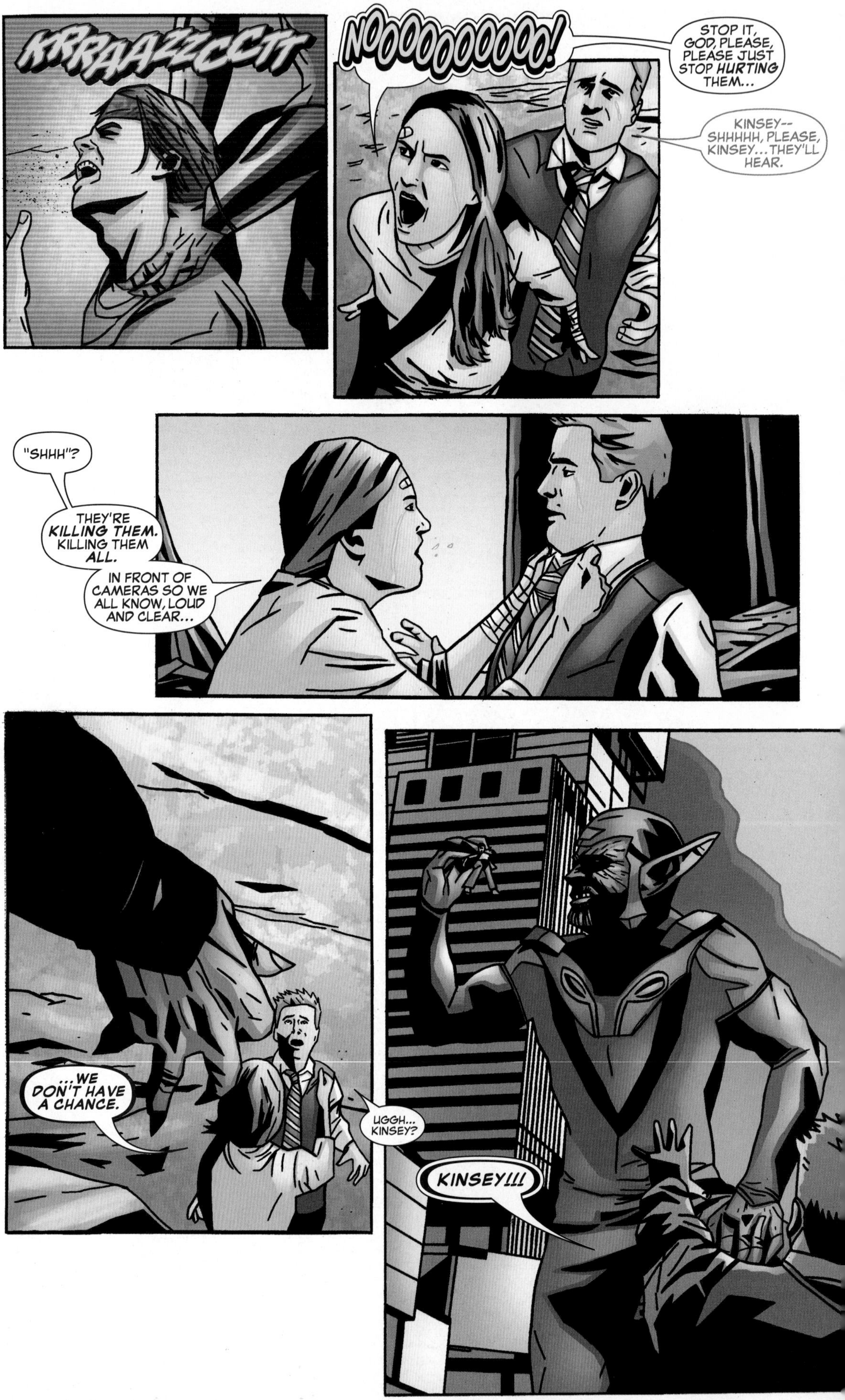
KRRAAZZCCTT
NOOOOOOOOOOO!
STOP IT, GOD, PLEASE, PLEASE JUST STOP HURTING THEM...
KINSEY-- SHHHHH, PLEASE, KINSEY... THEY'LL HEAR.
"SHHH"?
THEY'RE KILLING THEM. KILLING THEM ALL.
IN FRONT OF CAMERAS SO WE ALL KNOW, LOUD AND CLEAR...
...WE DON'T HAVE A CHANCE.
UGGH... KINSEY?
KINSEY!!!

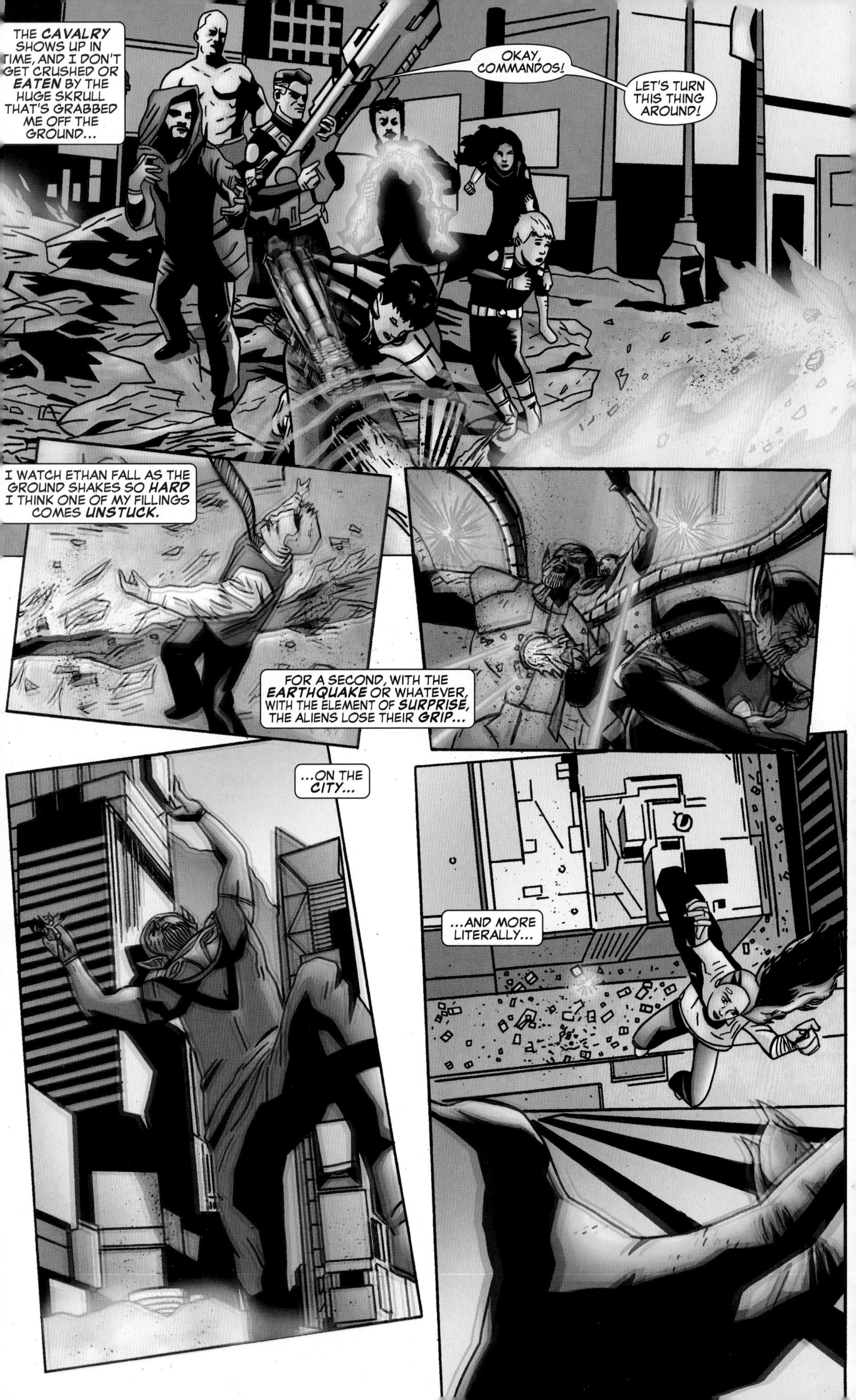
THE CAVALRY SHOWS UP IN TIME, AND I DON'T GET CRUSHED OR EATEN BY THE HUGE SKRULL THAT'S GRABBED ME OFF THE GROUND...
OKAY, COMMANDOS!
LET'S TURN THIS THING AROUND!
I WATCH ETHAN FALL AS THE GROUND SHAKES SO HARD I THINK ONE OF MY FILLINGS COMES UNSTUCK.
FOR A SECOND, WITH THE EARTHQUAKE OR WHATEVER, WITH THE ELEMENT OF SURPRISE, THE ALIENS LOSE THEIR GRIP...
...ON THE CITY...
...AND MORE LITERALLY...

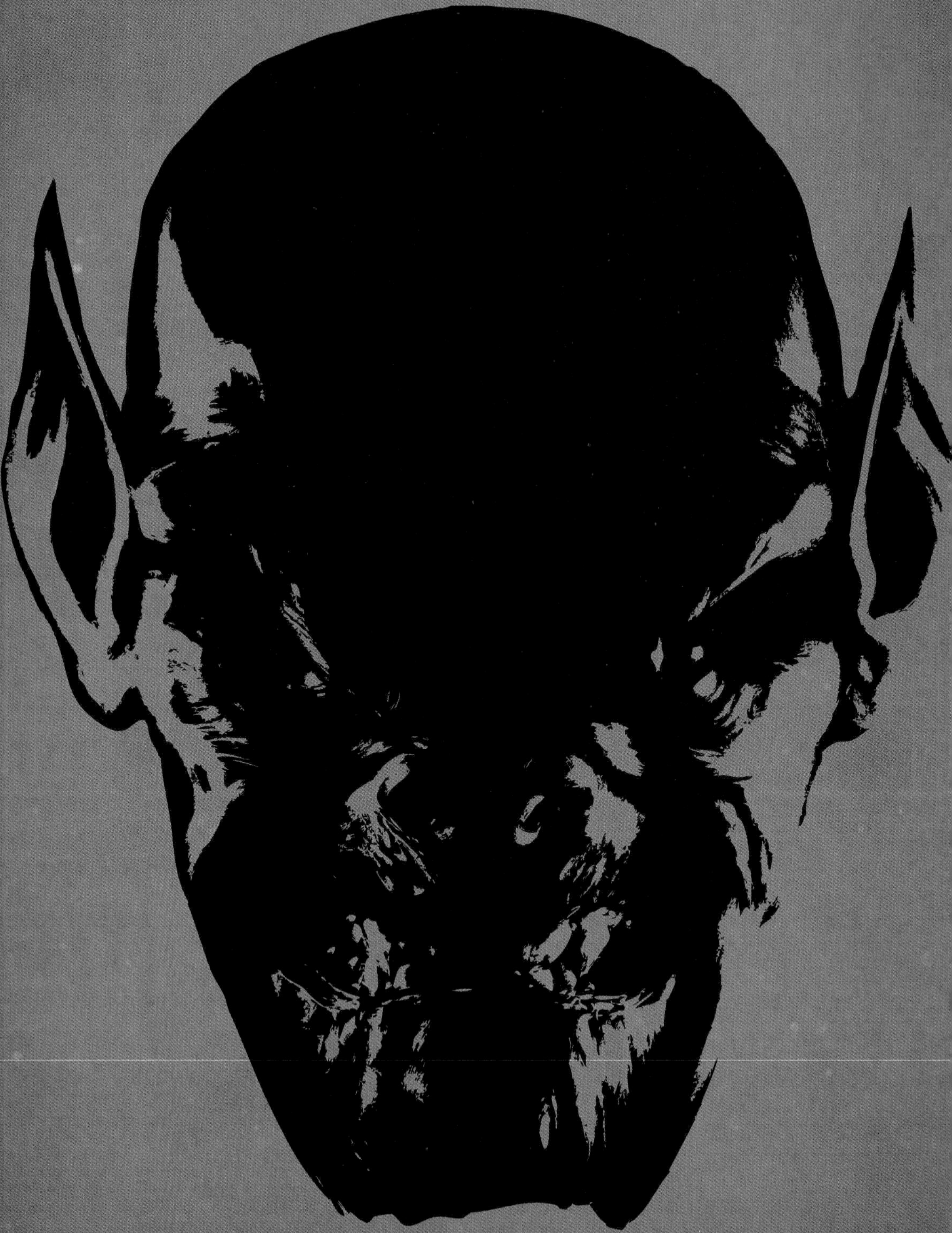

CHAPTER 4

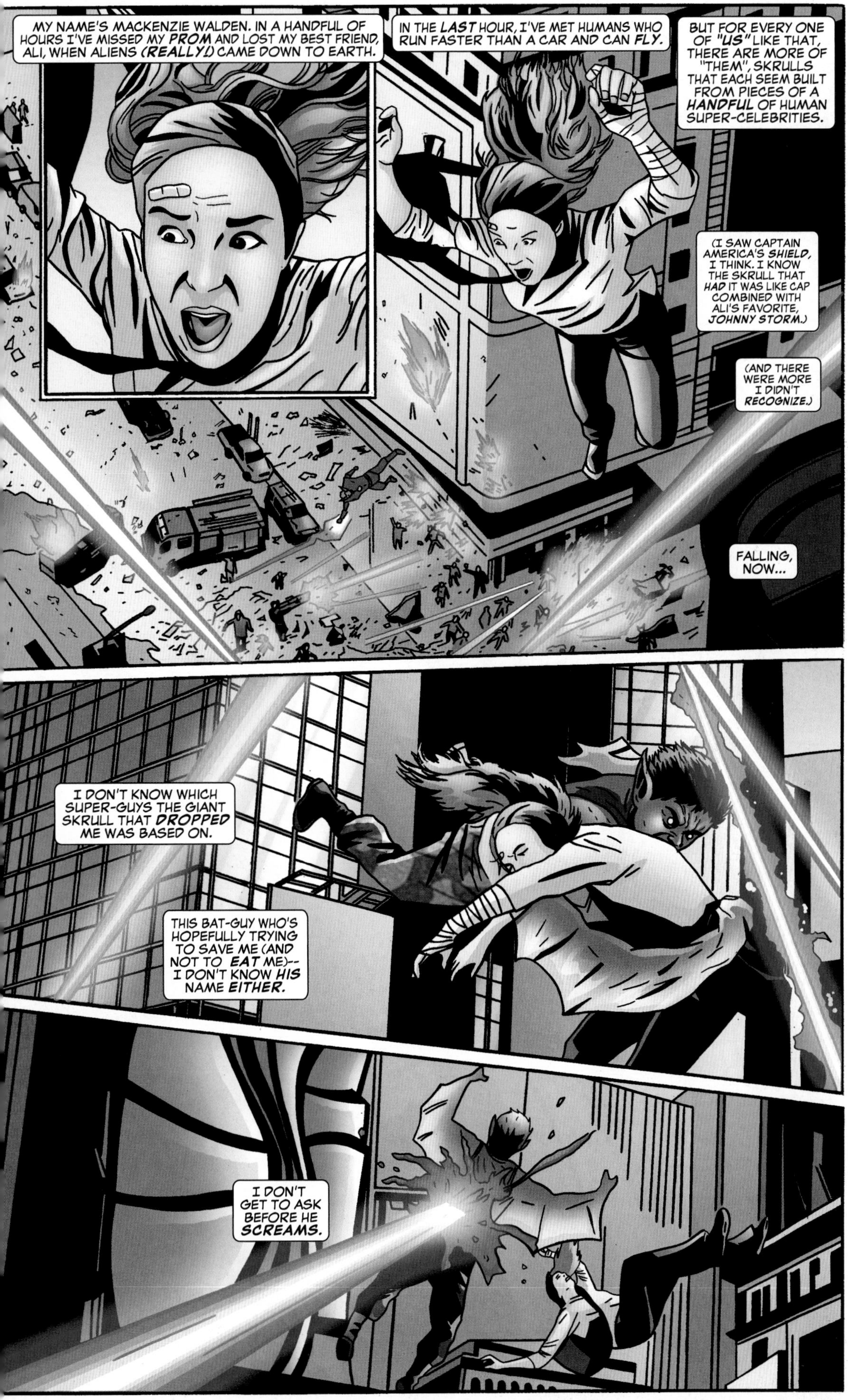
MY NAME'S MACKENZIE WALDEN. IN A HANDFUL OF HOURS I'VE MISSED MY PROM AND LOST MY BEST FRIEND, ALI, WHEN ALIENS (REALLY!) CAME DOWN TO EARTH.
IN THE LAST HOUR, I'VE MET HUMANS WHO RUN FASTER THAN A CAR AND CAN FLY.
BUT FOR EVERY ONE OF "US" LIKE THAT, THERE ARE MORE OF "THEM", SKRULLS THAT EACH SEEM BUILT FROM PIECES OF A HANDFUL OF HUMAN SUPER-CELEBRITIES.
(I SAW CAPTAIN AMERICA'S SHIELD, I THINK. I KNOW THE SKRULL THAT HAD IT WAS LIKE CAP COMBINED WITH ALI'S FAVORITE, JOHNNY STORM.)
(AND THERE WERE MORE I DIDN'T RECOGNIZE.)
FALLING, NOW...
I DON'T KNOW WHICH SUPER-GUYS THE GIANT SKRULL THAT DROPPED ME WAS BASED ON.
THIS BAT-GUY WHO'S HOPEFULLY TRYING TO SAVE ME (AND NOT TO EAT ME)-- I DON'T KNOW HIS NAME EITHER.
I DON'T GET TO ASK BEFORE HE SCREAMS.

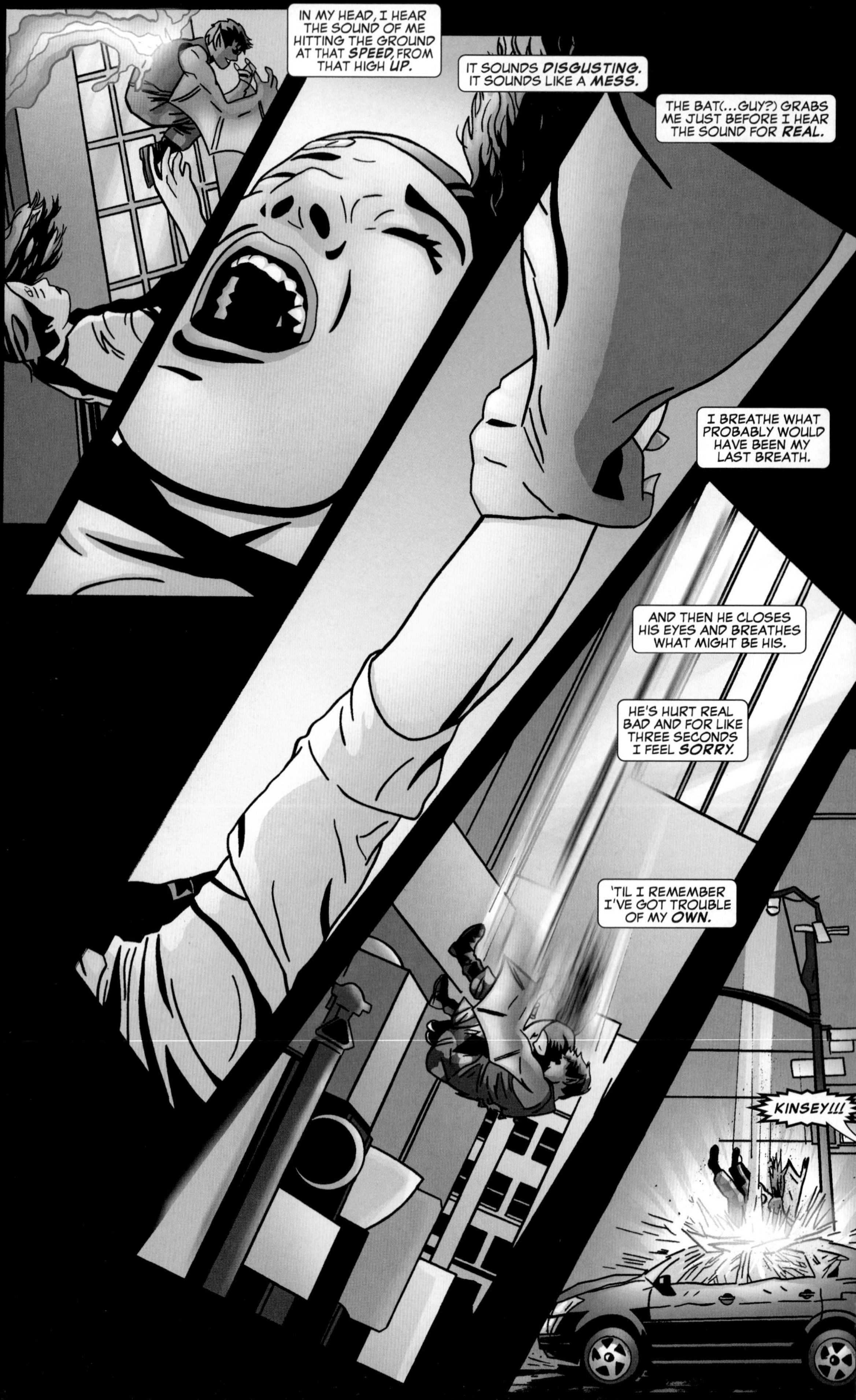
IN MY HEAD, I HEAR THE SOUND OF ME HITTING THE GROUND AT THAT SPEED, FROM THAT HIGH UP.
IT SOUNDS DISGUSTING. IT SOUNDS LIKE A MESS.
THE BAT(...GUY?) GRABS ME JUST BEFORE I HEAR THE SOUND FOR REAL.
I BREATHE WHAT PROBABLY WOULD HAVE BEEN MY LAST BREATH.
AND THEN HE CLOSES HIS EYES AND BREATHES WHAT MIGHT BE HIS.
HE'S HURT REAL BAD AND FOR LIKE THREE SECONDS I FEEL SORRY.
'TIL I REMEMBER I'VE GOT TROUBLE OF MY OWN.
KINSEY!!!

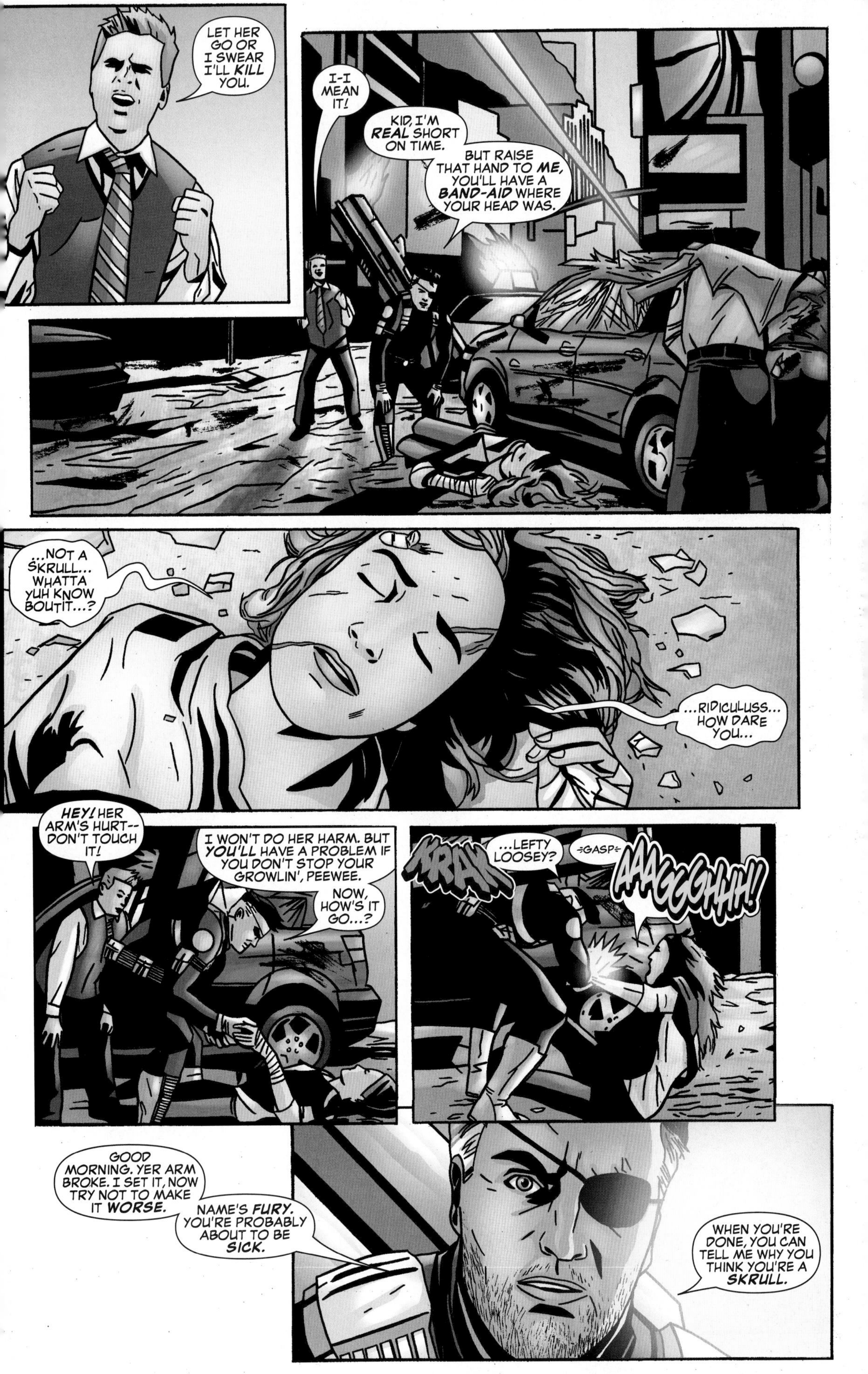

LET HER GO OR I SWEAR I'LL KILL YOU.
I-I MEAN IT!
KID, I'M REAL SHORT ON TIME.
BUT RAISE THAT HAND TO ME, YOU'LL HAVE A BAND-AID WHERE YOUR HEAD WAS.
...NOT A SKRULL... WHATTA YUH KNOW BOUTIT...?
...RIDICULUSS... HOW DARE YOU...
HEY! HER ARM'S HURT-- DON'T TOUCH IT!
I WON'T DO HER HARM. BUT YOU'LL HAVE A PROBLEM IF YOU DON'T STOP YOUR GROWLIN', PEEWEE.
NOW, HOW'S IT GO...?
KRAK
...LEFTY LOOSEY?
GASP
AAAGGGHHH!
GOOD MORNING. YER ARM BROKE. I SET IT, NOW TRY NOT TO MAKE IT WORSE.
NAME'S FURY. YOU'RE PROBABLY ABOUT TO BE SICK.
WHEN YOU'RE DONE, YOU CAN TELL ME WHY YOU THINK YOU'RE A SKRULL.

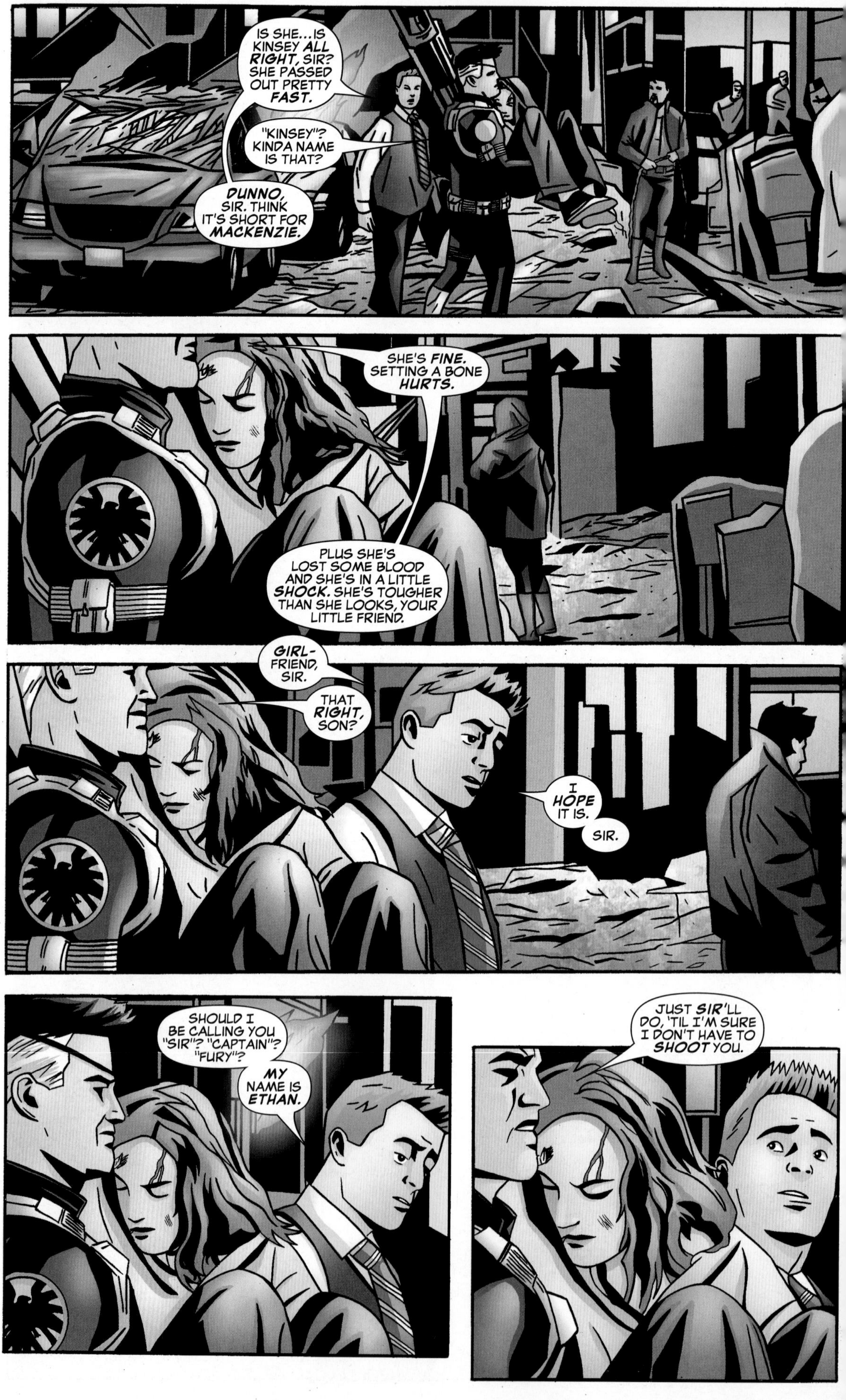
IS SHE...IS KINSEY ALL RIGHT, SIR? SHE PASSED OUT PRETTY FAST.
"KINSEY"? KINDA NAME IS THAT?
DUNNO, SIR. THINK IT'S SHORT FOR MACKENZIE.
SHE'S FINE. SETTING A BONE HURTS.
PLUS SHE'S LOST SOME BLOOD AND SHE'S IN A LITTLE SHOCK. SHE'S TOUGHER THAN SHE LOOKS, YOUR LITTLE FRIEND.
GIRL-FRIEND, SIR.
THAT RIGHT, SON?
I HOPE IT IS.
SIR.
SHOULD I BE CALLING YOU "SIR"? "CAPTAIN"? "FURY"?
MY NAME IS ETHAN.
JUST SIR'LL DO, 'TIL I'M SURE I DON'T HAVE TO SHOOT YOU.

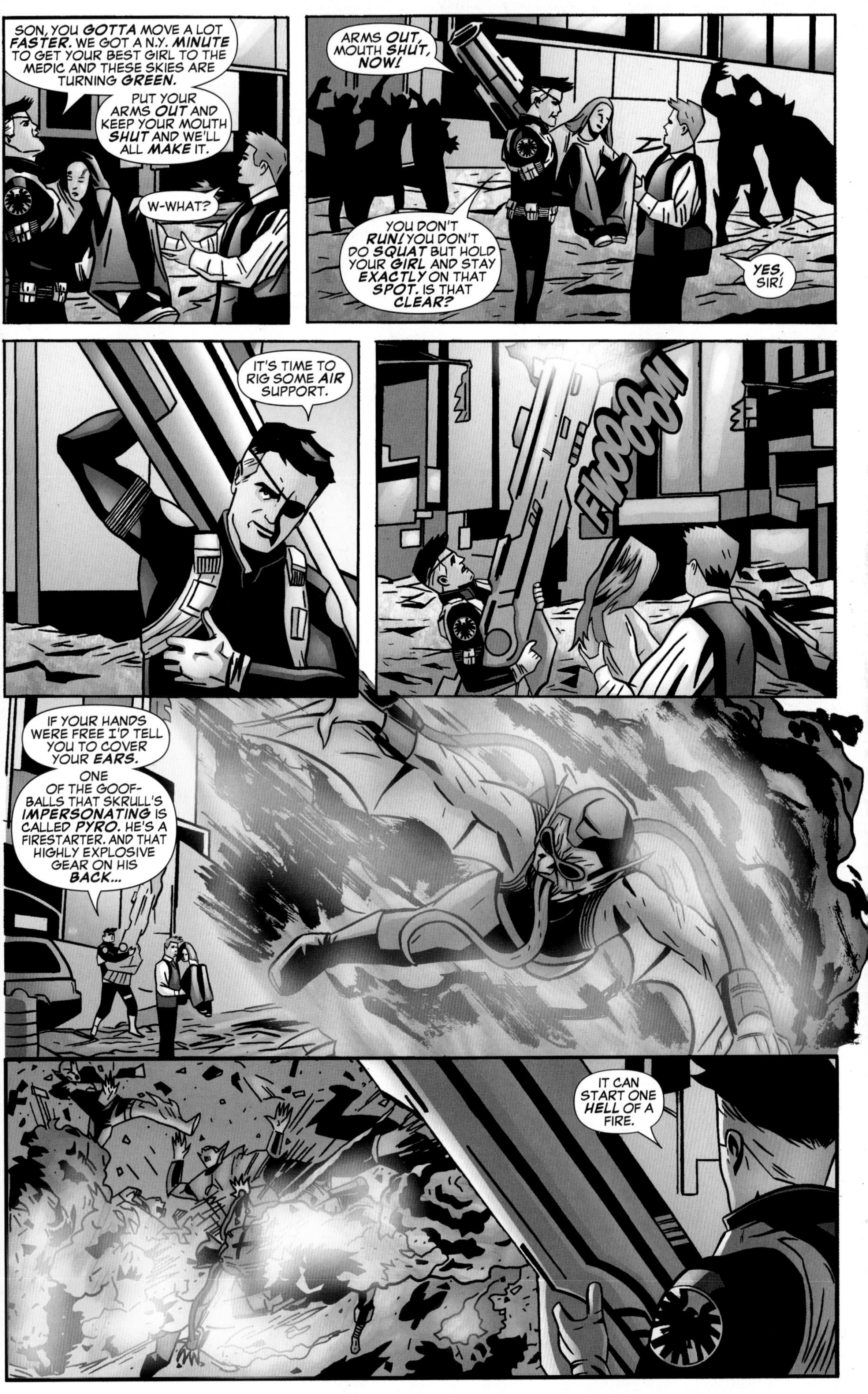
SON, YOU GOTTA MOVE A LOT FASTER. WE GOT A N.Y. MINUTE TO GET YOUR BEST GIRL TO THE MEDIC AND THESE SKIES ARE TURNING GREEN.
PUT YOUR ARMS OUT AND KEEP YOUR MOUTH SHUT AND WE'LL ALL MAKE IT.
W-WHAT?
ARMS OUT, MOUTH SHUT, NOW!
YOU DON'T RUN! YOU DON'T DO SQUAT BUT HOLD YOUR GIRL AND STAY EXACTLY ON THAT SPOT. IS THAT CLEAR?
YES, SIR!
IT'S TIME TO RIG SOME AIR SUPPORT.
FWOOOOM
IF YOUR HANDS WERE FREE I'D TELL YOU TO COVER YOUR EARS.
ONE OF THE GOOF-BALLS THAT SKRULL'S IMPERSONATING IS CALLED PYRO. HE'S A FIRESTARTER. AND THAT HIGHLY EXPLOSIVE GEAR ON HIS BACK...
IT CAN START ONE HELL OF A FIRE.

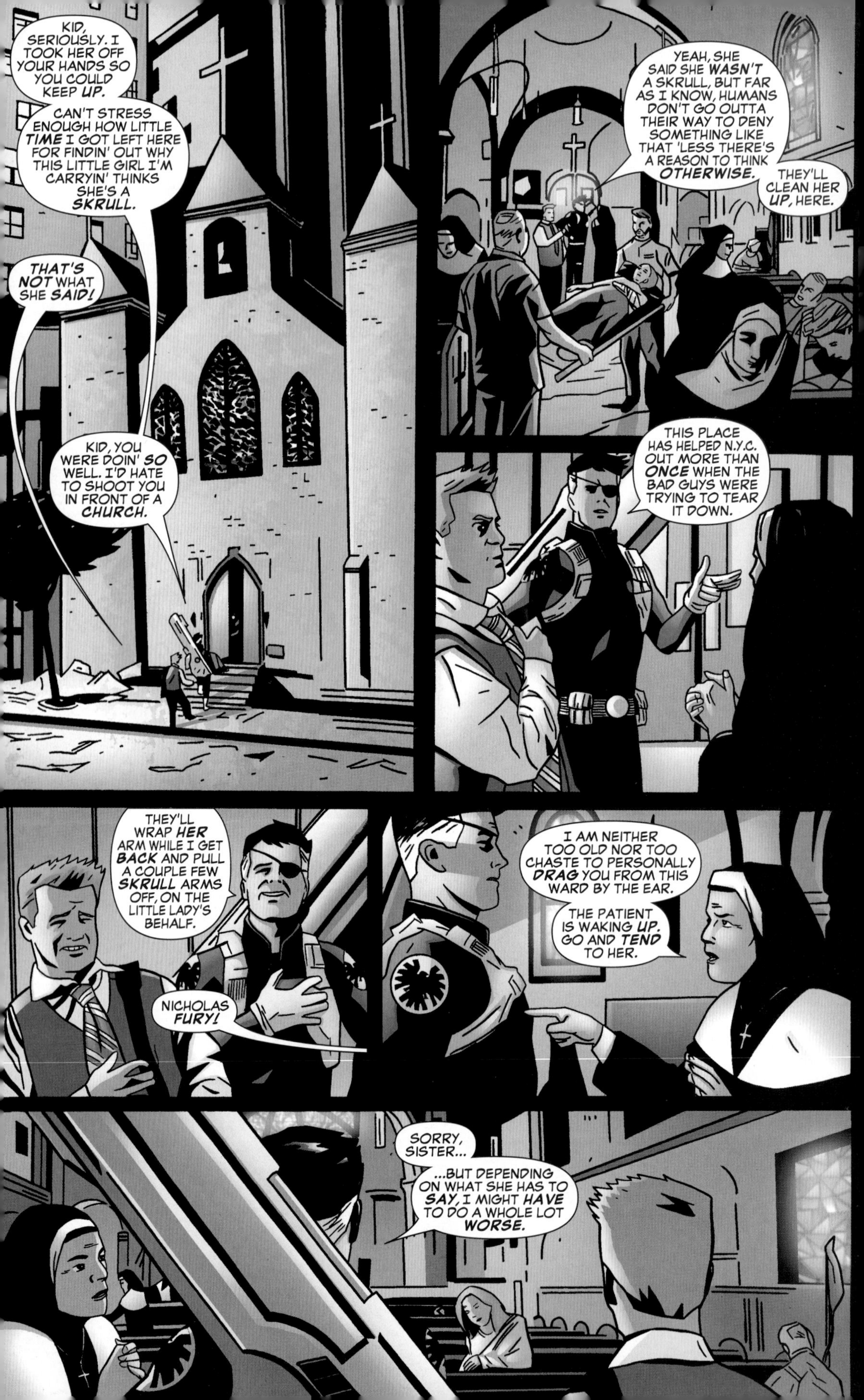
KID, SERIOUSLY. I TOOK HER OFF YOUR HANDS SO YOU COULD KEEP UP.
CAN'T STRESS ENOUGH HOW LITTLE TIME I GOT LEFT HERE FOR FINDIN' OUT WHY THIS LITTLE GIRL I'M CARRYIN' THINKS SHE'S A SKRULL.
THAT'S NOT WHAT SHE SAID!
KID, YOU WERE DOIN' SO WELL. I'D HATE TO SHOOT YOU IN FRONT OF A CHURCH.
YEAH, SHE SAID SHE WASN'T A SKRULL, BUT FAR AS I KNOW, HUMANS DON'T GO OUTTA THEIR WAY TO DENY SOMETHING LIKE THAT 'LESS THERE'S A REASON TO THINK OTHERWISE.
THEY'LL CLEAN HER UP, HERE.
THIS PLACE HAS HELPED N.Y.C. OUT MORE THAN ONCE WHEN THE BAD GUYS WERE TRYING TO TEAR IT DOWN.
THEY'LL WRAP HER ARM WHILE I GET BACK AND PULL A COUPLE FEW SKRULL ARMS OFF, ON THE LITTLE LADY'S BEHALF.
NICHOLAS FURY!
I AM NEITHER TOO OLD NOR TOO CHASTE TO PERSONALLY DRAG YOU FROM THIS WARD BY THE EAR.
THE PATIENT IS WAKING UP. GO AND TEND TO HER.
SORRY, SISTER...
...BUT DEPENDING ON WHAT SHE HAS TO SAY, I MIGHT HAVE TO DO A WHOLE LOT WORSE.

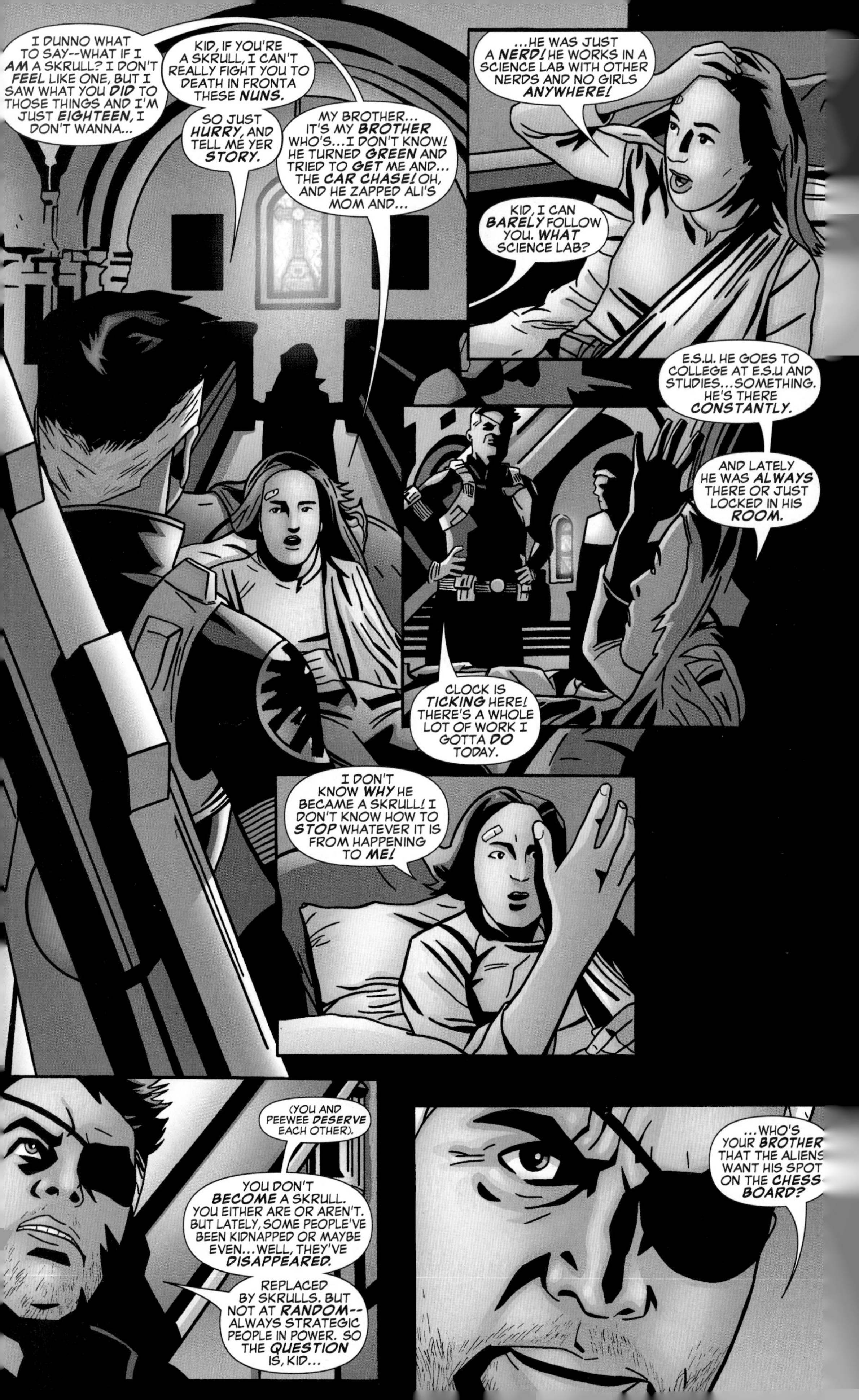
I DUNNO WHAT TO SAY--WHAT IF I **AM** A SKRULL? I DON'T **FEEL** LIKE ONE, BUT I SAW WHAT YOU **DID** TO THOSE THINGS AND I'M JUST **EIGHTEEN**, I DON'T WANNA...
KID, IF YOU'RE A SKRULL, I CAN'T REALLY FIGHT YOU TO DEATH IN FRONTA THESE **NUNS.**
SO JUST **HURRY**, AND TELL ME YER **STORY.**
MY BROTHER... IT'S MY **BROTHER** WHO'S...I DON'T KNOW! HE TURNED **GREEN** AND TRIED TO **GET** ME AND... THE **CAR CHASE!** OH, AND HE ZAPPED ALI'S MOM AND...
...HE WAS JUST A **NERD!** HE WORKS IN A SCIENCE LAB WITH OTHER NERDS AND NO GIRLS **ANYWHERE!**
KID, I CAN **BARELY** FOLLOW YOU. **WHAT** SCIENCE LAB?
E.S.U. HE GOES TO COLLEGE AT E.S.U AND STUDIES...SOMETHING. HE'S THERE **CONSTANTLY.**
AND LATELY HE WAS **ALWAYS** THERE OR JUST LOCKED IN HIS **ROOM.**
CLOCK IS **TICKING** HERE! THERE'S A WHOLE LOT OF WORK I GOTTA **DO** TODAY.
I DON'T KNOW **WHY** HE BECAME A SKRULL! I DON'T KNOW HOW TO **STOP** WHATEVER IT IS FROM HAPPENING TO **ME!**
(YOU AND PEEWEE **DESERVE** EACH OTHER).
YOU DON'T **BECOME** A SKRULL. YOU EITHER ARE OR AREN'T. BUT LATELY, SOME PEOPLE'VE BEEN KIDNAPPED OR MAYBE EVEN...WELL, THEY'VE **DISAPPEARED.**
REPLACED BY SKRULLS. BUT NOT AT **RANDOM**--ALWAYS STRATEGIC PEOPLE IN POWER. SO THE **QUESTION** IS, KID...
...WHO'S YOUR **BROTHER** THAT THE ALIENS WANT HIS SPOT ON THE **CHESS-BOARD?**

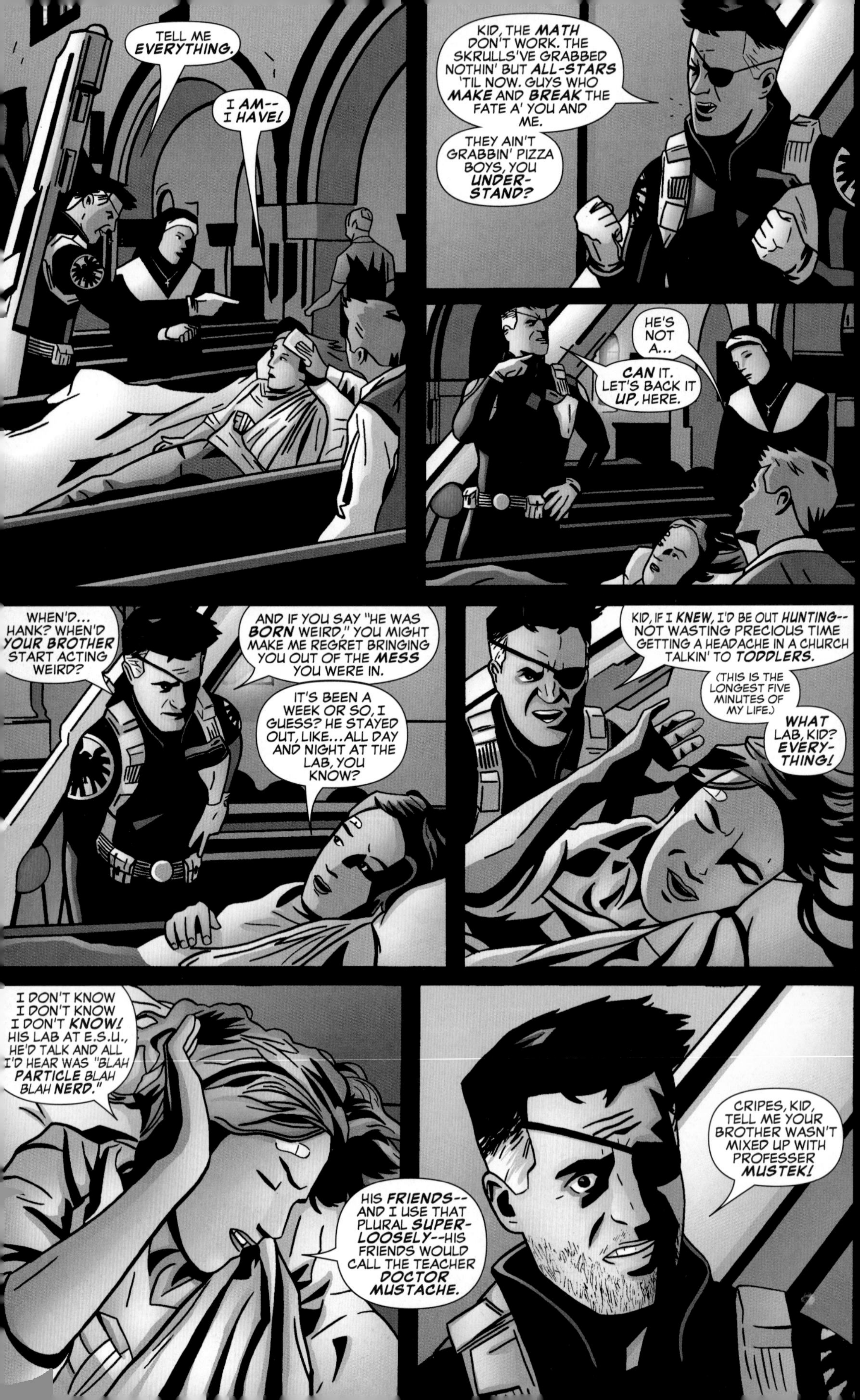
TELL ME EVERYTHING.
I AM-- I HAVE!
KID, THE MATH DON'T WORK. THE SKRULLS'VE GRABBED NOTHIN' BUT ALL-STARS 'TIL NOW. GUYS WHO MAKE AND BREAK THE FATE A' YOU AND ME.
THEY AIN'T GRABBIN' PIZZA BOYS, YOU UNDER-STAND?
HE'S NOT A...
CAN IT. LET'S BACK IT UP, HERE.
WHEN'D... HANK? WHEN'D YOUR BROTHER START ACTING WEIRD?
AND IF YOU SAY "HE WAS BORN WEIRD," YOU MIGHT MAKE ME REGRET BRINGING YOU OUT OF THE MESS YOU WERE IN.
IT'S BEEN A WEEK OR SO, I GUESS? HE STAYED OUT, LIKE...ALL DAY AND NIGHT AT THE LAB, YOU KNOW?
KID, IF I KNEW, I'D BE OUT HUNTING--NOT WASTING PRECIOUS TIME GETTING A HEADACHE IN A CHURCH TALKIN' TO TODDLERS.
(THIS IS THE LONGEST FIVE MINUTES OF MY LIFE.)
WHAT LAB, KID? EVERY-THING!
I DON'T KNOW I DON'T KNOW I DON'T KNOW! HIS LAB AT E.S.U., HE'D TALK AND ALL I'D HEAR WAS "BLAH PARTICLE BLAH BLAH NERD."
HIS FRIENDS--AND I USE THAT PLURAL SUPER-LOOSELY--HIS FRIENDS WOULD CALL THE TEACHER DOCTOR MUSTACHE.
CRIPES, KID, TELL ME YOUR BROTHER WASN'T MIXED UP WITH PROFESSER MUSTEK!

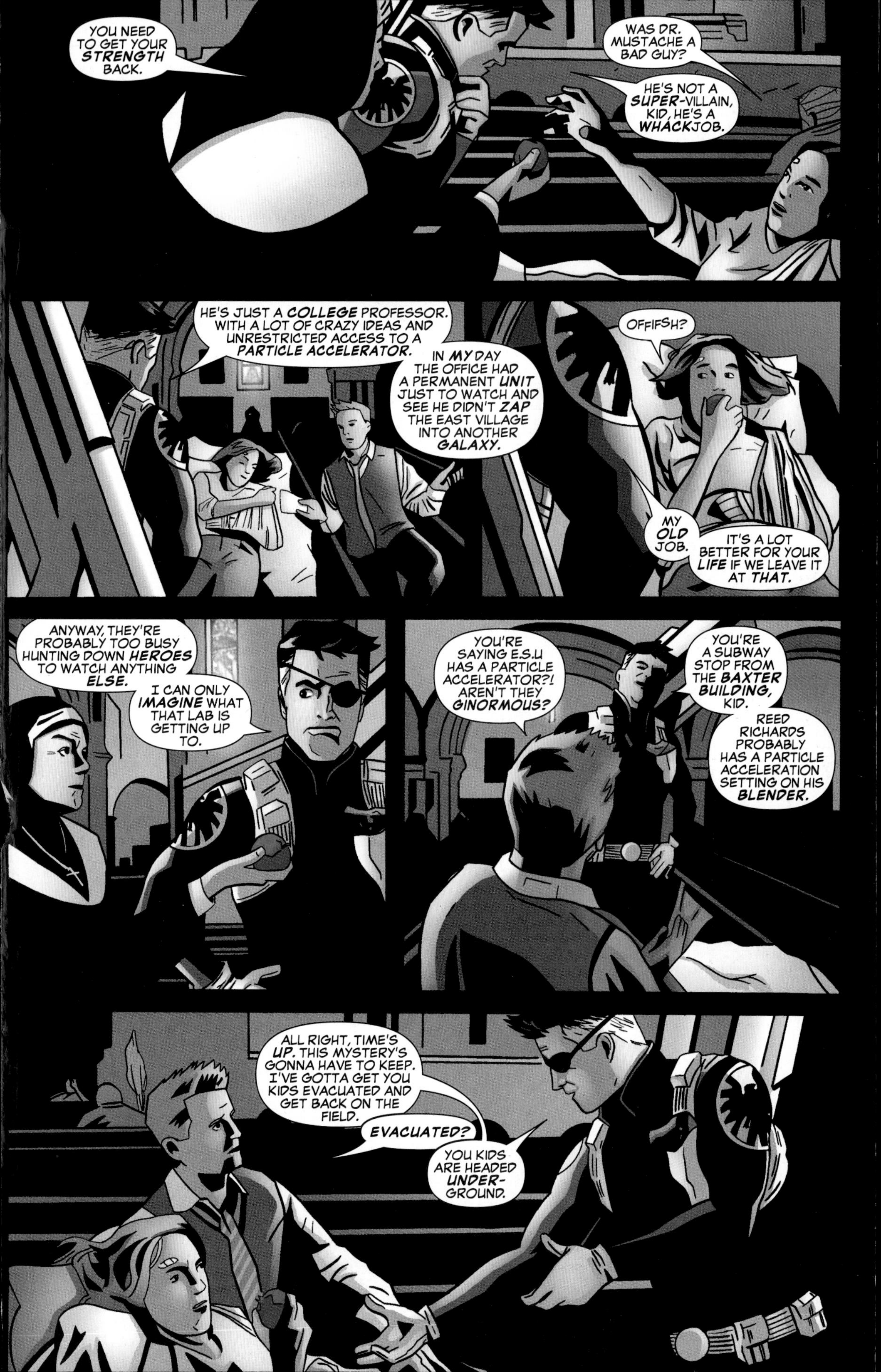

YOU NEED TO GET YOUR STRENGTH BACK.
WAS DR. MUSTACHE A BAD GUY?
HE'S NOT A SUPER-VILLAIN, KID, HE'S A WHACKJOB.
HE'S JUST A COLLEGE PROFESSOR. WITH A LOT OF CRAZY IDEAS AND UNRESTRICTED ACCESS TO A PARTICLE ACCELERATOR.
IN MY DAY THE OFFICE HAD A PERMANENT UNIT JUST TO WATCH AND SEE HE DIDN'T ZAP THE EAST VILLAGE INTO ANOTHER GALAXY.
OFFIFSH?
MY OLD JOB.
IT'S A LOT BETTER FOR YOUR LIFE IF WE LEAVE IT AT THAT.
ANYWAY, THEY'RE PROBABLY TOO BUSY HUNTING DOWN HEROES TO WATCH ANYTHING ELSE.
I CAN ONLY IMAGINE WHAT THAT LAB IS GETTING UP TO.
YOU'RE SAYING E.S.U HAS A PARTICLE ACCELERATOR?! AREN'T THEY GINORMOUS?
YOU'RE A SUBWAY STOP FROM THE BAXTER BUILDING, KID.
REED RICHARDS PROBABLY HAS A PARTICLE ACCELERATION SETTING ON HIS BLENDER.
ALL RIGHT, TIME'S UP. THIS MYSTERY'S GONNA HAVE TO KEEP. I'VE GOTTA GET YOU KIDS EVACUATED AND GET BACK ON THE FIELD.
EVACUATED?
YOU KIDS ARE HEADED UNDER-GROUND.

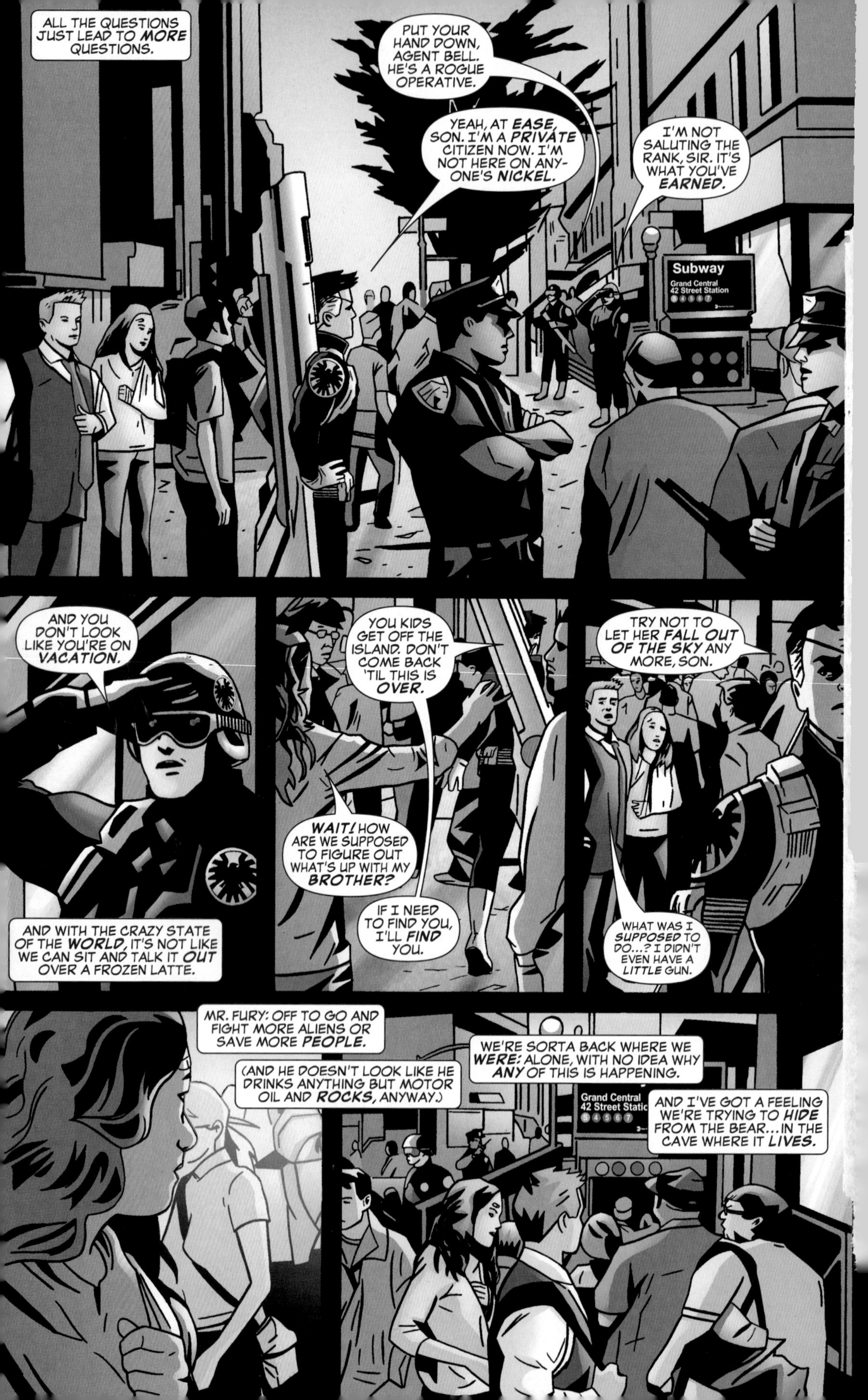
ALL THE QUESTIONS JUST LEAD TO MORE QUESTIONS.
PUT YOUR HAND DOWN, AGENT BELL. HE'S A ROGUE OPERATIVE.
YEAH, AT EASE, SON. I'M A PRIVATE CITIZEN NOW. I'M NOT HERE ON ANY-ONE'S NICKEL.
I'M NOT SALUTING THE RANK, SIR. IT'S WHAT YOU'VE EARNED.
Subway
Grand Central 42 Street Station
S 4 5 6 7
AND YOU DON'T LOOK LIKE YOU'RE ON VACATION.
AND WITH THE CRAZY STATE OF THE WORLD, IT'S NOT LIKE WE CAN SIT AND TALK IT OUT OVER A FROZEN LATTE.
YOU KIDS GET OFF THE ISLAND. DON'T COME BACK 'TIL THIS IS OVER.
WAIT! HOW ARE WE SUPPOSED TO FIGURE OUT WHAT'S UP WITH MY BROTHER?
IF I NEED TO FIND YOU, I'LL FIND YOU.
TRY NOT TO LET HER FALL OUT OF THE SKY ANY MORE, SON.
WHAT WAS I SUPPOSED TO DO...? I DIDN'T EVEN HAVE A LITTLE GUN.
MR. FURY: OFF TO GO AND FIGHT MORE ALIENS OR SAVE MORE PEOPLE.
(AND HE DOESN'T LOOK LIKE HE DRINKS ANYTHING BUT MOTOR OIL AND ROCKS, ANYWAY.)
WE'RE SORTA BACK WHERE WE WERE: ALONE, WITH NO IDEA WHY ANY OF THIS IS HAPPENING.
Grand Central 42 Street Static
S 4 5 6 7
AND I'VE GOT A FEELING WE'RE TRYING TO HIDE FROM THE BEAR...IN THE CAVE WHERE IT LIVES.

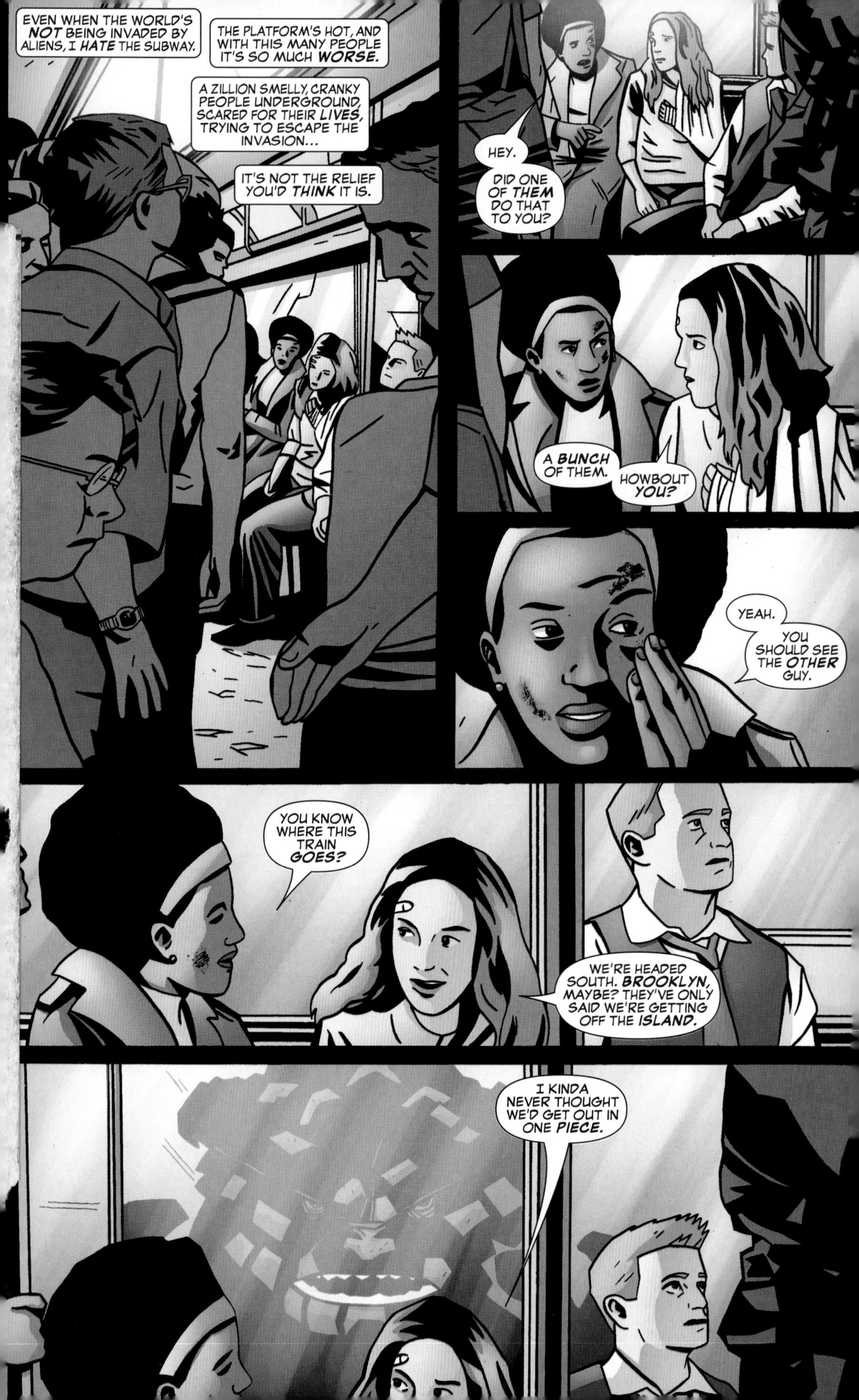
EVEN WHEN THE WORLD'S NOT BEING INVADED BY ALIENS, I HATE THE SUBWAY.
THE PLATFORM'S HOT, AND WITH THIS MANY PEOPLE IT'S SO MUCH WORSE.
A ZILLION SMELLY, CRANKY PEOPLE UNDERGROUND, SCARED FOR THEIR LIVES, TRYING TO ESCAPE THE INVASION...
IT'S NOT THE RELIEF YOU'D THINK IT IS.
HEY.
DID ONE OF THEM DO THAT TO YOU?
A BUNCH OF THEM.
HOWBOUT YOU?
YEAH.
YOU SHOULD SEE THE OTHER GUY.
YOU KNOW WHERE THIS TRAIN GOES?
WE'RE HEADED SOUTH. BROOKLYN, MAYBE? THEY'VE ONLY SAID WE'RE GETTING OFF THE ISLAND.
I KINDA NEVER THOUGHT WE'D GET OUT IN ONE PIECE.

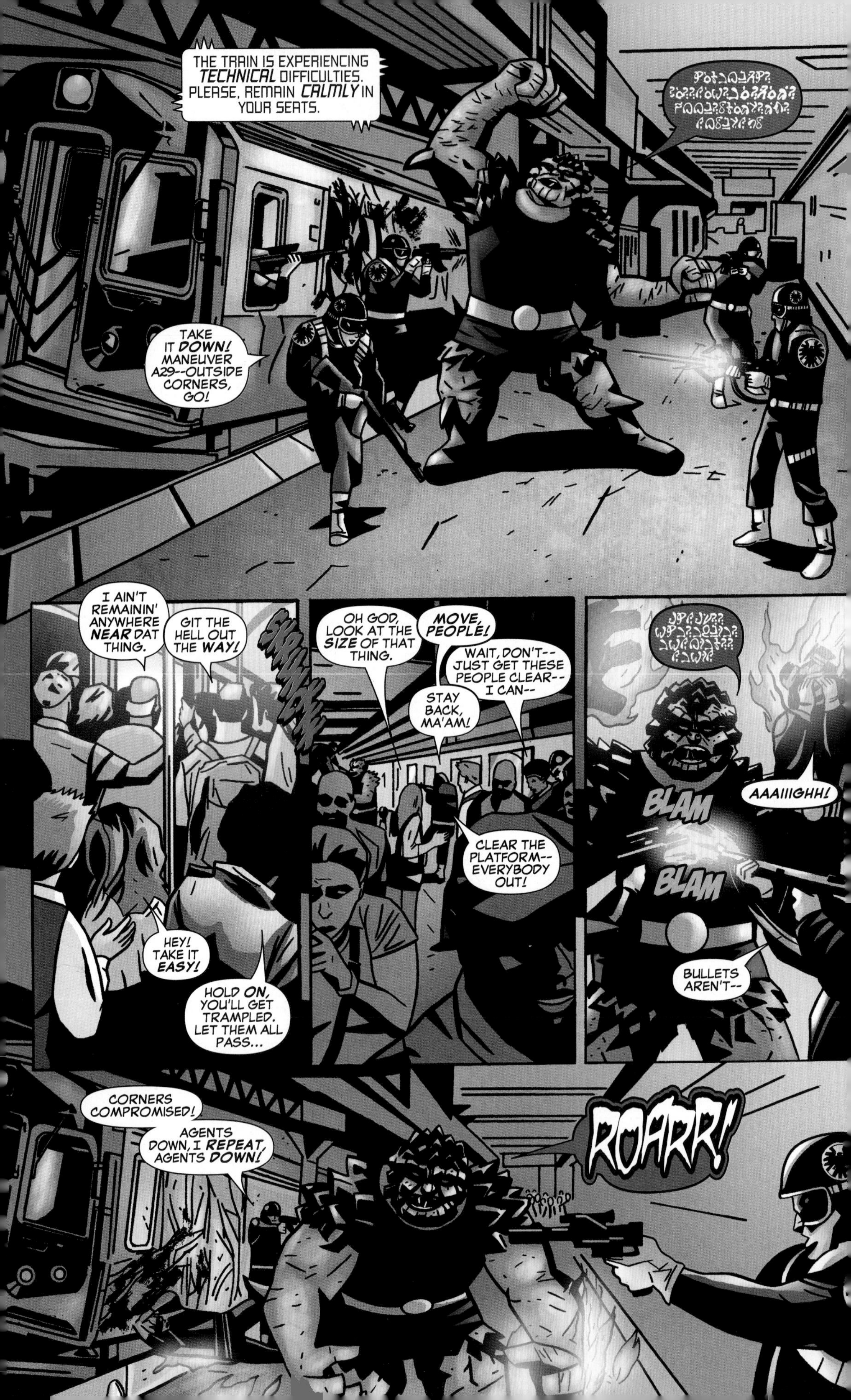

THE TRAIN IS EXPERIENCING TECHNICAL DIFFICULTIES. PLEASE, REMAIN CALMLY IN YOUR SEATS.
TAKE IT DOWN! MANEUVER A29--OUTSIDE CORNERS, GO!
I AIN'T REMAININ' ANYWHERE NEAR DAT THING.
GIT THE HELL OUT THE WAY!
SKRUNCH
HEY! TAKE IT EASY!
HOLD ON, YOU'LL GET TRAMPLED. LET THEM ALL PASS...
OH GOD, LOOK AT THE SIZE OF THAT THING.
MOVE, PEOPLE!
WAIT, DON'T-- JUST GET THESE PEOPLE CLEAR-- I CAN--
STAY BACK, MA'AM!
CLEAR THE PLATFORM-- EVERYBODY OUT!
AAAIIIGHH!
BLAM
BLAM
BULLETS AREN'T--
CORNERS COMPROMISED!
AGENTS DOWN, I REPEAT, AGENTS DOWN!
ROARR!

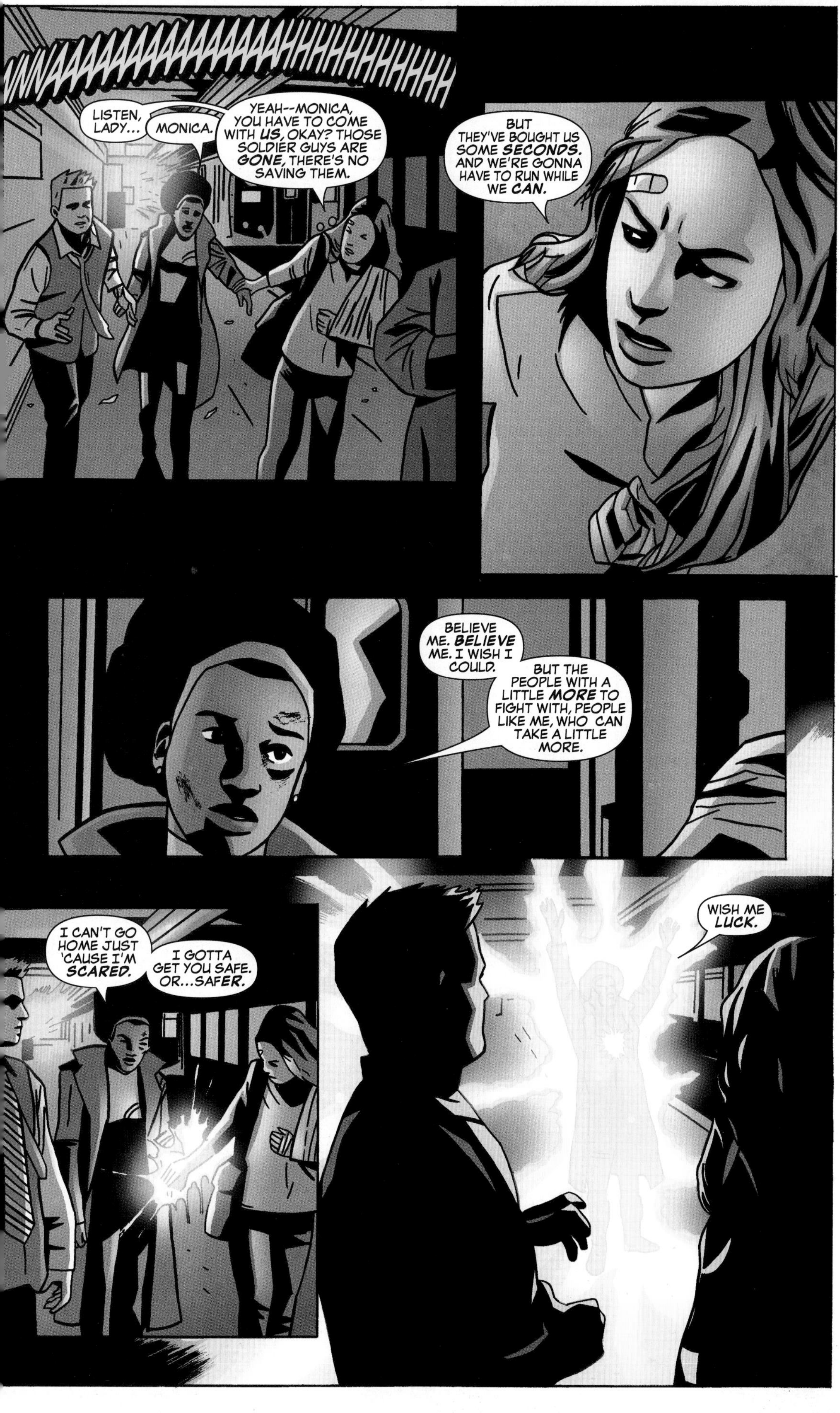
AAAAAAAAAAAAAAAAAAHHHHHHHHHH
LISTEN, LADY...
MONICA.
YEAH--MONICA, YOU HAVE TO COME WITH US, OKAY? THOSE SOLDIER GUYS ARE GONE, THERE'S NO SAVING THEM.
BUT THEY'VE BOUGHT US SOME SECONDS. AND WE'RE GONNA HAVE TO RUN WHILE WE CAN.
BELIEVE ME. BELIEVE ME. I WISH I COULD.
BUT THE PEOPLE WITH A LITTLE MORE TO FIGHT WITH, PEOPLE LIKE ME, WHO CAN TAKE A LITTLE MORE.
I CAN'T GO HOME JUST 'CAUSE I'M SCARED.
I GOTTA GET YOU SAFE. OR...SAFER.
WISH ME LUCK.

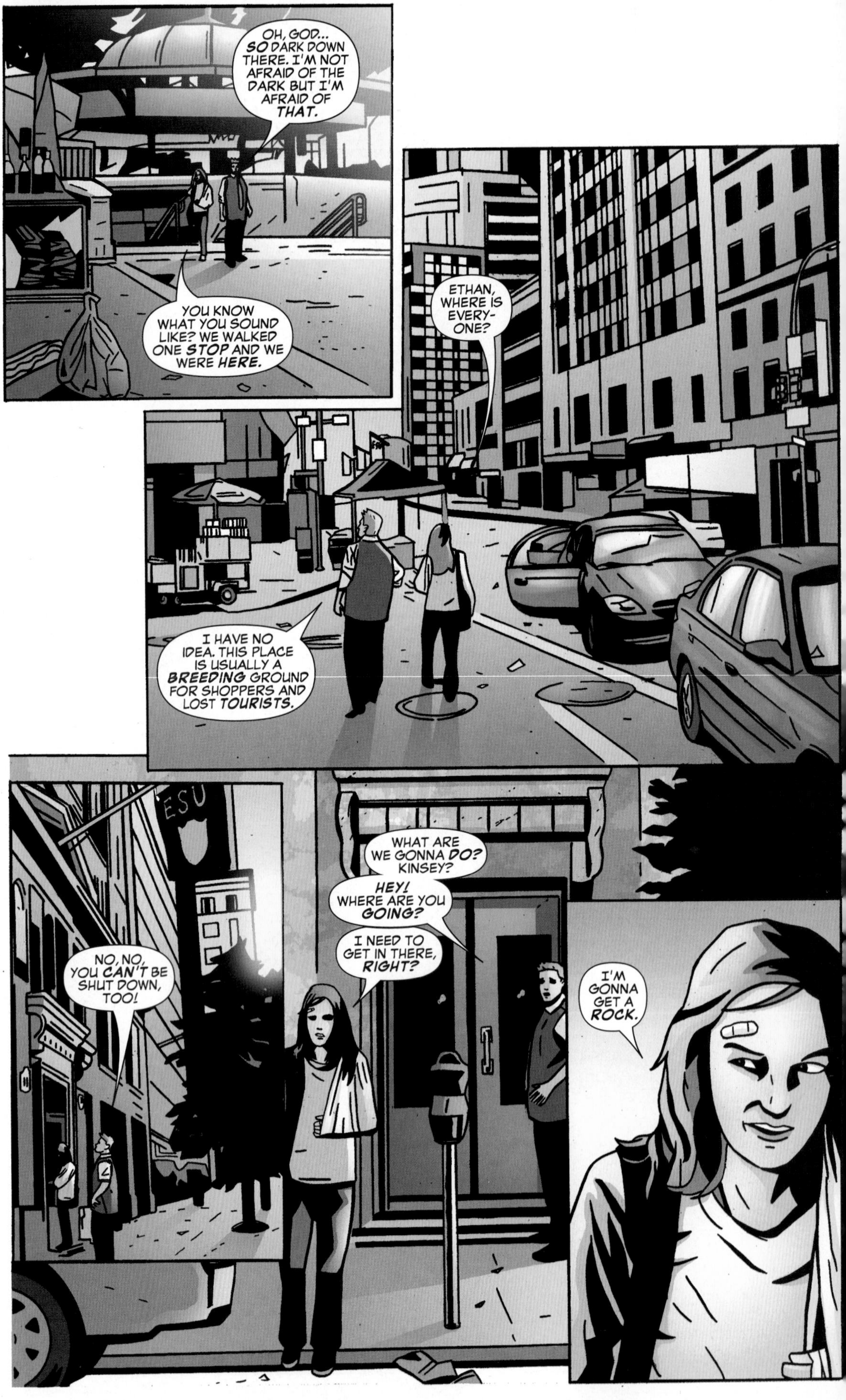
OH, GOD... SO DARK DOWN THERE. I'M NOT AFRAID OF THE DARK BUT I'M AFRAID OF THAT.
YOU KNOW WHAT YOU SOUND LIKE? WE WALKED ONE STOP AND WE WERE HERE.
ETHAN, WHERE IS EVERY-ONE?
I HAVE NO IDEA. THIS PLACE IS USUALLY A BREEDING GROUND FOR SHOPPERS AND LOST TOURISTS.
ESU
NO, NO, YOU CAN'T BE SHUT DOWN, TOO!
WHAT ARE WE GONNA DO? KINSEY?
HEY! WHERE ARE YOU GOING?
I NEED TO GET IN THERE, RIGHT?
I'M GONNA GET A ROCK.

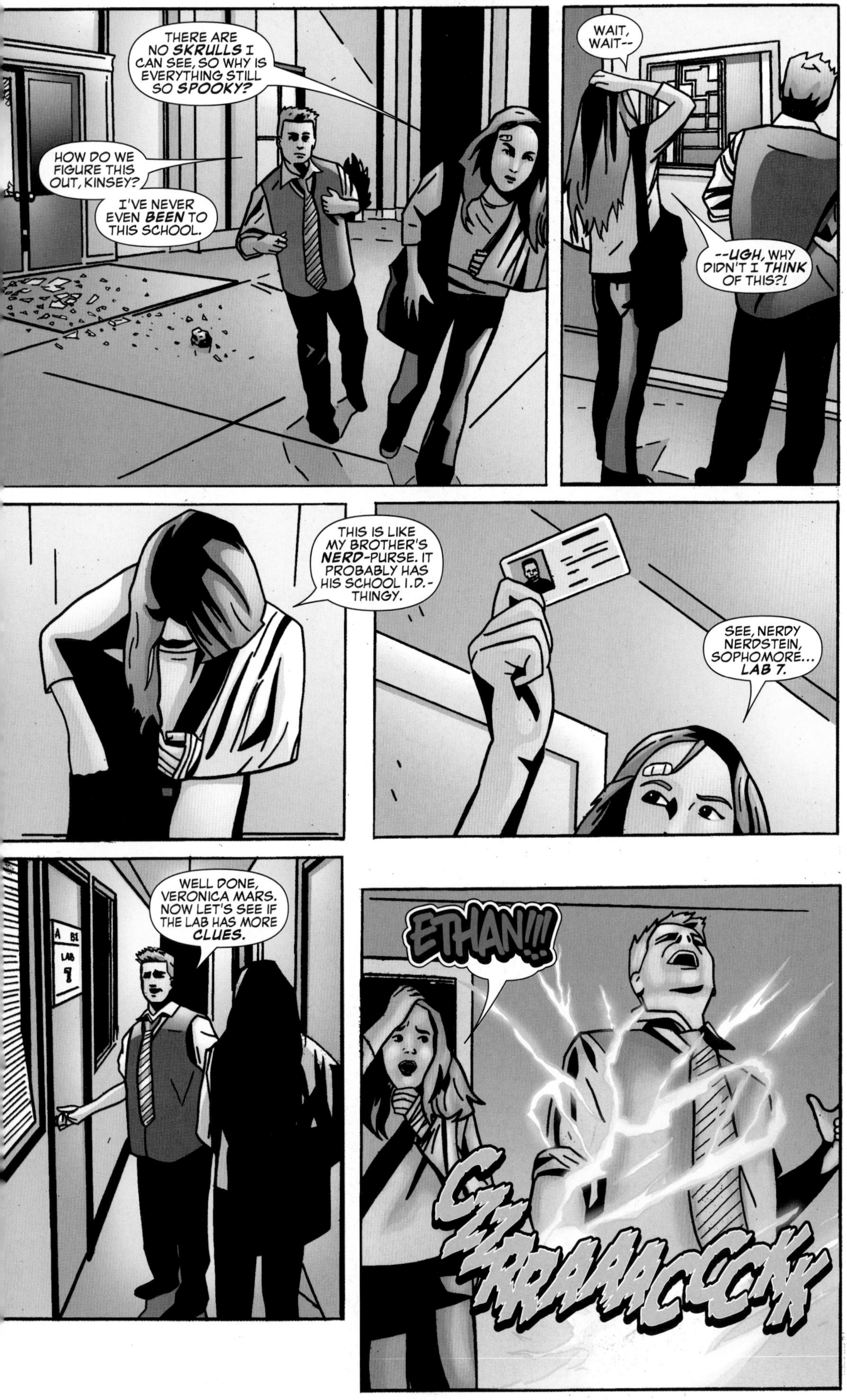
THERE ARE NO SKRULLS I CAN SEE, SO WHY IS EVERYTHING STILL SO SPOOKY?
HOW DO WE FIGURE THIS OUT, KINSEY?
I'VE NEVER EVEN BEEN TO THIS SCHOOL.
WAIT, WAIT--
--UGH, WHY DIDN'T I THINK OF THIS?!
THIS IS LIKE MY BROTHER'S NERD-PURSE. IT PROBABLY HAS HIS SCHOOL I.D.-THINGY.
SEE, NERDY NERDSTEIN, SOPHOMORE... LAB 7.
WELL DONE, VERONICA MARS. NOW LET'S SEE IF THE LAB HAS MORE CLUES.
ETHAN!!!
CZZRRAAAACCCK

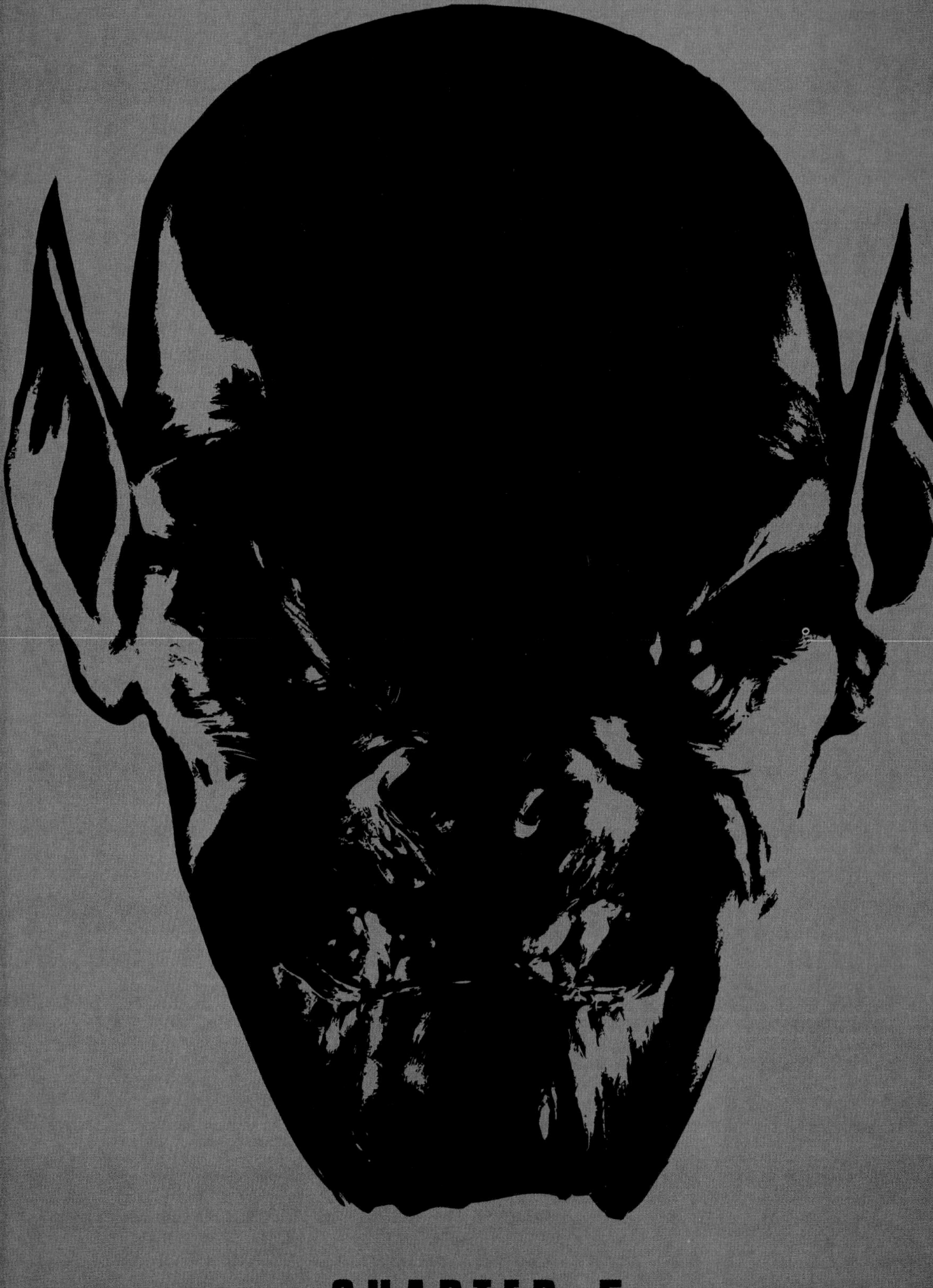

CHAPTER 5

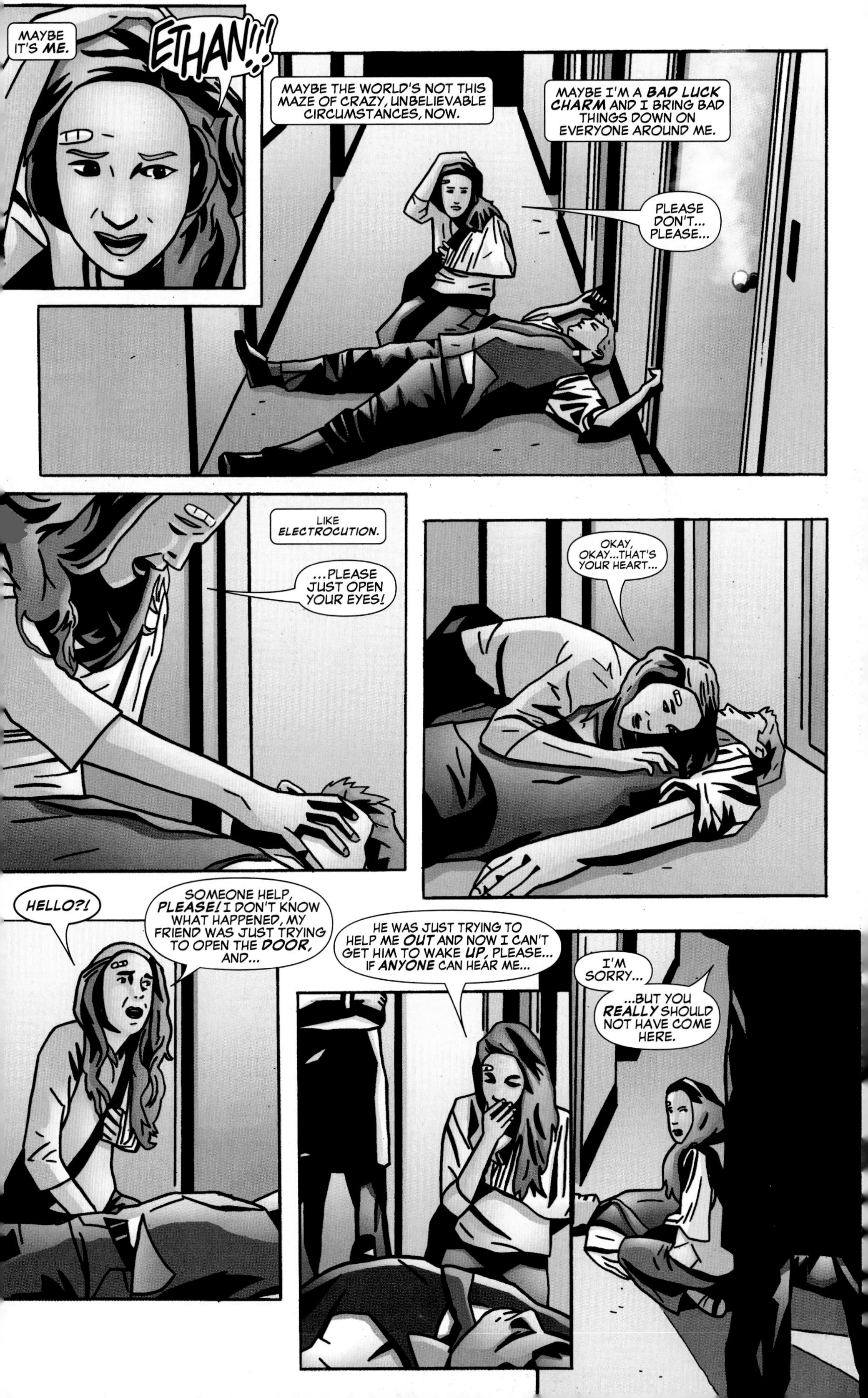
MAYBE IT'S ME.
ETHAN!!!
MAYBE THE WORLD'S NOT THIS MAZE OF CRAZY, UNBELIEVABLE CIRCUMSTANCES, NOW.
MAYBE I'M A BAD LUCK CHARM AND I BRING BAD THINGS DOWN ON EVERYONE AROUND ME.
PLEASE DON'T... PLEASE...
LIKE ELECTROCUTION.
...PLEASE JUST OPEN YOUR EYES!
OKAY, OKAY...THAT'S YOUR HEART...
HELLO?!
SOMEONE HELP, PLEASE! I DON'T KNOW WHAT HAPPENED, MY FRIEND WAS JUST TRYING TO OPEN THE DOOR, AND...
HE WAS JUST TRYING TO HELP ME OUT AND NOW I CAN'T GET HIM TO WAKE UP, PLEASE... IF ANYONE CAN HEAR ME...
I'M SORRY...
...BUT YOU REALLY SHOULD NOT HAVE COME HERE.

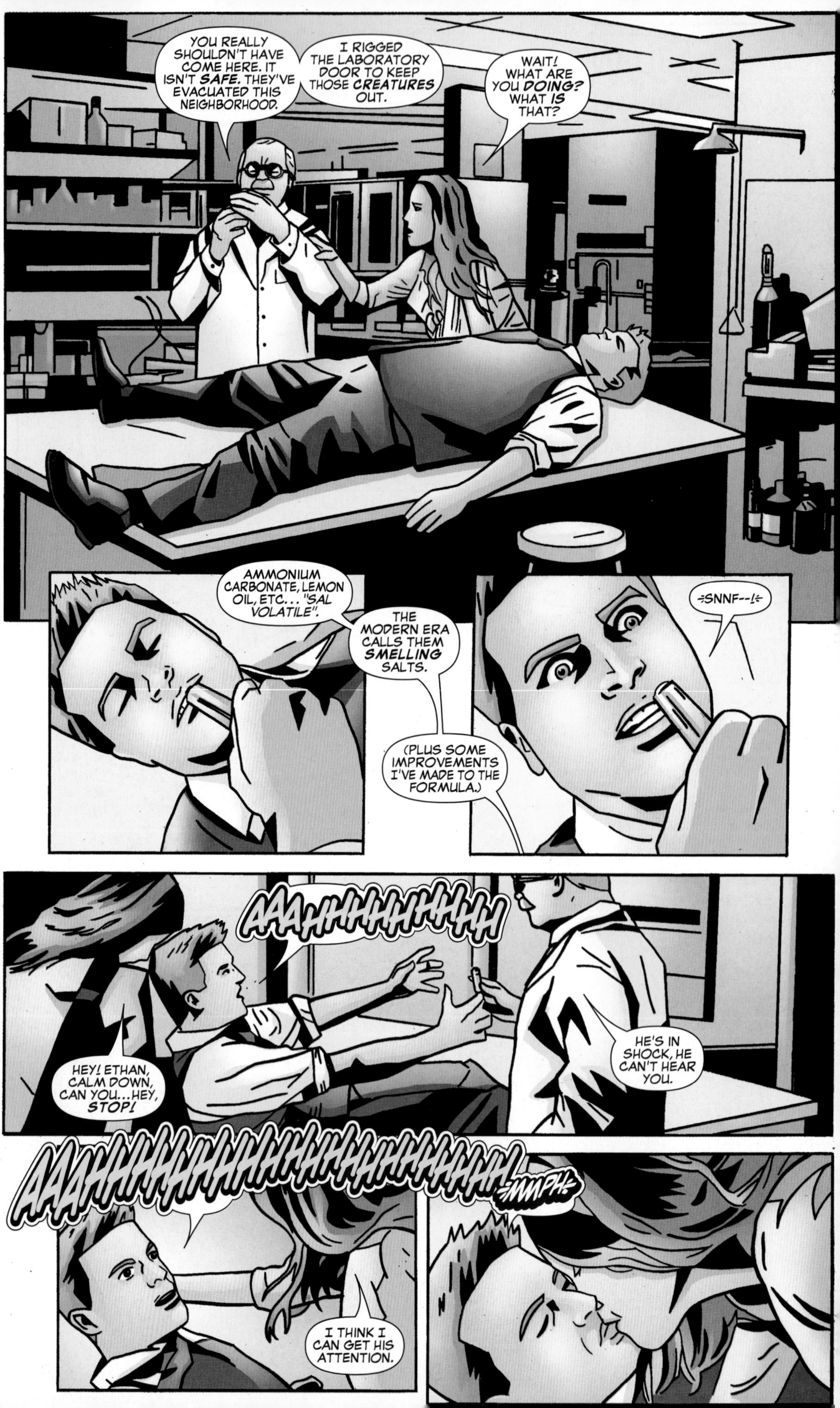
YOU REALLY SHOULDN'T HAVE COME HERE. IT ISN'T SAFE. THEY'VE EVACUATED THIS NEIGHBORHOOD.
I RIGGED THE LABORATORY DOOR TO KEEP THOSE CREATURES OUT.
WAIT! WHAT ARE YOU DOING? WHAT IS THAT?
AMMONIUM CARBONATE, LEMON OIL, ETC... "SAL VOLATILE".
THE MODERN ERA CALLS THEM SMELLING SALTS.
(PLUS SOME IMPROVEMENTS I'VE MADE TO THE FORMULA.)
SNNF--!
AAAHHHHHHHHHH
HEY! ETHAN, CALM DOWN, CAN YOU...HEY, STOP!
HE'S IN SHOCK, HE CAN'T HEAR YOU.
AAAHHHHHHHHHHHHHHHHHHHHHHHHHH-MMPH!
I THINK I CAN GET HIS ATTENTION.

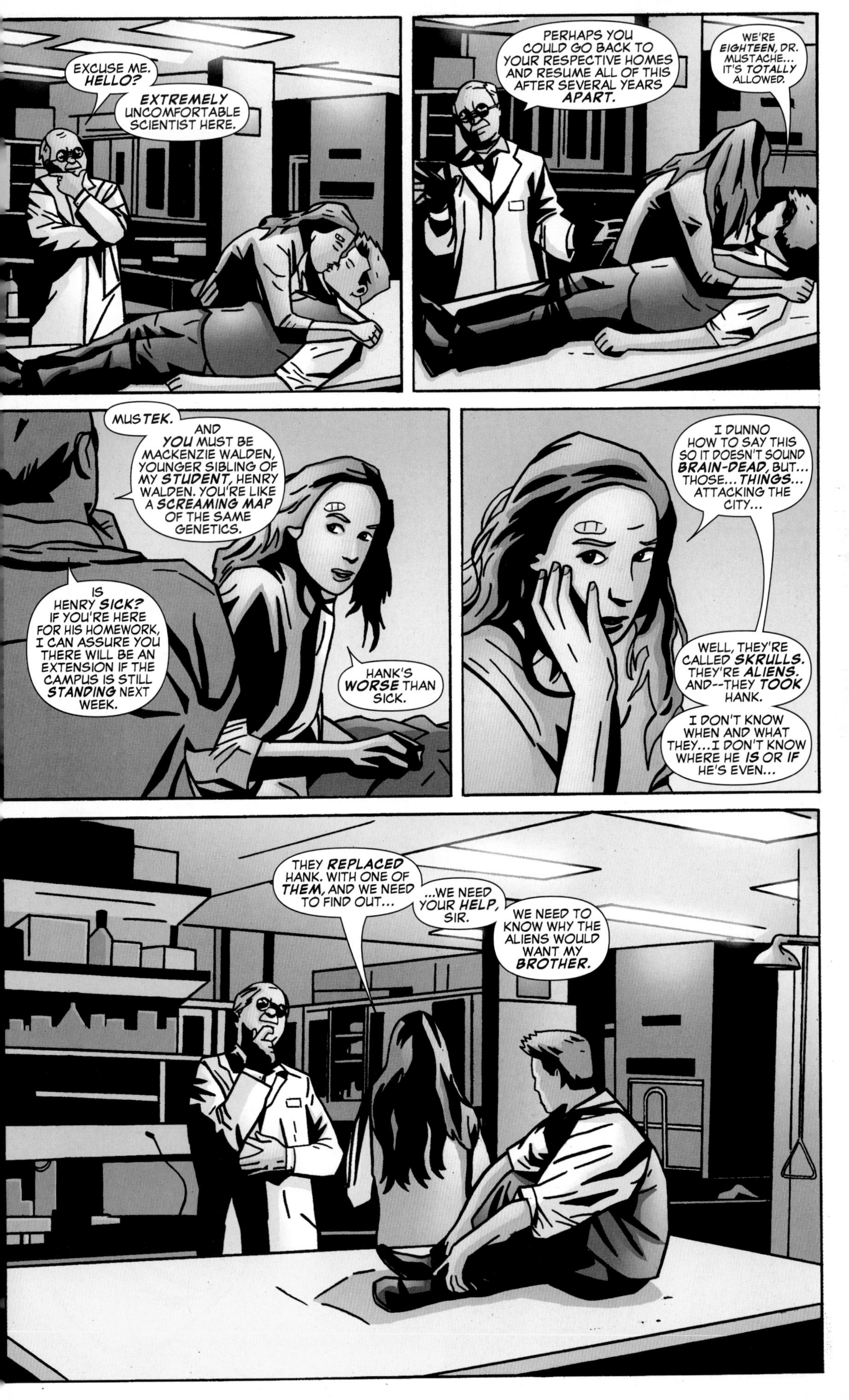
EXCUSE ME. HELLO?
EXTREMELY UNCOMFORTABLE SCIENTIST HERE.
PERHAPS YOU COULD GO BACK TO YOUR RESPECTIVE HOMES AND RESUME ALL OF THIS AFTER SEVERAL YEARS APART.
WE'RE EIGHTEEN, DR. MUSTACHE... IT'S TOTALLY ALLOWED.
MUSTEK.
AND YOU MUST BE MACKENZIE WALDEN, YOUNGER SIBLING OF MY STUDENT, HENRY WALDEN. YOU'RE LIKE A SCREAMING MAP OF THE SAME GENETICS.
IS HENRY SICK? IF YOU'RE HERE FOR HIS HOMEWORK, I CAN ASSURE YOU THERE WILL BE AN EXTENSION IF THE CAMPUS IS STILL STANDING NEXT WEEK.
HANK'S WORSE THAN SICK.
I DUNNO HOW TO SAY THIS SO IT DOESN'T SOUND BRAIN-DEAD, BUT... THOSE... THINGS... ATTACKING THE CITY...
WELL, THEY'RE CALLED SKRULLS. THEY'RE ALIENS. AND--THEY TOOK HANK.
I DON'T KNOW WHEN AND WHAT THEY... I DON'T KNOW WHERE HE IS OR IF HE'S EVEN...
THEY REPLACED HANK. WITH ONE OF THEM, AND WE NEED TO FIND OUT...
...WE NEED YOUR HELP, SIR.
WE NEED TO KNOW WHY THE ALIENS WOULD WANT MY BROTHER.

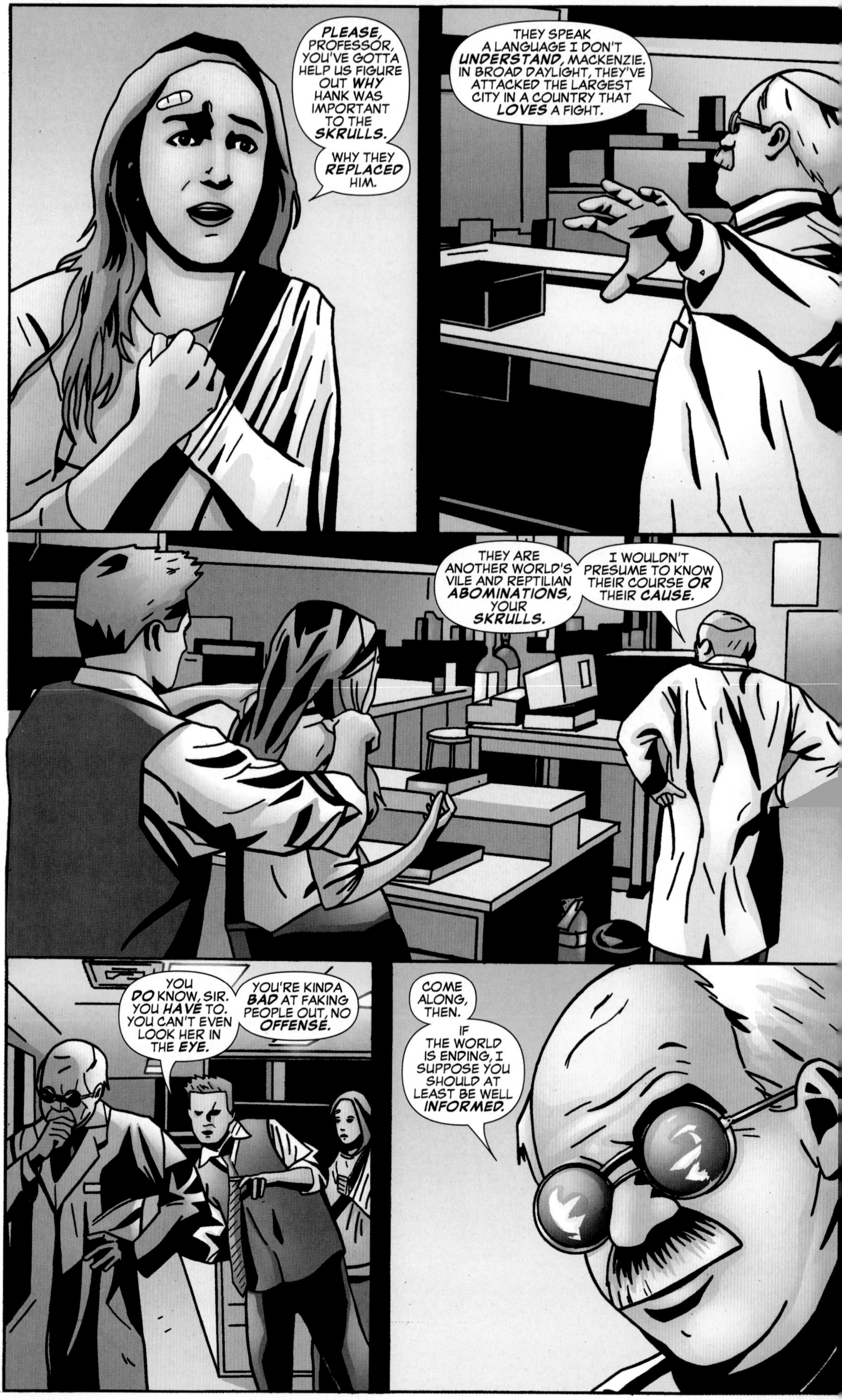
PLEASE, PROFESSOR, YOU'VE GOTTA HELP US FIGURE OUT WHY HANK WAS IMPORTANT TO THE SKRULLS.
WHY THEY REPLACED HIM.
THEY SPEAK A LANGUAGE I DON'T UNDERSTAND, MACKENZIE. IN BROAD DAYLIGHT, THEY'VE ATTACKED THE LARGEST CITY IN A COUNTRY THAT LOVES A FIGHT.
THEY ARE ANOTHER WORLD'S VILE AND REPTILIAN ABOMINATIONS, YOUR SKRULLS.
I WOULDN'T PRESUME TO KNOW THEIR COURSE OR THEIR CAUSE.
YOU DO KNOW, SIR. YOU HAVE TO. YOU CAN'T EVEN LOOK HER IN THE EYE.
YOU'RE KINDA BAD AT FAKING PEOPLE OUT, NO OFFENSE.
COME ALONG, THEN.
IF THE WORLD IS ENDING, I SUPPOSE YOU SHOULD AT LEAST BE WELL INFORMED.

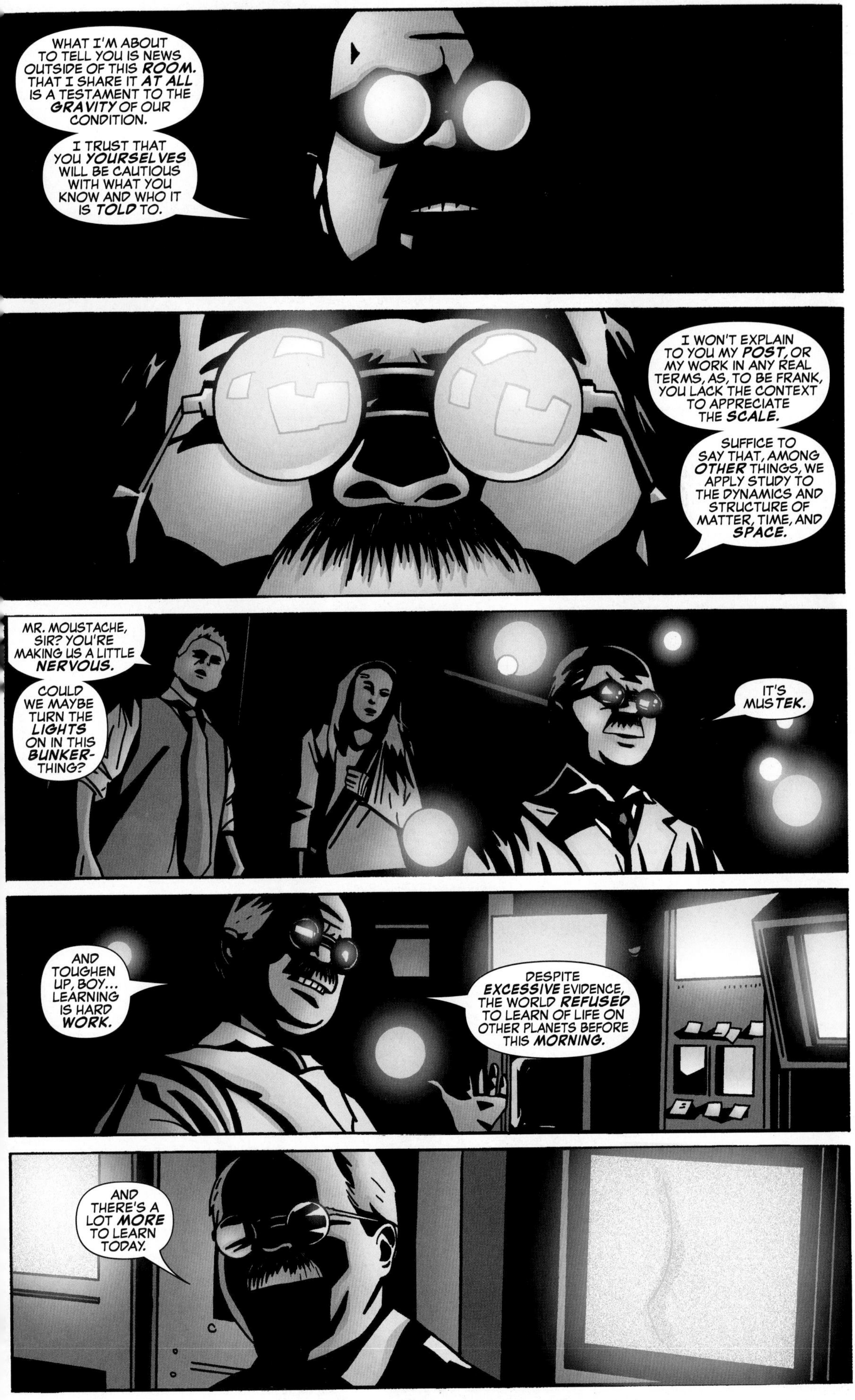
WHAT I'M ABOUT TO TELL YOU IS NEWS OUTSIDE OF THIS ROOM. THAT I SHARE IT AT ALL IS A TESTAMENT TO THE GRAVITY OF OUR CONDITION.
I TRUST THAT YOU YOURSELVES WILL BE CAUTIOUS WITH WHAT YOU KNOW AND WHO IT IS TOLD TO.
I WON'T EXPLAIN TO YOU MY POST, OR MY WORK IN ANY REAL TERMS, AS, TO BE FRANK, YOU LACK THE CONTEXT TO APPRECIATE THE SCALE.
SUFFICE TO SAY THAT, AMONG OTHER THINGS, WE APPLY STUDY TO THE DYNAMICS AND STRUCTURE OF MATTER, TIME, AND SPACE.
MR. MOUSTACHE, SIR? YOU'RE MAKING US A LITTLE NERVOUS.
COULD WE MAYBE TURN THE LIGHTS ON IN THIS BUNKER-THING?
IT'S MUSTEK.
AND TOUGHEN UP, BOY... LEARNING IS HARD WORK.
DESPITE EXCESSIVE EVIDENCE, THE WORLD REFUSED TO LEARN OF LIFE ON OTHER PLANETS BEFORE THIS MORNING.
AND THERE'S A LOT MORE TO LEARN TODAY.

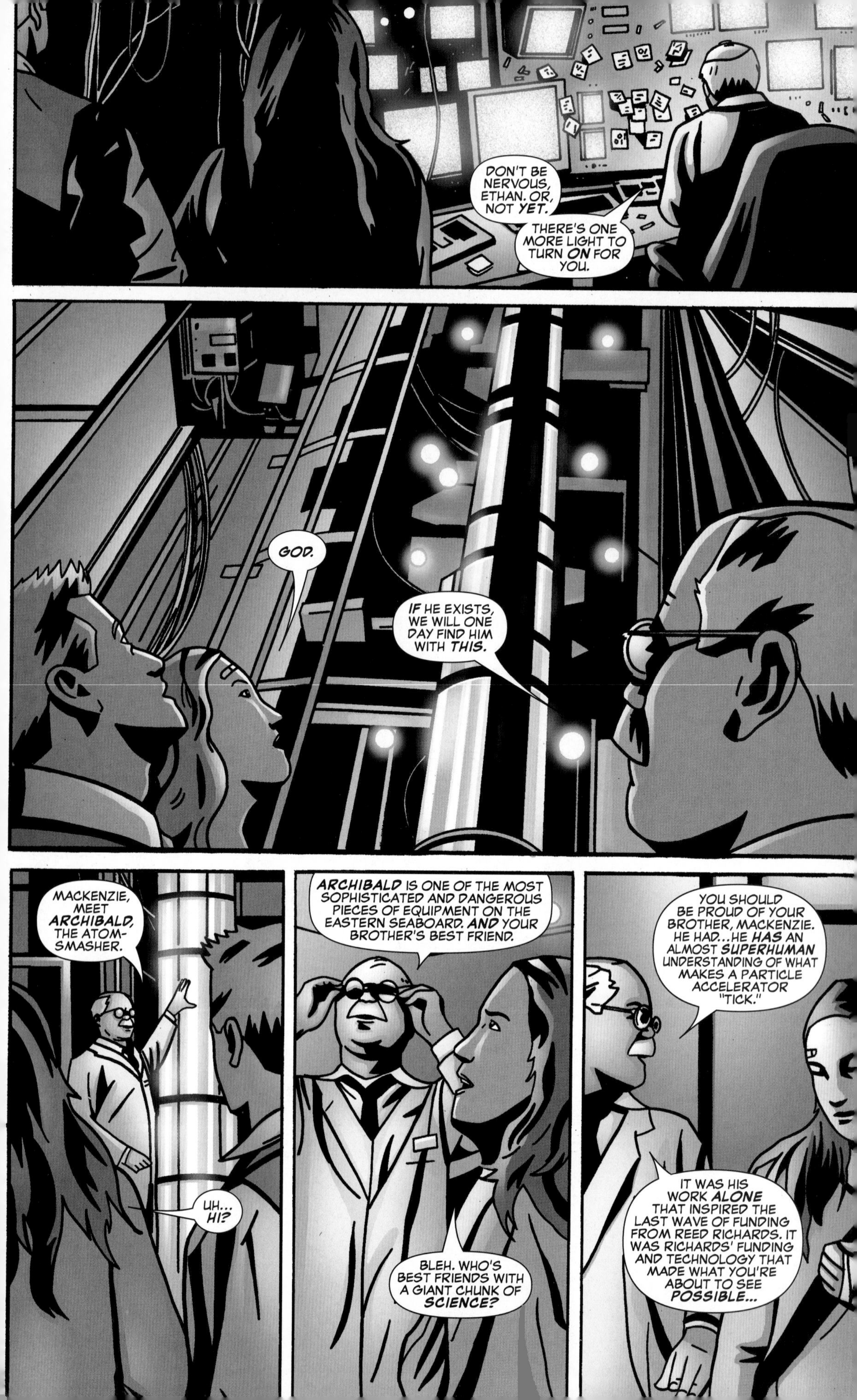

DON'T BE NERVOUS, ETHAN. OR, NOT YET.
THERE'S ONE MORE LIGHT TO TURN ON FOR YOU.
GOD.
IF HE EXISTS, WE WILL ONE DAY FIND HIM WITH THIS.
MACKENZIE, MEET ARCHIBALD, THE ATOM-SMASHER.
UH... HI?
ARCHIBALD IS ONE OF THE MOST SOPHISTICATED AND DANGEROUS PIECES OF EQUIPMENT ON THE EASTERN SEABOARD. AND YOUR BROTHER'S BEST FRIEND.
BLEH. WHO'S BEST FRIENDS WITH A GIANT CHUNK OF SCIENCE?
YOU SHOULD BE PROUD OF YOUR BROTHER, MACKENZIE. HE HAD...HE HAS AN ALMOST SUPERHUMAN UNDERSTANDING OF WHAT MAKES A PARTICLE ACCELERATOR "TICK."
IT WAS HIS WORK ALONE THAT INSPIRED THE LAST WAVE OF FUNDING FROM REED RICHARDS. IT WAS RICHARDS' FUNDING AND TECHNOLOGY THAT MADE WHAT YOU'RE ABOUT TO SEE POSSIBLE...

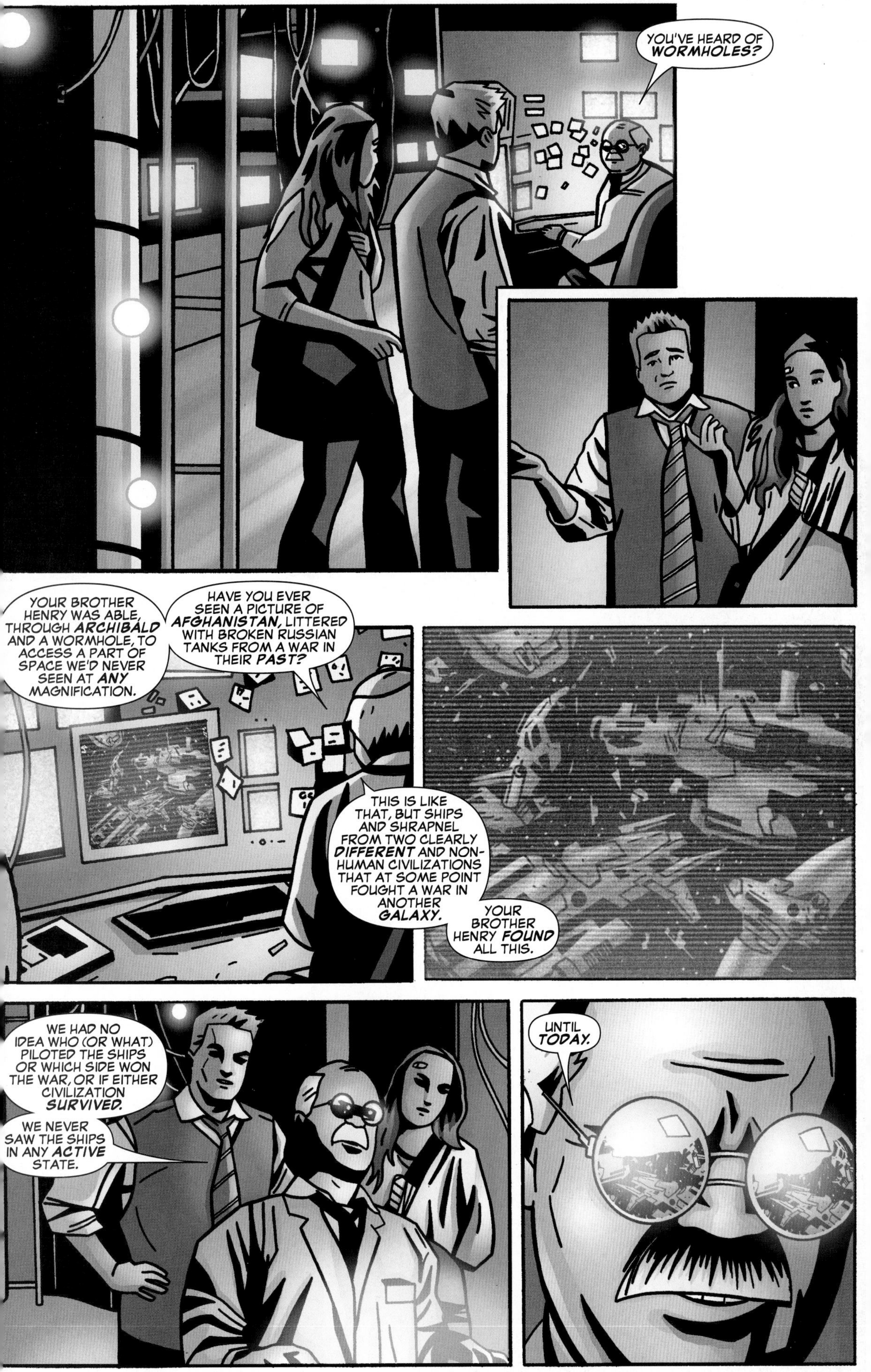
YOU'VE HEARD OF WORMHOLES?
YOUR BROTHER HENRY WAS ABLE, THROUGH ARCHIBALD AND A WORMHOLE, TO ACCESS A PART OF SPACE WE'D NEVER SEEN AT ANY MAGNIFICATION.
HAVE YOU EVER SEEN A PICTURE OF AFGHANISTAN, LITTERED WITH BROKEN RUSSIAN TANKS FROM A WAR IN THEIR PAST?
THIS IS LIKE THAT, BUT SHIPS AND SHRAPNEL FROM TWO CLEARLY DIFFERENT AND NON-HUMAN CIVILIZATIONS THAT AT SOME POINT FOUGHT A WAR IN ANOTHER GALAXY.
YOUR BROTHER HENRY FOUND ALL THIS.
WE HAD NO IDEA WHO (OR WHAT) PILOTED THE SHIPS OR WHICH SIDE WON THE WAR, OR IF EITHER CIVILIZATION SURVIVED.
WE NEVER SAW THE SHIPS IN ANY ACTIVE STATE.
UNTIL TODAY.

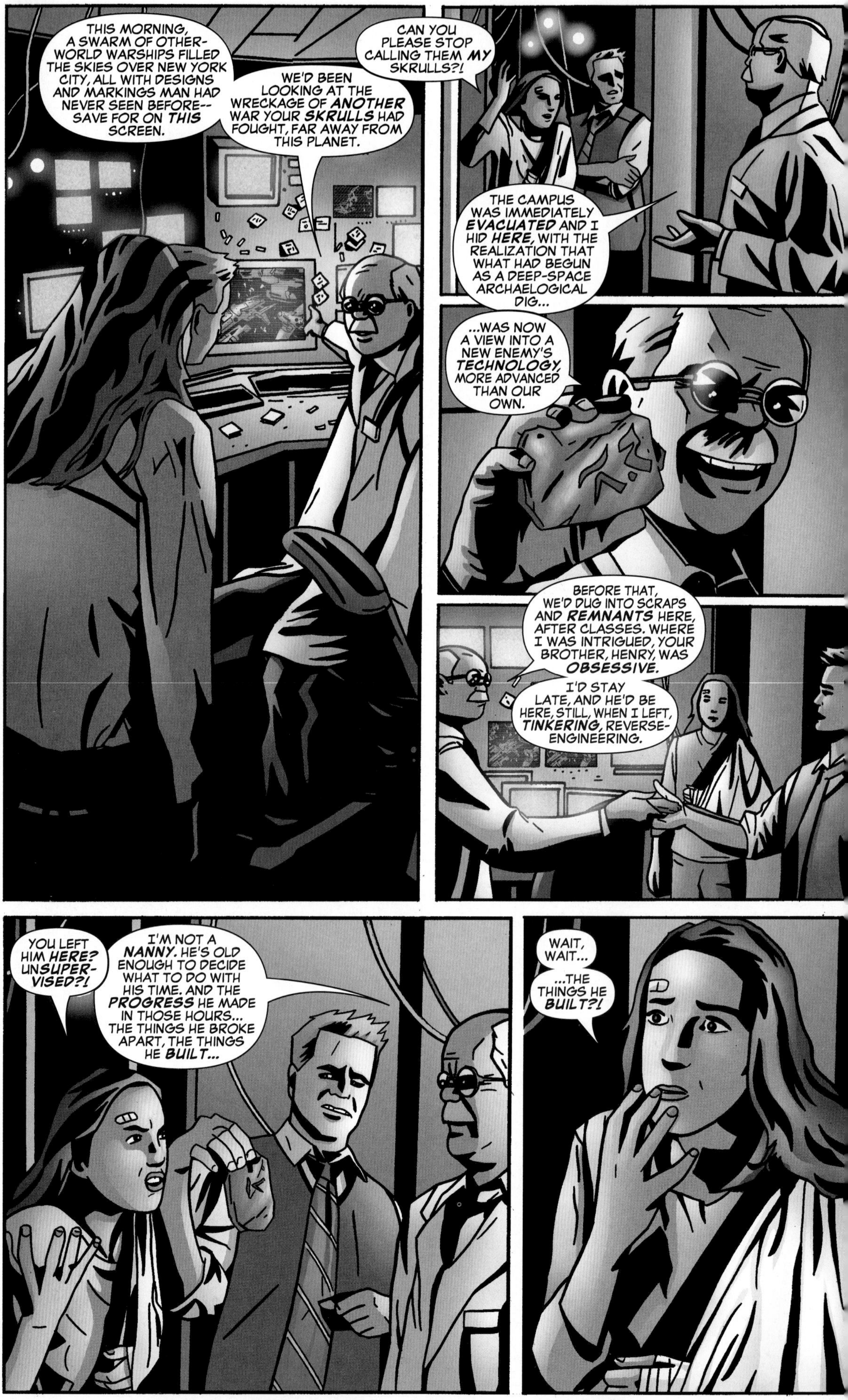

THIS MORNING, A SWARM OF OTHER-WORLD WARSHIPS FILLED THE SKIES OVER NEW YORK CITY, ALL WITH DESIGNS AND MARKINGS MAN HAD NEVER SEEN BEFORE-- SAVE FOR ON THIS SCREEN.
WE'D BEEN LOOKING AT THE WRECKAGE OF ANOTHER WAR YOUR SKRULLS HAD FOUGHT, FAR AWAY FROM THIS PLANET.
CAN YOU PLEASE STOP CALLING THEM MY SKRULLS?!
THE CAMPUS WAS IMMEDIATELY EVACUATED AND I HID HERE, WITH THE REALIZATION THAT WHAT HAD BEGUN AS A DEEP-SPACE ARCHAELOGICAL DIG...
...WAS NOW A VIEW INTO A NEW ENEMY'S TECHNOLOGY, MORE ADVANCED THAN OUR OWN.
BEFORE THAT, WE'D DUG INTO SCRAPS AND REMNANTS HERE, AFTER CLASSES. WHERE I WAS INTRIGUED, YOUR BROTHER, HENRY, WAS OBSESSIVE.
I'D STAY LATE, AND HE'D BE HERE, STILL, WHEN I LEFT, TINKERING, REVERSE-ENGINEERING.
YOU LEFT HIM HERE? UNSUPERVISED?!
I'M NOT A NANNY. HE'S OLD ENOUGH TO DECIDE WHAT TO DO WITH HIS TIME. AND THE PROGRESS HE MADE IN THOSE HOURS... THE THINGS HE BROKE APART, THE THINGS HE BUILT...
WAIT, WAIT...
...THE THINGS HE BUILT?!

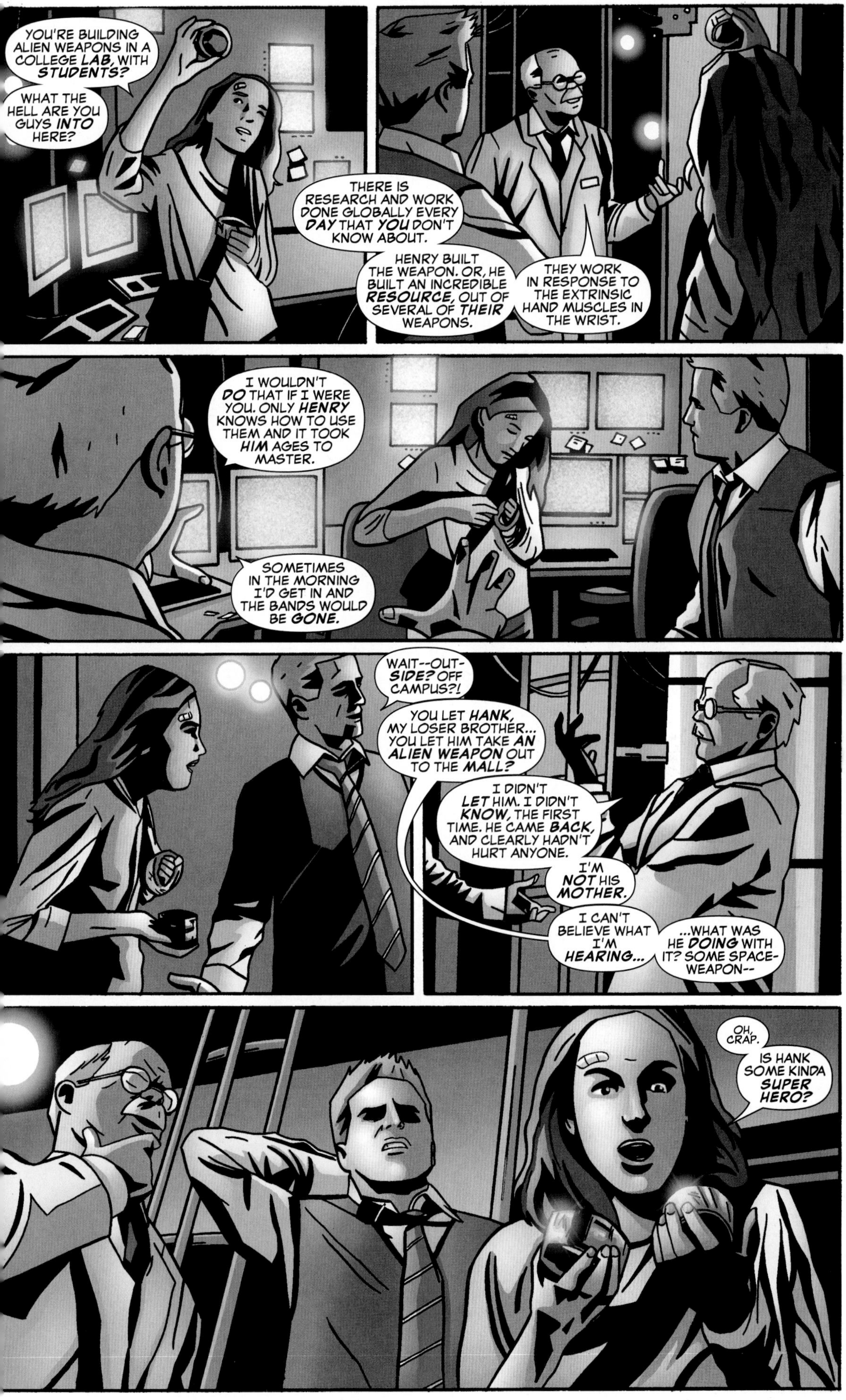

YOU'RE BUILDING ALIEN WEAPONS IN A COLLEGE LAB, WITH STUDENTS?
WHAT THE HELL ARE YOU GUYS INTO HERE?
THERE IS RESEARCH AND WORK DONE GLOBALLY EVERY DAY THAT YOU DON'T KNOW ABOUT.
HENRY BUILT THE WEAPON. OR, HE BUILT AN INCREDIBLE RESOURCE, OUT OF SEVERAL OF THEIR WEAPONS.
THEY WORK IN RESPONSE TO THE EXTRINSIC HAND MUSCLES IN THE WRIST.
I WOULDN'T DO THAT IF I WERE YOU. ONLY HENRY KNOWS HOW TO USE THEM AND IT TOOK HIM AGES TO MASTER.
SOMETIMES IN THE MORNING I'D GET IN AND THE BANDS WOULD BE GONE.
WAIT--OUT-SIDE? OFF CAMPUS?!
YOU LET HANK, MY LOSER BROTHER... YOU LET HIM TAKE AN ALIEN WEAPON OUT TO THE MALL?
I DIDN'T LET HIM. I DIDN'T KNOW, THE FIRST TIME. HE CAME BACK, AND CLEARLY HADN'T HURT ANYONE.
I'M NOT HIS MOTHER.
I CAN'T BELIEVE WHAT I'M HEARING...
...WHAT WAS HE DOING WITH IT? SOME SPACE-WEAPON--
OH, CRAP.
IS HANK SOME KINDA SUPER HERO?

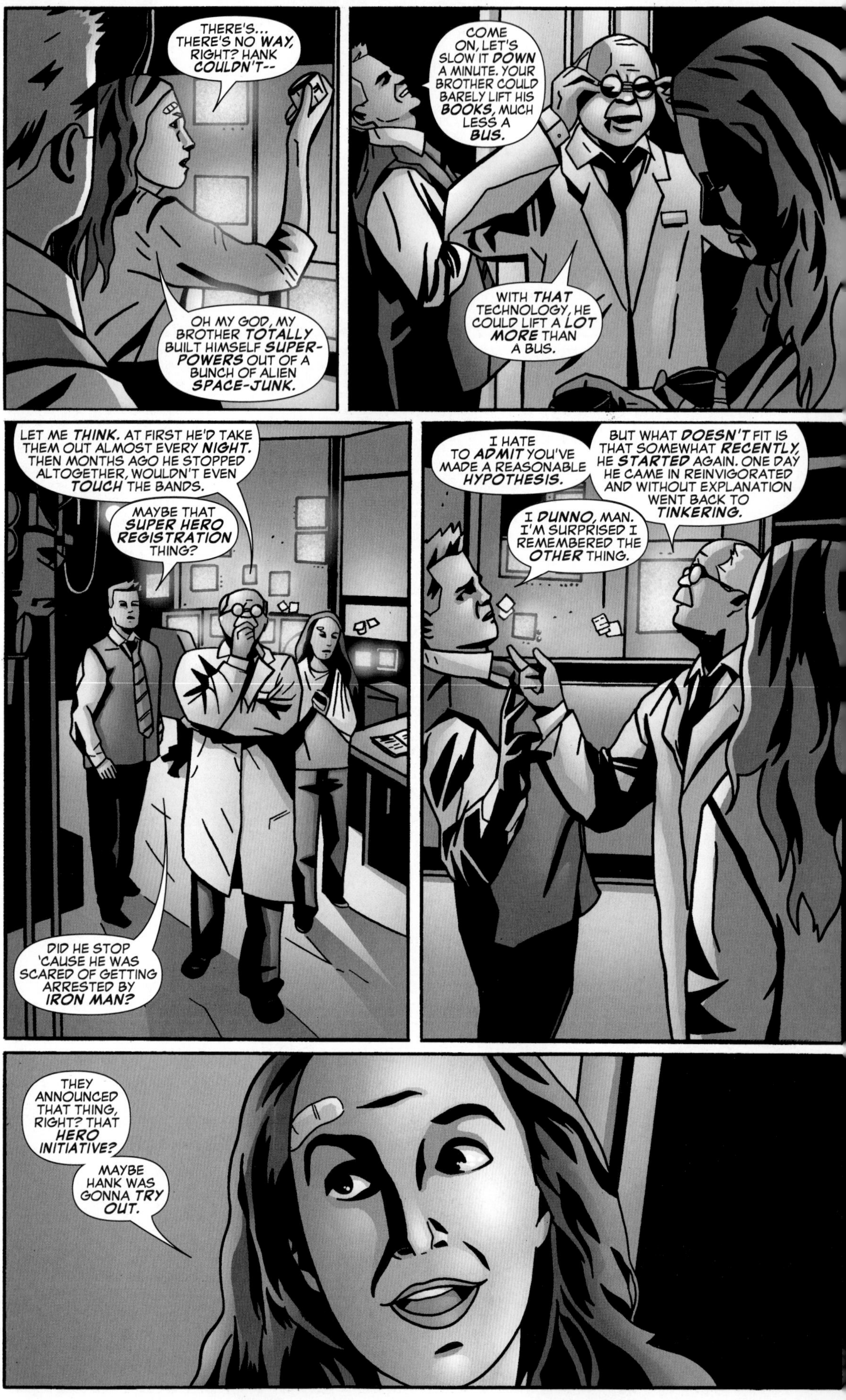
THERE'S... THERE'S NO WAY, RIGHT? HANK COULDN'T--
OH MY GOD, MY BROTHER TOTALLY BUILT HIMSELF SUPER-POWERS OUT OF A BUNCH OF ALIEN SPACE-JUNK.
COME ON, LET'S SLOW IT DOWN A MINUTE. YOUR BROTHER COULD BARELY LIFT HIS BOOKS, MUCH LESS A BUS.
WITH THAT TECHNOLOGY, HE COULD LIFT A LOT MORE THAN A BUS.
LET ME THINK. AT FIRST HE'D TAKE THEM OUT ALMOST EVERY NIGHT. THEN MONTHS AGO HE STOPPED ALTOGETHER, WOULDN'T EVEN TOUCH THE BANDS.
MAYBE THAT SUPER HERO REGISTRATION THING?
DID HE STOP 'CAUSE HE WAS SCARED OF GETTING ARRESTED BY IRON MAN?
I HATE TO ADMIT YOU'VE MADE A REASONABLE HYPOTHESIS.
BUT WHAT DOESN'T FIT IS THAT SOMEWHAT RECENTLY, HE STARTED AGAIN. ONE DAY HE CAME IN REINVIGORATED AND WITHOUT EXPLANATION WENT BACK TO TINKERING.
I DUNNO, MAN. I'M SURPRISED I REMEMBERED THE OTHER THING.
THEY ANNOUNCED THAT THING, RIGHT? THAT HERO INITIATIVE?
MAYBE HANK WAS GONNA TRY OUT.

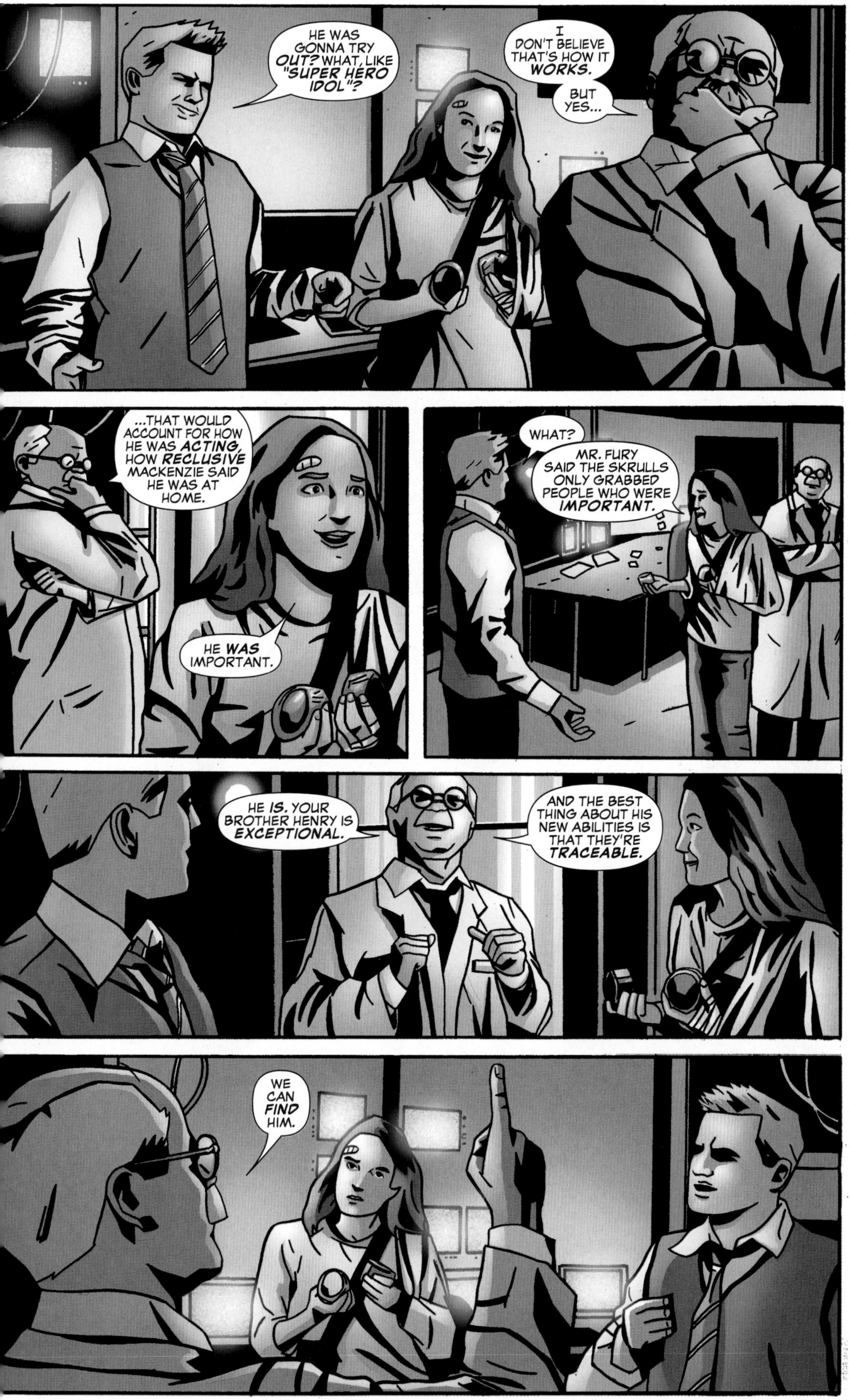
HE WAS GONNA TRY OUT? WHAT, LIKE "SUPER HERO IDOL"?
I DON'T BELIEVE THAT'S HOW IT WORKS.
BUT YES...
...THAT WOULD ACCOUNT FOR HOW HE WAS ACTING, HOW RECLUSIVE MACKENZIE SAID HE WAS AT HOME.
HE WAS IMPORTANT.
WHAT?
MR. FURY SAID THE SKRULLS ONLY GRABBED PEOPLE WHO WERE IMPORTANT.
HE IS. YOUR BROTHER HENRY IS EXCEPTIONAL.
AND THE BEST THING ABOUT HIS NEW ABILITIES IS THAT THEY'RE TRACEABLE.
WE CAN FIND HIM.

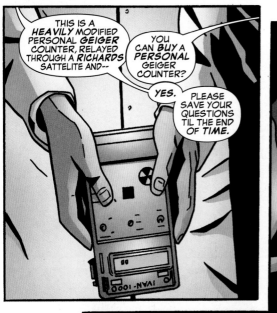

THIS IS A *HEAVILY* MODIFIED PERSONAL *GEIGER* COUNTER, RELAYED THROUGH A *RICHARDS* SATELLITE AND--

YOU CAN *BUY* A *PERSONAL* GEIGER COUNTER?

YES.

PLEASE SAVE YOUR QUESTIONS TIL THE END OF *TIME.*

THE ALIEN TECHNOLOGY EMITS A SORT OF *RADIATION* WHEN USED. NON-TOXIC TO *HUMANS,* BUT IT LEAVES A *RESIDUE,* LIKE A HANDGUN WOULD LEAVE TRACES OF *POWDER.*

HENRY USED TO SET IT *OFF,* WHEN WE WERE LOOKING FOR DEBRIS.

IF HE'S WITHIN THE *CITY LIMITS,* THIS DEVICE WILL SHOW HIS GENERAL *WHEREABOUTS.*

IT WON'T BE *EASY.* YOU'VE GOT A FLEET OF *SKRULL* VEHICLES EMITTING *SIMILAR* TRACES OVER MIDTOWN.

BUT HANK'S SIGNAL IS *UNIQUE.* THE TECH HE'S USING IS ALSO DERIVED FROM THAT *OTHER* ALIEN RACE. FIND *THIS* SIGNATURE, YOU FIND YOUR *BROTHER.*

DR. MUSTEK, *PLEASE...JUST* TELL ME HOW TO *USE* THE THING.

EXIT

THIS IS JUST LIKE "ALIENS." GAME OVER, MAN!

WHIIIIIIRRRRRRRRRR CLICK

EXIT

WHA--

EXIT

DR. MUSTEK, *PLEASE! ENOUGH* WITH THE DRAMATIC LIGHTING!

I'M *SORRY,* CHILDREN...

BUT I'M AFRAID *SOMETHING ELSE* HAS CUT THE POWER.

BEEP BEEP BEEP BEEP

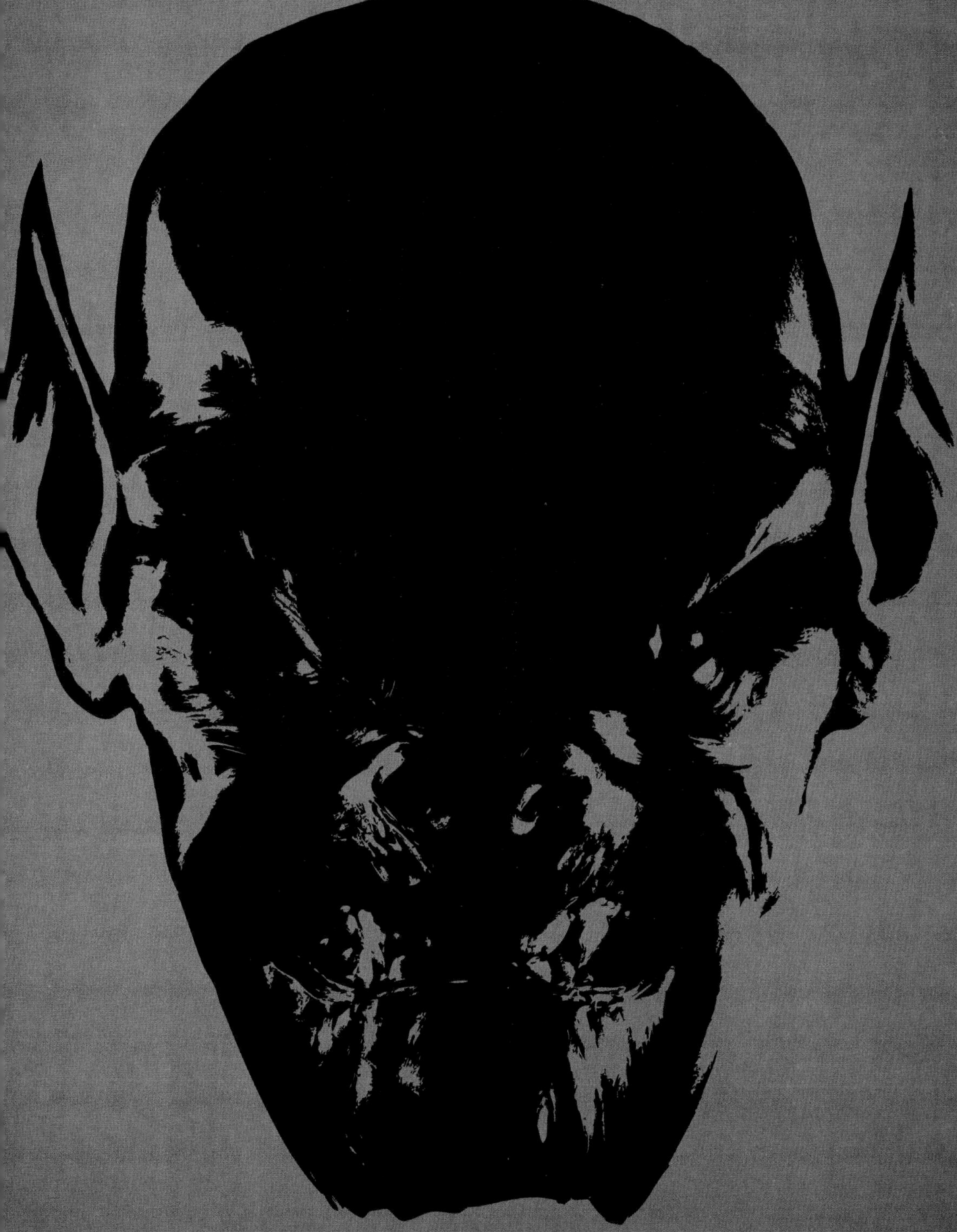

CHAPTER 6

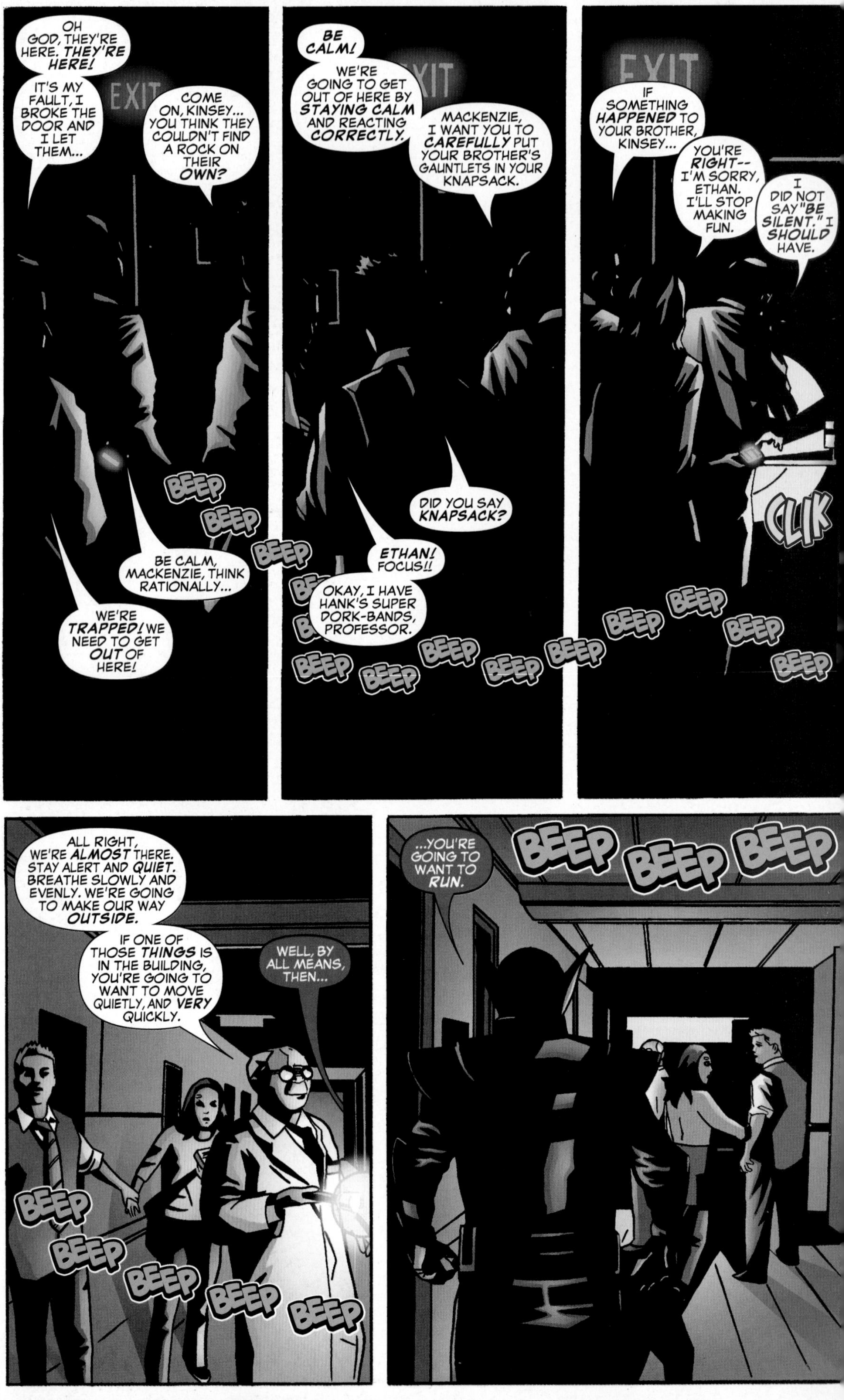
OH GOD, THEY'RE HERE. THEY'RE HERE!
IT'S MY FAULT, I BROKE THE DOOR AND I LET THEM...
EXIT
COME ON, KINSEY... YOU THINK THEY COULDN'T FIND A ROCK ON THEIR OWN?
BEEP
BEEP
BE CALM, MACKENZIE, THINK RATIONALLY...
WE'RE TRAPPED! WE NEED TO GET OUT OF HERE!
BE CALM!
WE'RE GOING TO GET OUT OF HERE BY STAYING CALM AND REACTING CORRECTLY.
EXIT
MACKENZIE, I WANT YOU TO CAREFULLY PUT YOUR BROTHER'S GAUNTLETS IN YOUR KNAPSACK.
DID YOU SAY KNAPSACK?
ETHAN! FOCUS!!
OKAY, I HAVE HANK'S SUPER DORK-BANDS, PROFESSOR.
BEEP
BEEP
BEEP
EXIT
IF SOMETHING HAPPENED TO YOUR BROTHER, KINSEY...
YOU'RE RIGHT-- I'M SORRY, ETHAN. I'LL STOP MAKING FUN.
I DID NOT SAY "BE SILENT." I SHOULD HAVE.
CLIK
BEEP
BEEP
BEEP
BEEP
BEEP
BEEP
ALL RIGHT, WE'RE ALMOST THERE. STAY ALERT AND QUIET. BREATHE SLOWLY AND EVENLY. WE'RE GOING TO MAKE OUR WAY OUTSIDE.
IF ONE OF THOSE THINGS IS IN THE BUILDING, YOU'RE GOING TO WANT TO MOVE QUIETLY, AND VERY QUICKLY.
WELL, BY ALL MEANS, THEN...
BEEP
BEEP
BEEP
BEEP
BEEP
...YOU'RE GOING TO WANT TO RUN.
BEEP
BEEP
BEEP

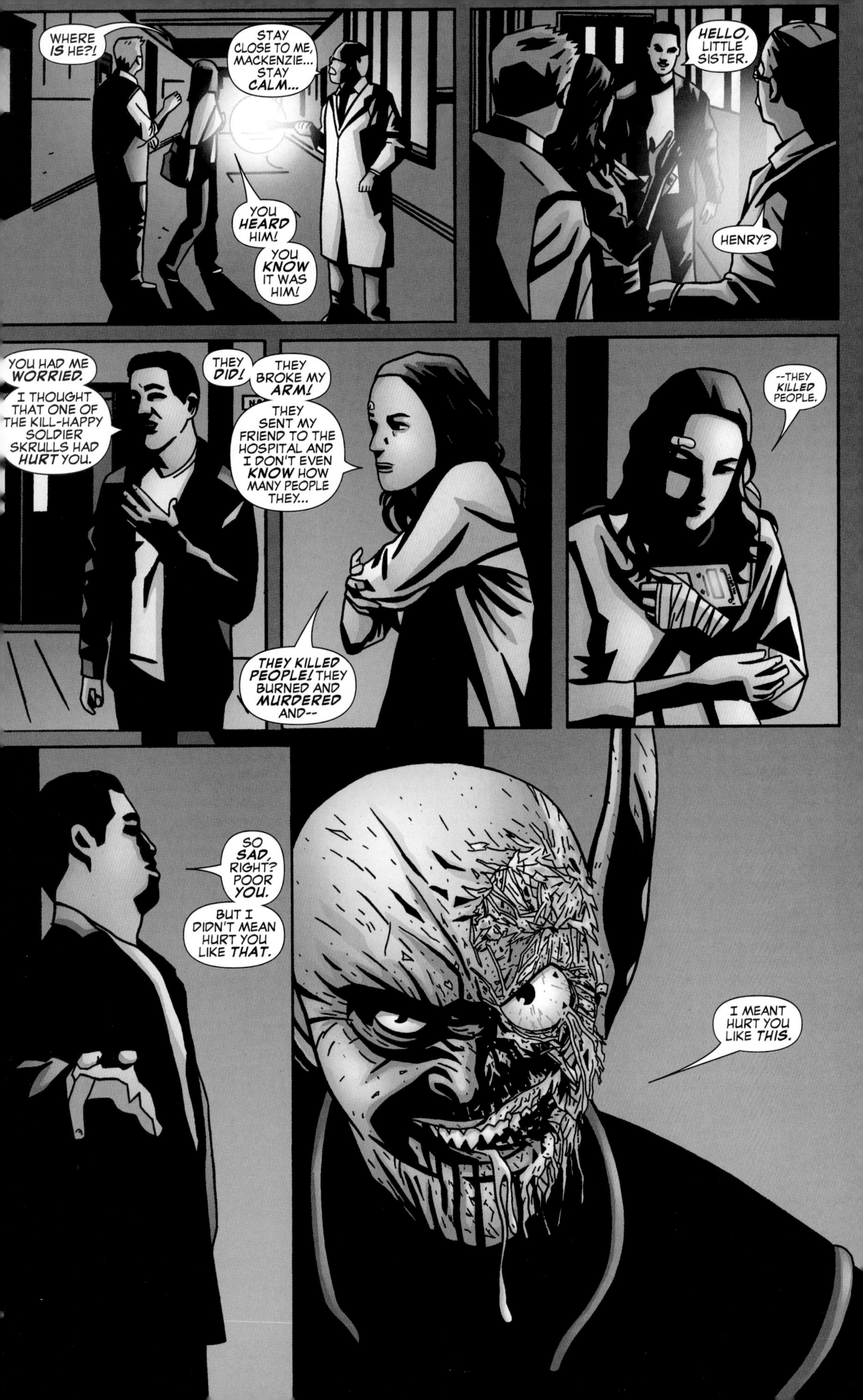
WHERE IS HE?!
STAY CLOSE TO ME, MACKENZIE... STAY CALM...
YOU HEARD HIM!
YOU KNOW IT WAS HIM!
HELLO, LITTLE SISTER.
HENRY?
YOU HAD ME WORRIED.
I THOUGHT THAT ONE OF THE KILL-HAPPY SOLDIER SKRULLS HAD HURT YOU.
THEY DID!
THEY BROKE MY ARM!
THEY SENT MY FRIEND TO THE HOSPITAL AND I DON'T EVEN KNOW HOW MANY PEOPLE THEY...
THEY KILLED PEOPLE! THEY BURNED AND MURDERED AND--
--THEY KILLED PEOPLE.
SO SAD, RIGHT? POOR YOU.
BUT I DIDN'T MEAN HURT YOU LIKE THAT.
I MEANT HURT YOU LIKE THIS.

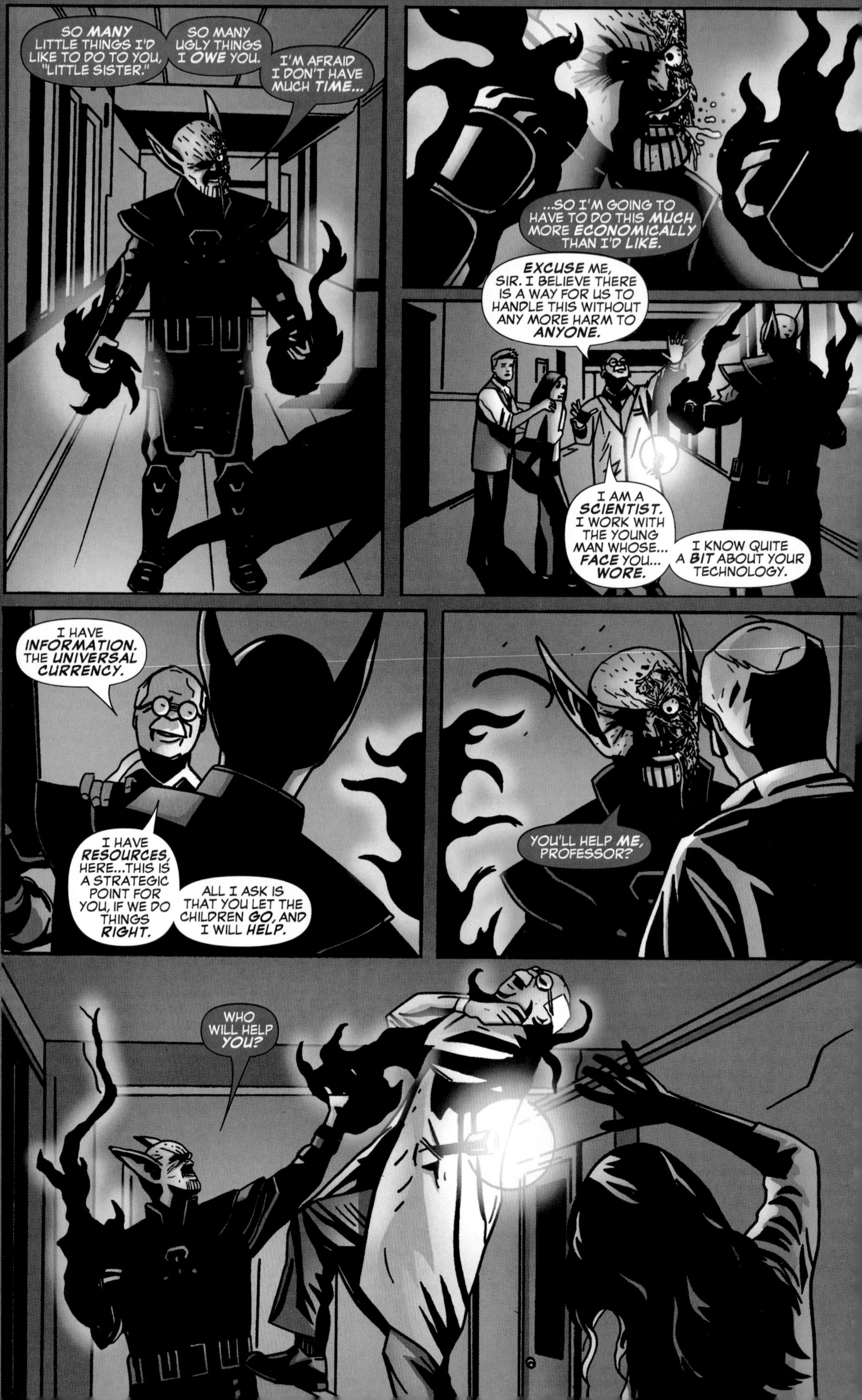
SO MANY LITTLE THINGS I'D LIKE TO DO TO YOU, "LITTLE SISTER."
SO MANY UGLY THINGS I OWE YOU.
I'M AFRAID I DON'T HAVE MUCH TIME...
...SO I'M GOING TO HAVE TO DO THIS MUCH MORE ECONOMICALLY THAN I'D LIKE.
EXCUSE ME, SIR. I BELIEVE THERE IS A WAY FOR US TO HANDLE THIS WITHOUT ANY MORE HARM TO ANYONE.
I AM A SCIENTIST. I WORK WITH THE YOUNG MAN WHOSE... FACE YOU... WORE.
I KNOW QUITE A BIT ABOUT YOUR TECHNOLOGY.
I HAVE INFORMATION. THE UNIVERSAL CURRENCY.
I HAVE RESOURCES, HERE...THIS IS A STRATEGIC POINT FOR YOU, IF WE DO THINGS RIGHT.
ALL I ASK IS THAT YOU LET THE CHILDREN GO, AND I WILL HELP.
YOU'LL HELP ME, PROFESSOR?
WHO WILL HELP YOU?

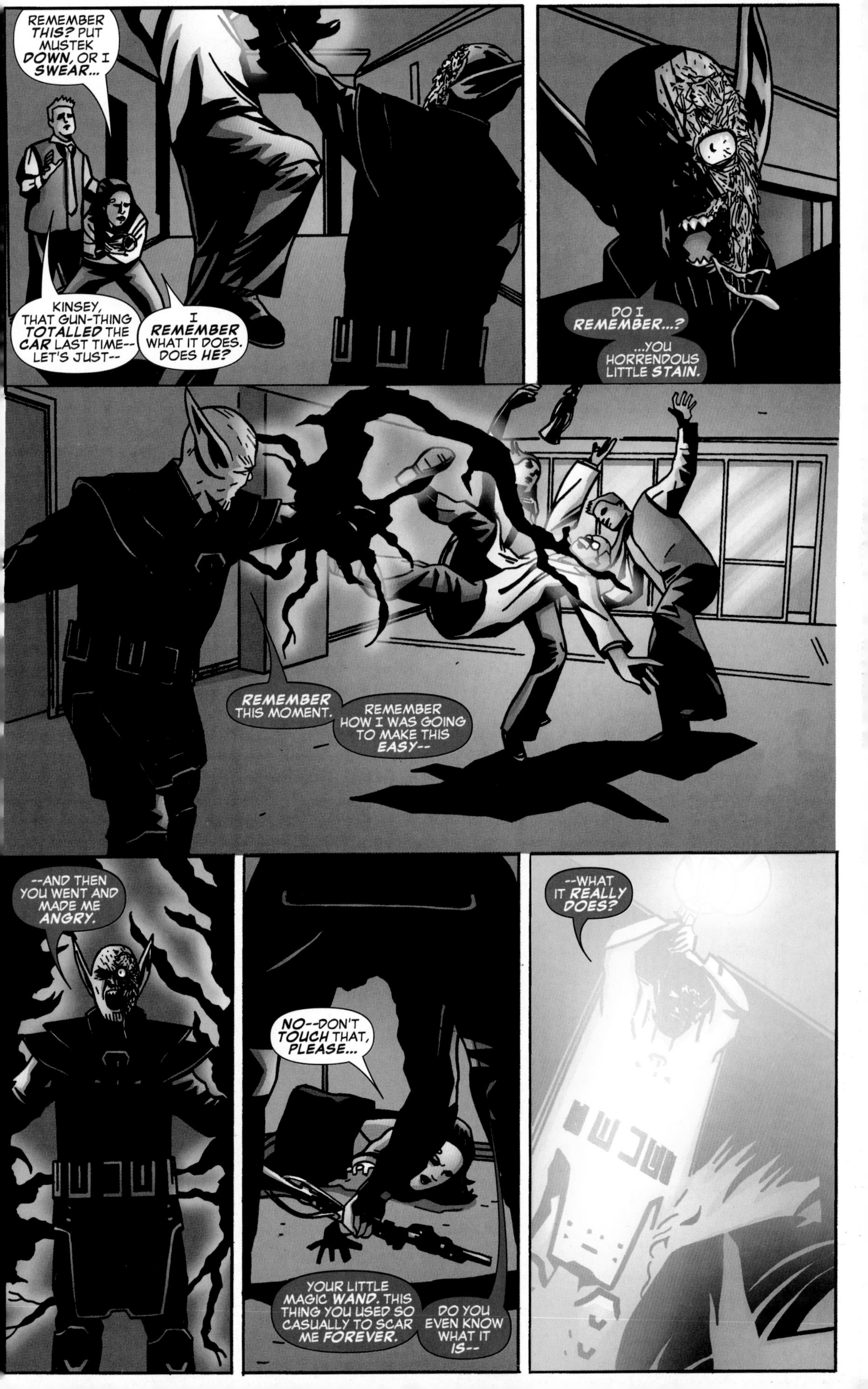
REMEMBER THIS? PUT MUSTEK DOWN, OR I SWEAR...
KINSEY, THAT GUN-THING TOTALLED THE CAR LAST TIME-- LET'S JUST--
I REMEMBER WHAT IT DOES. DOES HE?
DO I REMEMBER...?
...YOU HORRENDOUS LITTLE STAIN.
REMEMBER THIS MOMENT.
REMEMBER HOW I WAS GOING TO MAKE THIS EASY--
--AND THEN YOU WENT AND MADE ME ANGRY.
NO--DON'T TOUCH THAT, PLEASE...
YOUR LITTLE MAGIC WAND. THIS THING YOU USED SO CASUALLY TO SCAR ME FOREVER.
DO YOU EVEN KNOW WHAT IT IS--
--WHAT IT REALLY DOES?

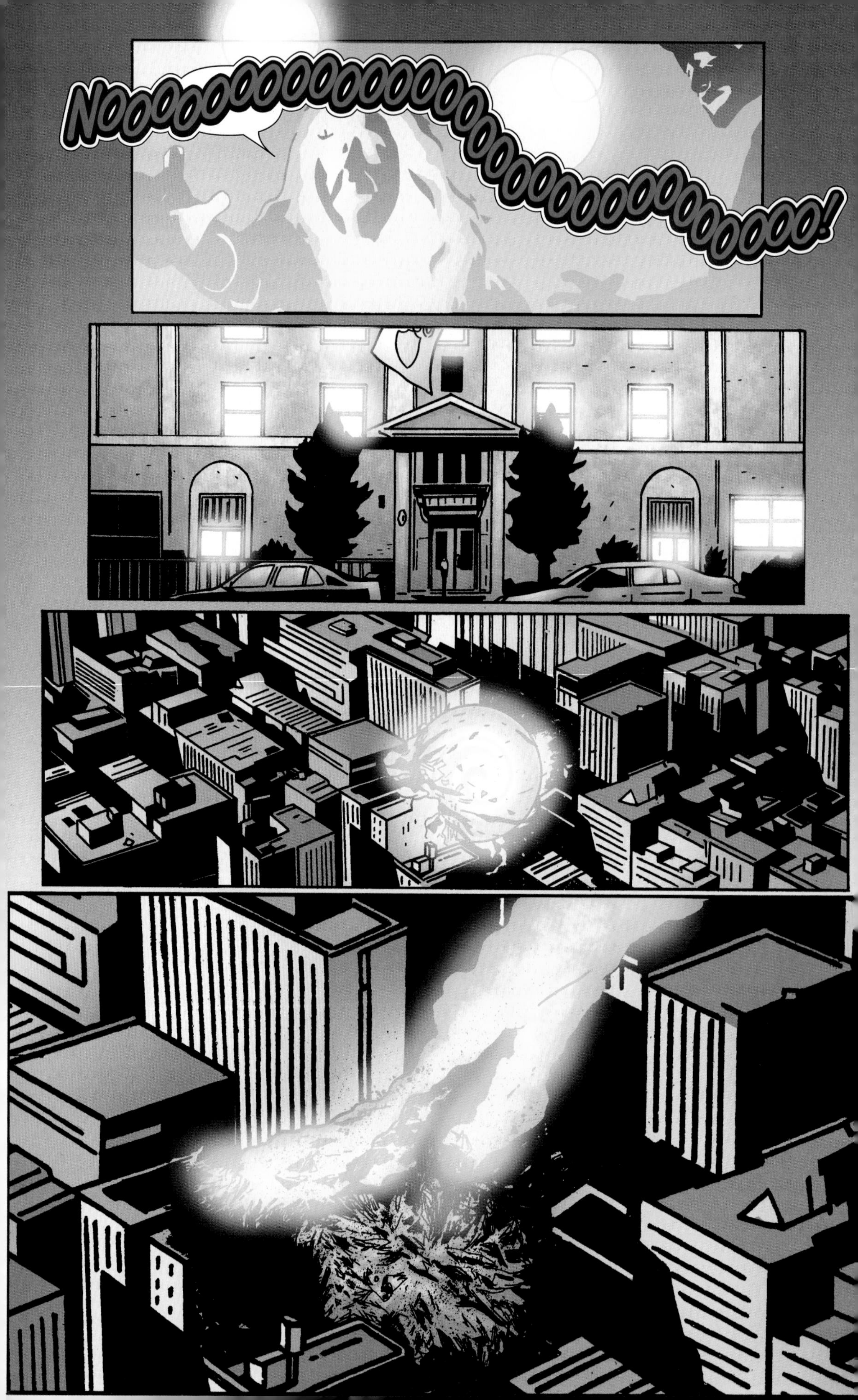
NOOOOOOOOOOOOOOOOOOOOOOOOOOOOOOOOOOOOOOOOOOOOO!

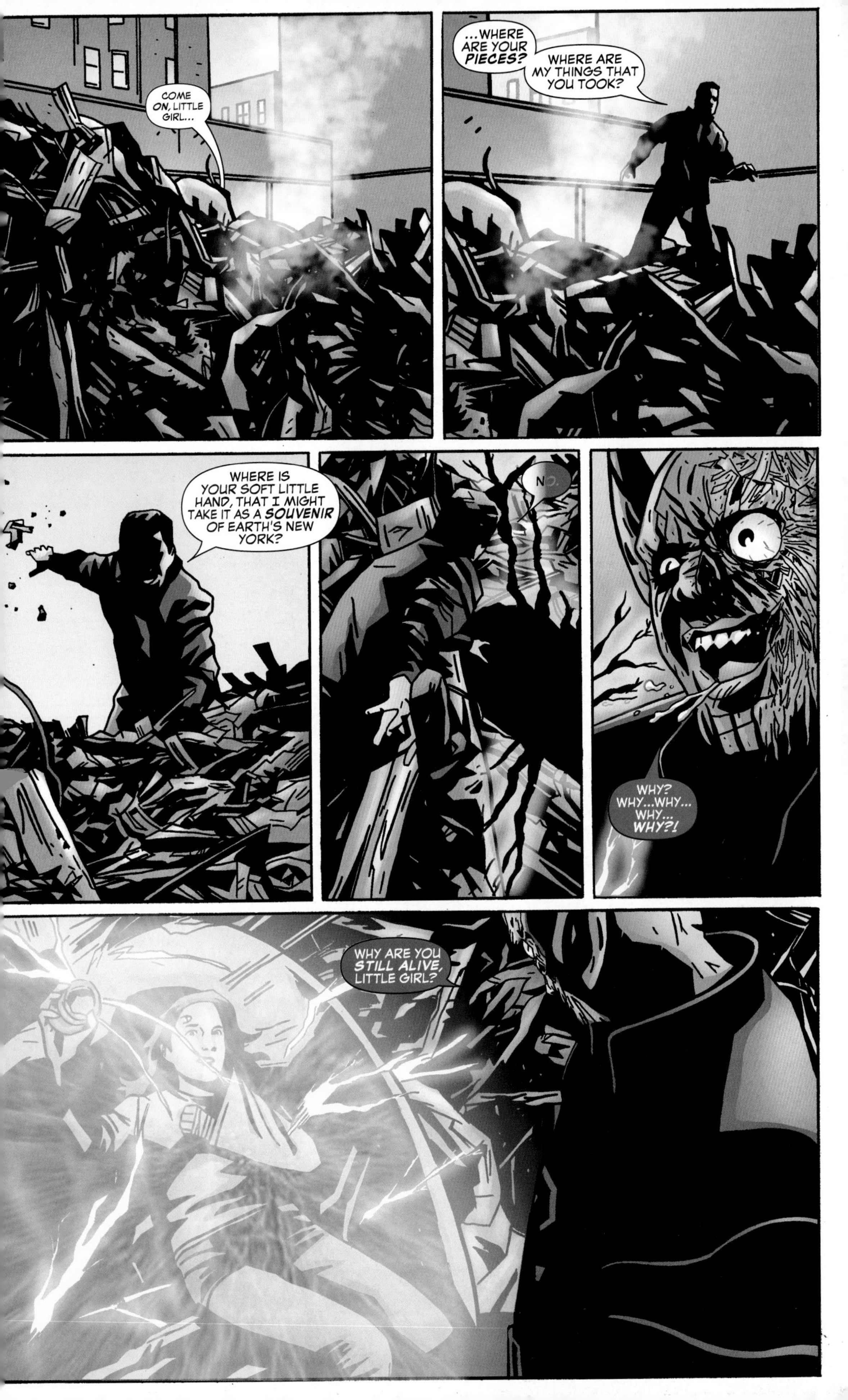
COME ON, LITTLE GIRL...
...WHERE ARE YOUR PIECES?
WHERE ARE MY THINGS THAT YOU TOOK?
WHERE IS YOUR SOFT LITTLE HAND, THAT I MIGHT TAKE IT AS A SOUVENIR OF EARTH'S NEW YORK?
NO.
WHY? WHY...WHY... WHY... WHY?!
WHY ARE YOU STILL ALIVE, LITTLE GIRL?

IN MY MIND I'VE KILLED YOU *SO MANY* TIMES. IT'S *AMAZING.* IT'S SO EASY AND SO... *FULFILLING.*

I'VE NEVER WANTED ANYTHING *MORE.*

LET *GO.* ALL OF THIS WILL *PASS!* DO YOU UNDER-STAND? IT WILL ALL FINALLY BE *OVER.*

FIGHTING IS SO MUCH HARDER THAN LETTING GO...

JUST BREATHE...

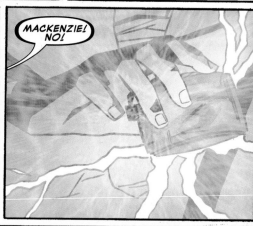
MACKENZIE! NO!

THERE'S STILL A LOT OF *WORK* FOR YOU TO DO.

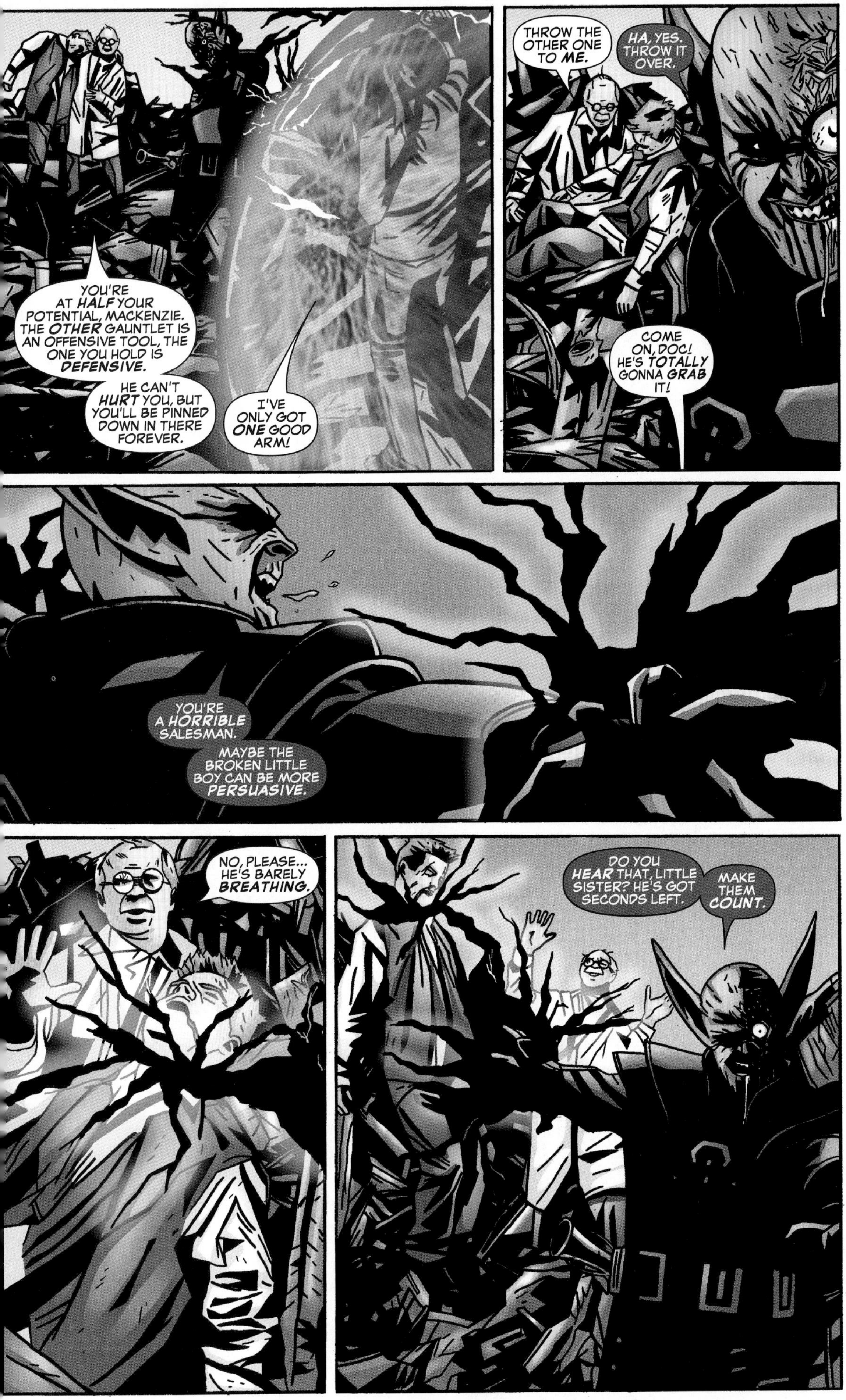

YOU'RE AT HALF YOUR POTENTIAL, MACKENZIE. THE OTHER GAUNTLET IS AN OFFENSIVE TOOL, THE ONE YOU HOLD IS DEFENSIVE.
HE CAN'T HURT YOU, BUT YOU'LL BE PINNED DOWN IN THERE FOREVER.
I'VE ONLY GOT ONE GOOD ARM!
THROW THE OTHER ONE TO ME.
HA, YES. THROW IT OVER.
COME ON, DOC! HE'S TOTALLY GONNA GRAB IT!
YOU'RE A HORRIBLE SALESMAN.
MAYBE THE BROKEN LITTLE BOY CAN BE MORE PERSUASIVE.
NO, PLEASE... HE'S BARELY BREATHING.
DO YOU HEAR THAT, LITTLE SISTER? HE'S GOT SECONDS LEFT.
MAKE THEM COUNT.

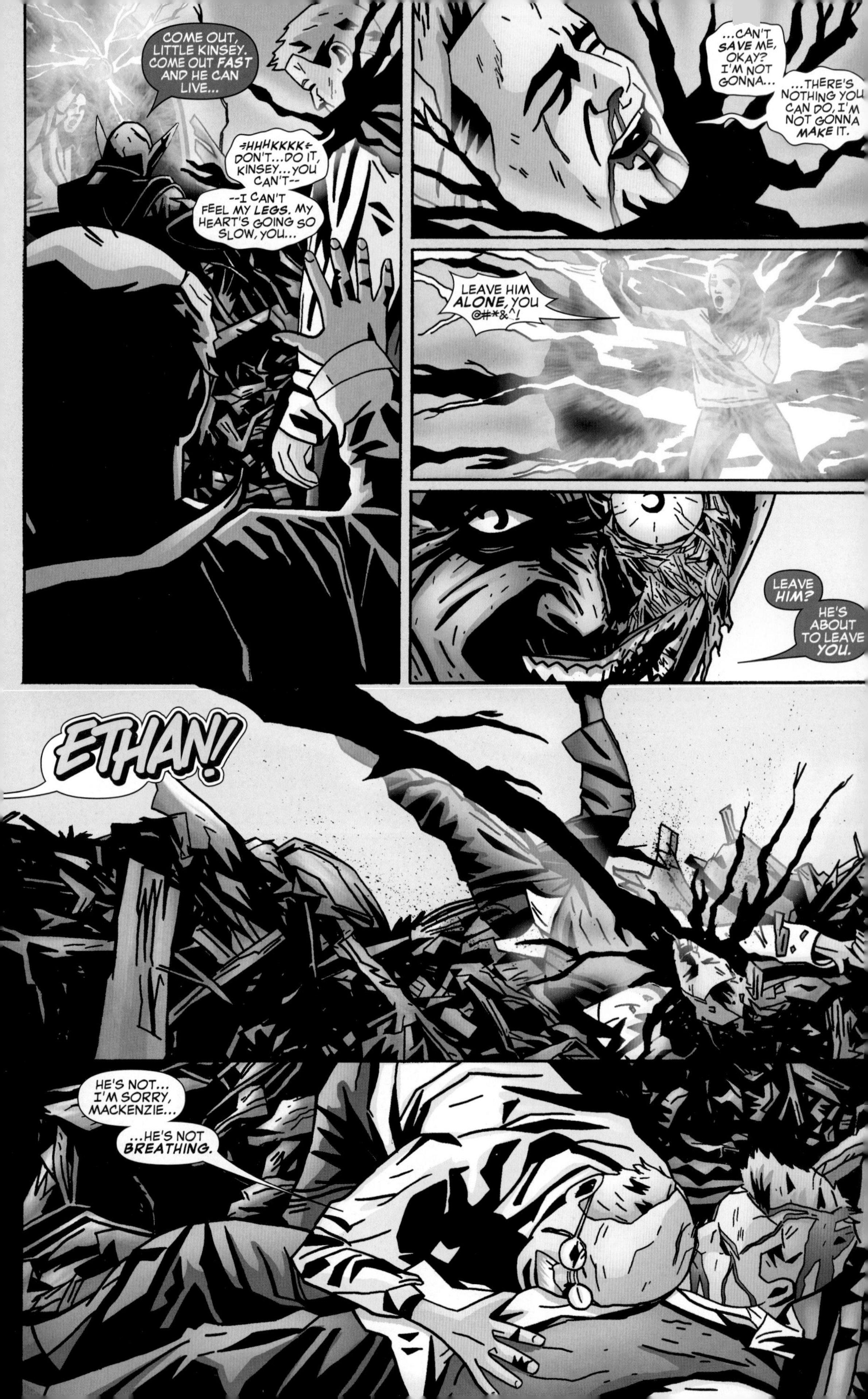
COME OUT, LITTLE KINSEY. COME OUT FAST AND HE CAN LIVE...
=HHHKKKK= DON'T...DO IT, KINSEY...YOU CAN'T--
--I CAN'T FEEL MY LEGS. MY HEART'S GOING SO SLOW, YOU...
...CAN'T SAVE ME, OKAY? I'M NOT GONNA...
...THERE'S NOTHING YOU CAN DO, I'M NOT GONNA MAKE IT.
LEAVE HIM ALONE, YOU @#*&^!
LEAVE HIM?
HE'S ABOUT TO LEAVE YOU.
ETHAN!
HE'S NOT... I'M SORRY, MACKENZIE...
...HE'S NOT BREATHING.

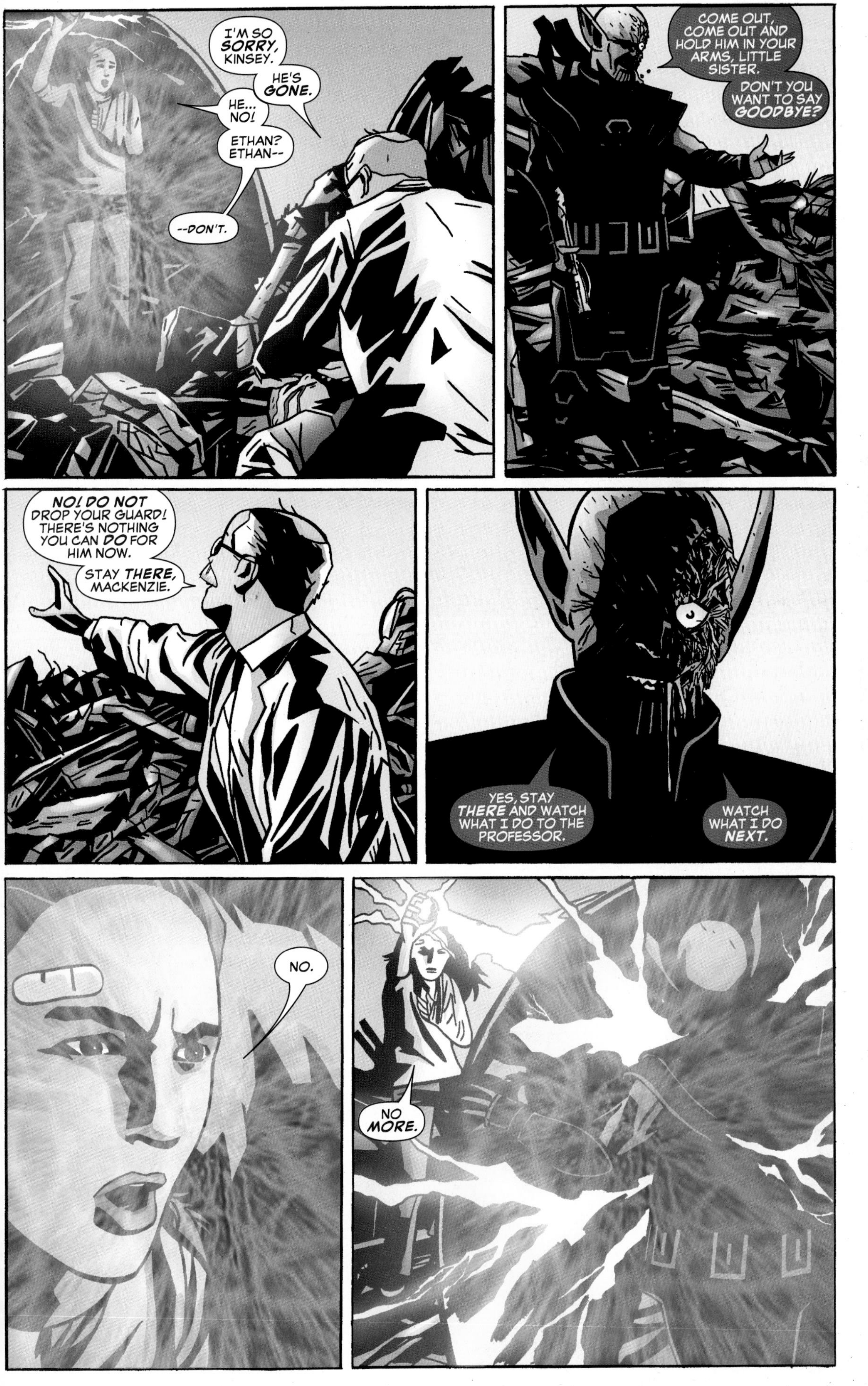
I'M SO SORRY, KINSEY.
HE'S GONE.
HE... NO!
ETHAN? ETHAN--
--DON'T.
COME OUT, COME OUT AND HOLD HIM IN YOUR ARMS, LITTLE SISTER.
DON'T YOU WANT TO SAY GOODBYE?
NO! DO NOT DROP YOUR GUARD! THERE'S NOTHING YOU CAN DO FOR HIM NOW.
STAY THERE, MACKENZIE.
YES, STAY THERE AND WATCH WHAT I DO TO THE PROFESSOR.
WATCH WHAT I DO NEXT.
NO.
NO MORE.

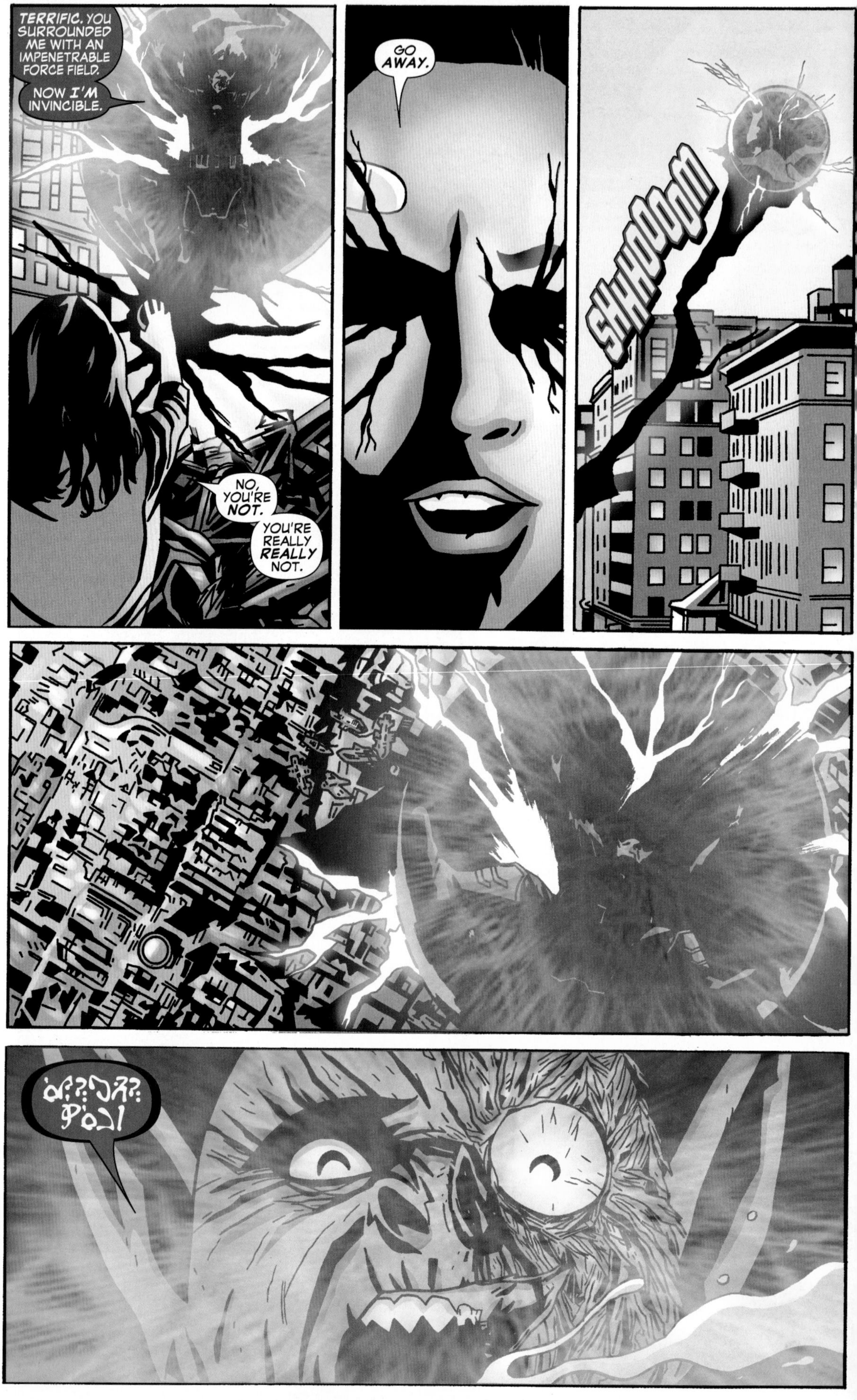
TERRIFIC. YOU SURROUNDED ME WITH AN IMPENETRABLE FORCE FIELD.
NOW I'M INVINCIBLE.
NO, YOU'RE NOT.
YOU'RE REALLY REALLY NOT.
GO AWAY.
SHHOOOM

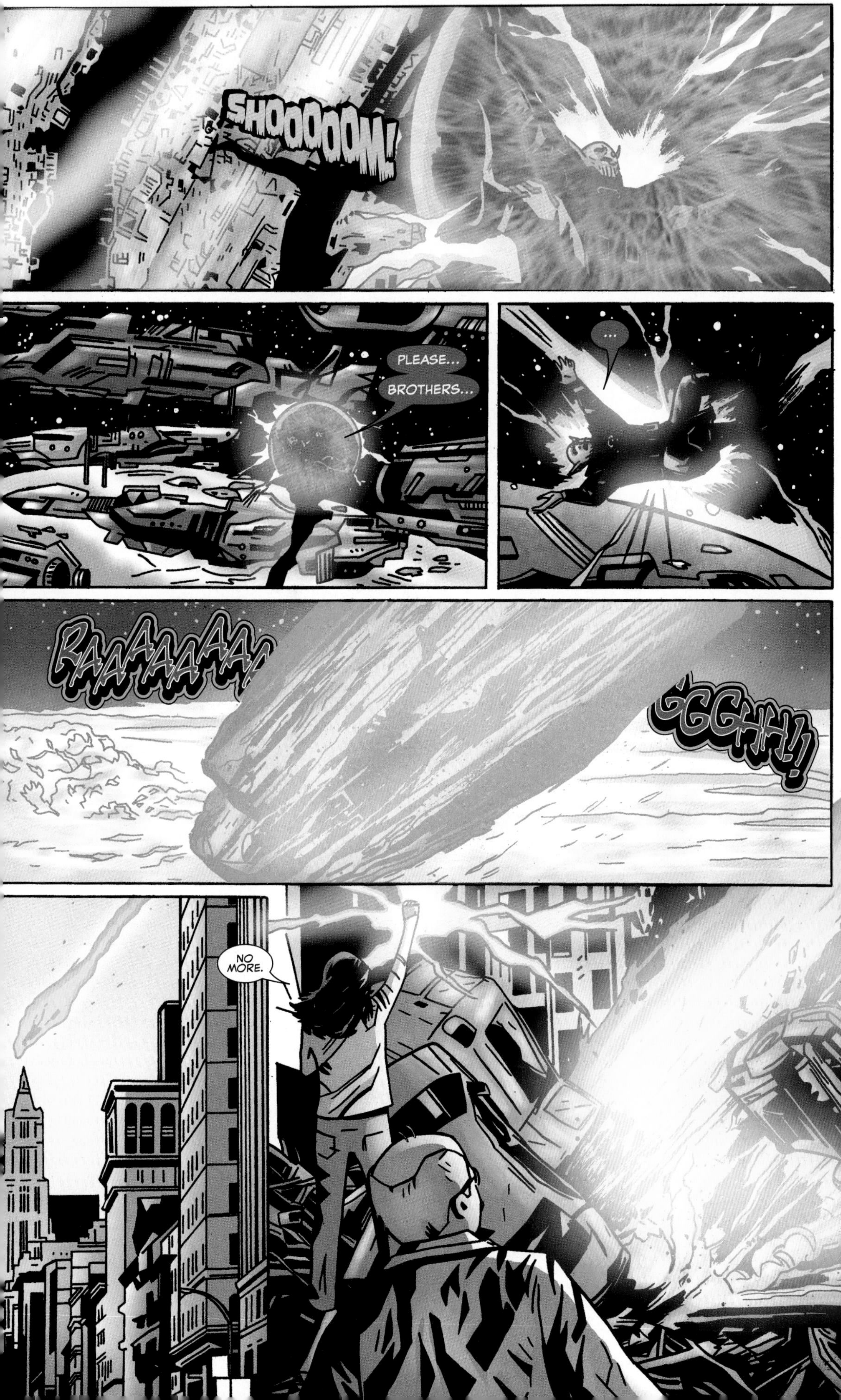
SHOOOOOM!
PLEASE...
BROTHERS...
...
RAAAAAAA
GGGHH!!
NO MORE.

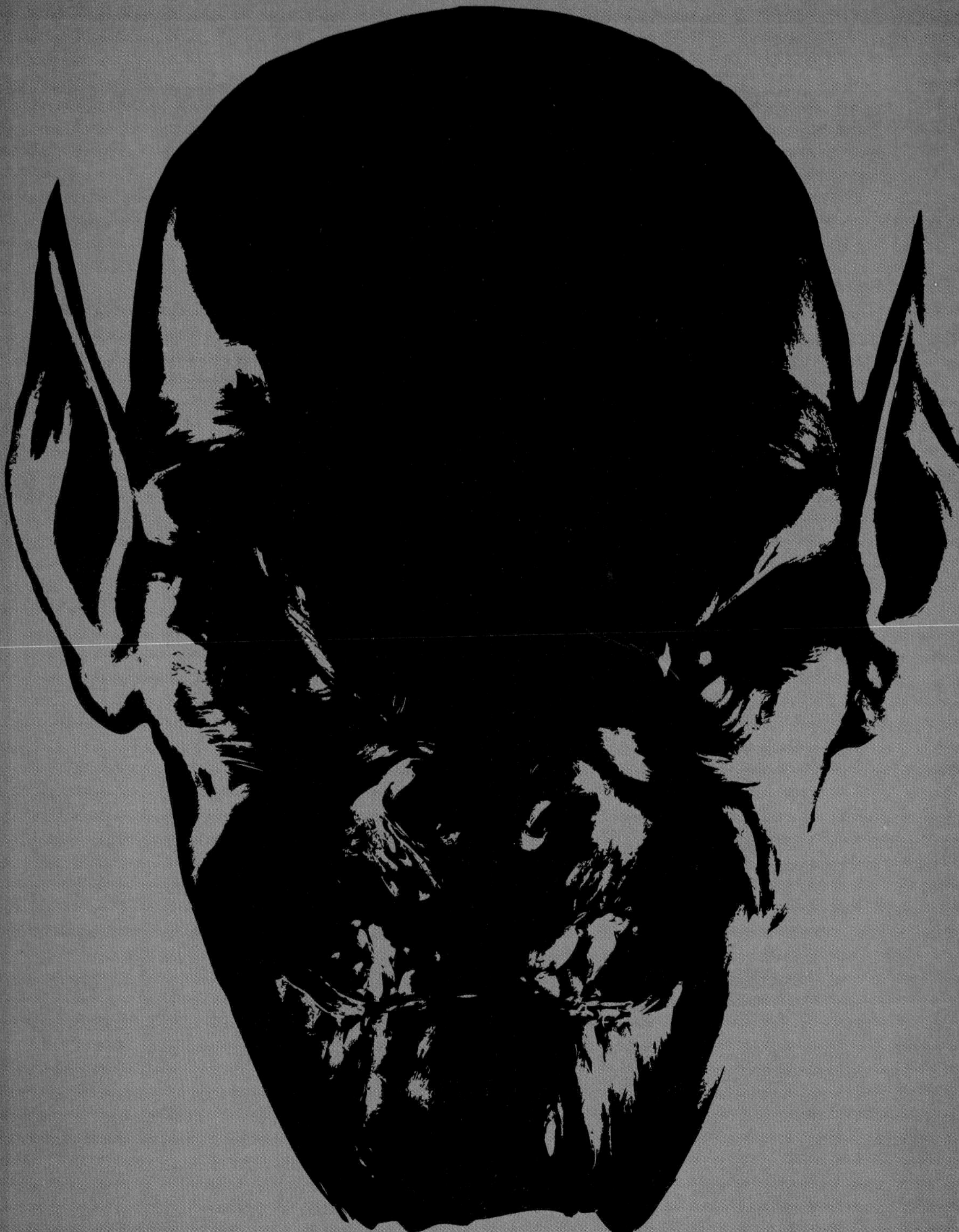

CHAPTER 7

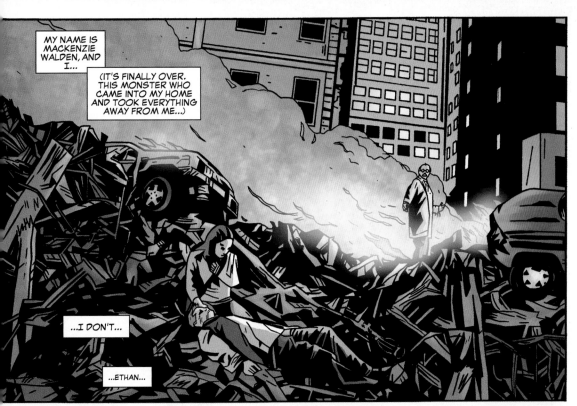

MY NAME IS MACKENZIE WALDEN, AND I...

(IT'S FINALLY OVER. THIS MONSTER WHO CAME INTO MY HOME AND TOOK EVERYTHING AWAY FROM ME...)

...I DON'T...

...ETHAN...

GOOD LORD.

IS IT DEAD, PROFESSOR?

IT LOOKS... IT NO LONGER WEARS YOUR BROTHER'S FACE.

IS IT DEAD?!

IT LOOKS VERY DEAD. I DON'T KNOW THE PHYSIOLOGY, IT COULD...

IT WAS A SHAPE-SHIFTER, MACKENZIE... IT LOOKS DEAD TO ME.

NOT GOOD ENOUGH.

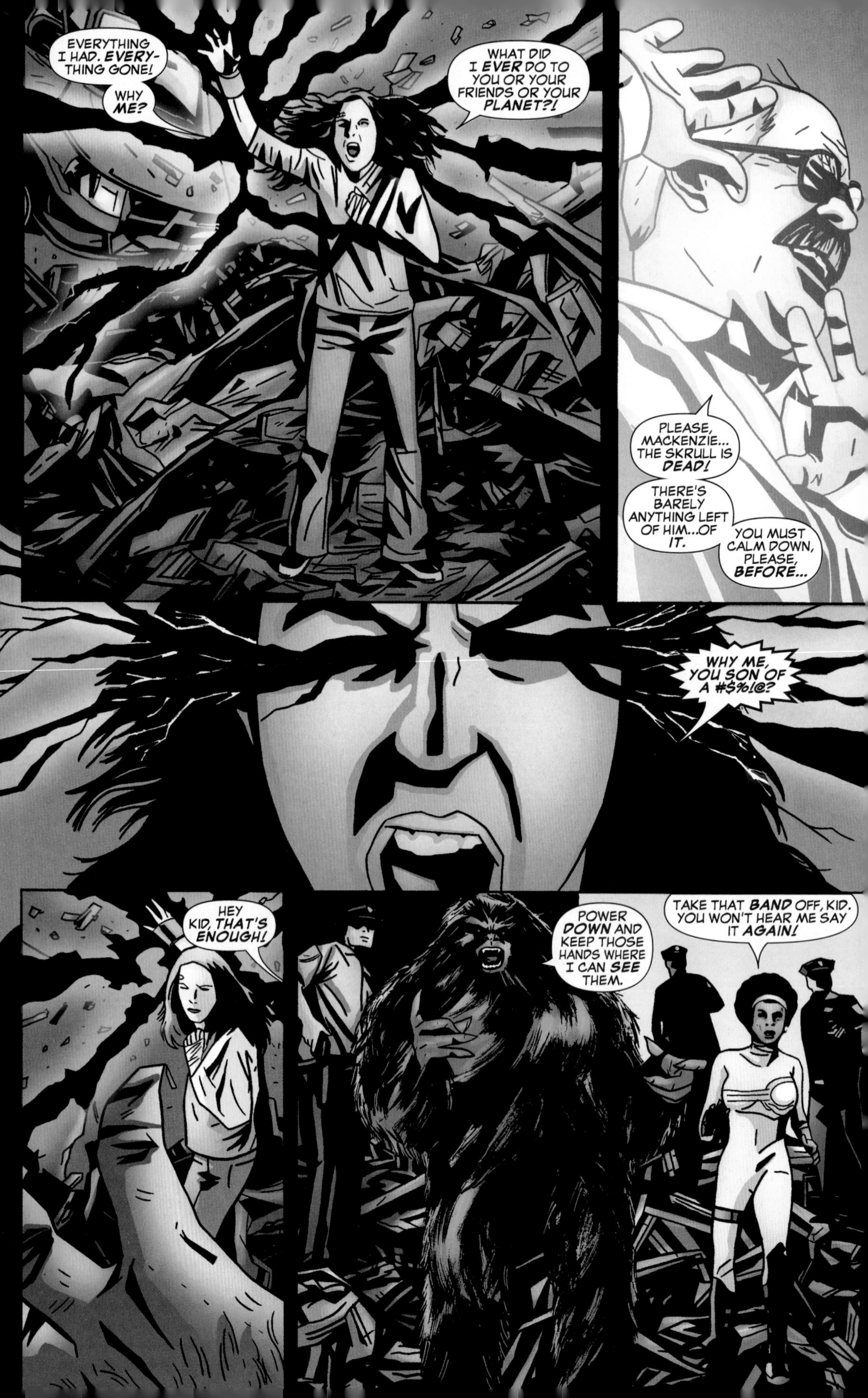
EVERYTHING I HAD. EVERY-THING GONE!
WHY ME?
WHAT DID I EVER DO TO YOU OR YOUR FRIENDS OR YOUR PLANET?!
PLEASE, MACKENZIE... THE SKRULL IS DEAD!
THERE'S BARELY ANYTHING LEFT OF HIM...OF IT.
YOU MUST CALM DOWN, PLEASE, BEFORE...
WHY ME, YOU SON OF A #$%!@?
HEY KID, THAT'S ENOUGH!
POWER DOWN AND KEEP THOSE HANDS WHERE I CAN SEE THEM.
TAKE THAT BAND OFF, KID. YOU WON'T HEAR ME SAY IT AGAIN!

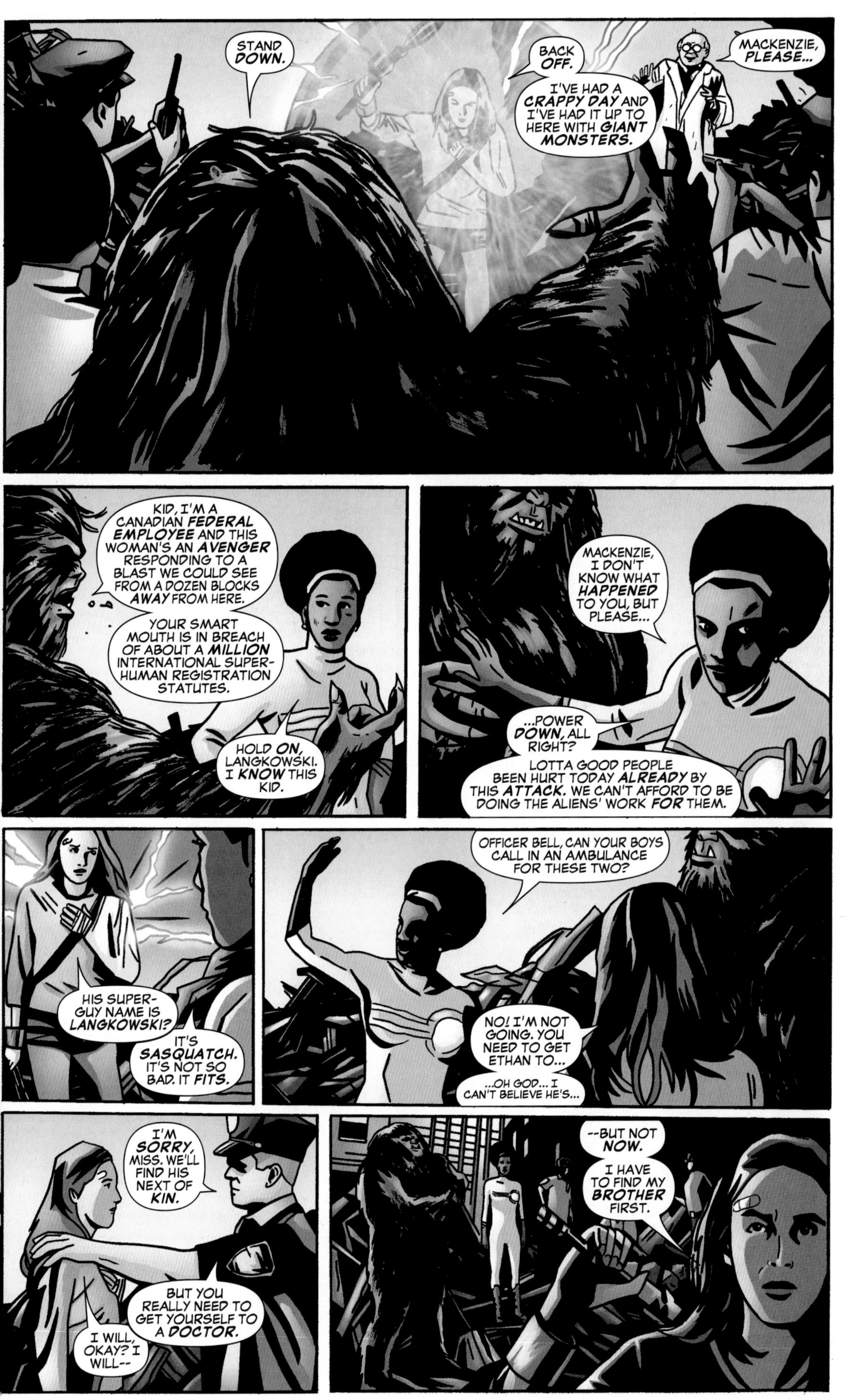
STAND DOWN.
BACK OFF.
I'VE HAD A CRAPPY DAY AND I'VE HAD IT UP TO HERE WITH GIANT MONSTERS.
MACKENZIE, PLEASE...
KID, I'M A CANADIAN FEDERAL EMPLOYEE AND THIS WOMAN'S AN AVENGER RESPONDING TO A BLAST WE COULD SEE FROM A DOZEN BLOCKS AWAY FROM HERE.
YOUR SMART MOUTH IS IN BREACH OF ABOUT A MILLION INTERNATIONAL SUPER-HUMAN REGISTRATION STATUTES.
HOLD ON, LANGKOWSKI. I KNOW THIS KID.
MACKENZIE, I DON'T KNOW WHAT HAPPENED TO YOU, BUT PLEASE...
...POWER DOWN, ALL RIGHT?
LOTTA GOOD PEOPLE BEEN HURT TODAY ALREADY BY THIS ATTACK. WE CAN'T AFFORD TO BE DOING THE ALIENS' WORK FOR THEM.
HIS SUPER-GUY NAME IS LANGKOWSKI?
IT'S SASQUATCH. IT'S NOT SO BAD. IT FITS.
OFFICER BELL, CAN YOUR BOYS CALL IN AN AMBULANCE FOR THESE TWO?
NO! I'M NOT GOING. YOU NEED TO GET ETHAN TO...
...OH GOD... I CAN'T BELIEVE HE'S...
I'M SORRY, MISS. WE'LL FIND HIS NEXT OF KIN.
BUT YOU REALLY NEED TO GET YOURSELF TO A DOCTOR.
I WILL, OKAY? I WILL--
--BUT NOT NOW.
I HAVE TO FIND MY BROTHER FIRST.

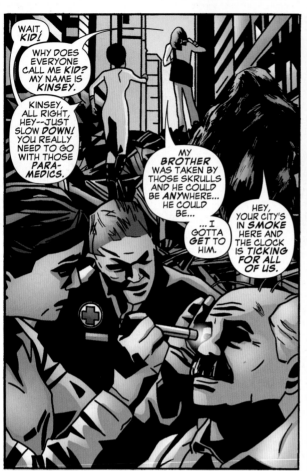

WAIT, KID!

WHY DOES EVERYONE CALL ME KID? MY NAME IS KINSEY.

KINSEY, ALL RIGHT, HEY--JUST SLOW DOWN! YOU REALLY NEED TO GO WITH THOSE PARAMEDICS.

MY BROTHER WAS TAKEN BY THOSE SKRULLS AND HE COULD BE ANYWHERE... HE COULD BE...

...I GOTTA GET TO HIM.

HEY, YOUR CITY'S IN SMOKE HERE AND THE CLOCK IS TICKING FOR ALL OF US.

WE'VE GOTTA GET BACK INTO IT AND LET HER DO WHAT SHE HAS TO.

SHE'S A KID!

I'M EIGHTEEN!

YOU SAW HER BUBBLE AND GLOW OVER THERE. SHE'S OBVIOUSLY GOT HER OWN POWERS.

YEAH, SHE'S SOME KINDA SUPER HERO, BUT EVEN AS SUCH...

...I'M NOT LETTING A ONE-ARMED HIGH SCHOOL GIRL WALK INTO A SKRULL PRISON LIKE SHE'S--

I CAN TAKE CARE OF MYSELF.

SEE?!?

AND I'M NOT A...

...SUPER...

SHE'S ONE OF US. I'M NOT LETTING HER WALK INTO THAT ALONE AND NEITHER ARE YOU, LANGKOWSKI.

AND IF IT'S A SKRULL BASE, I BET THERE ARE MORE THAN ENOUGH SKRULLS THERE FOR YOU TO FIGHT.

NYC
AMBUL

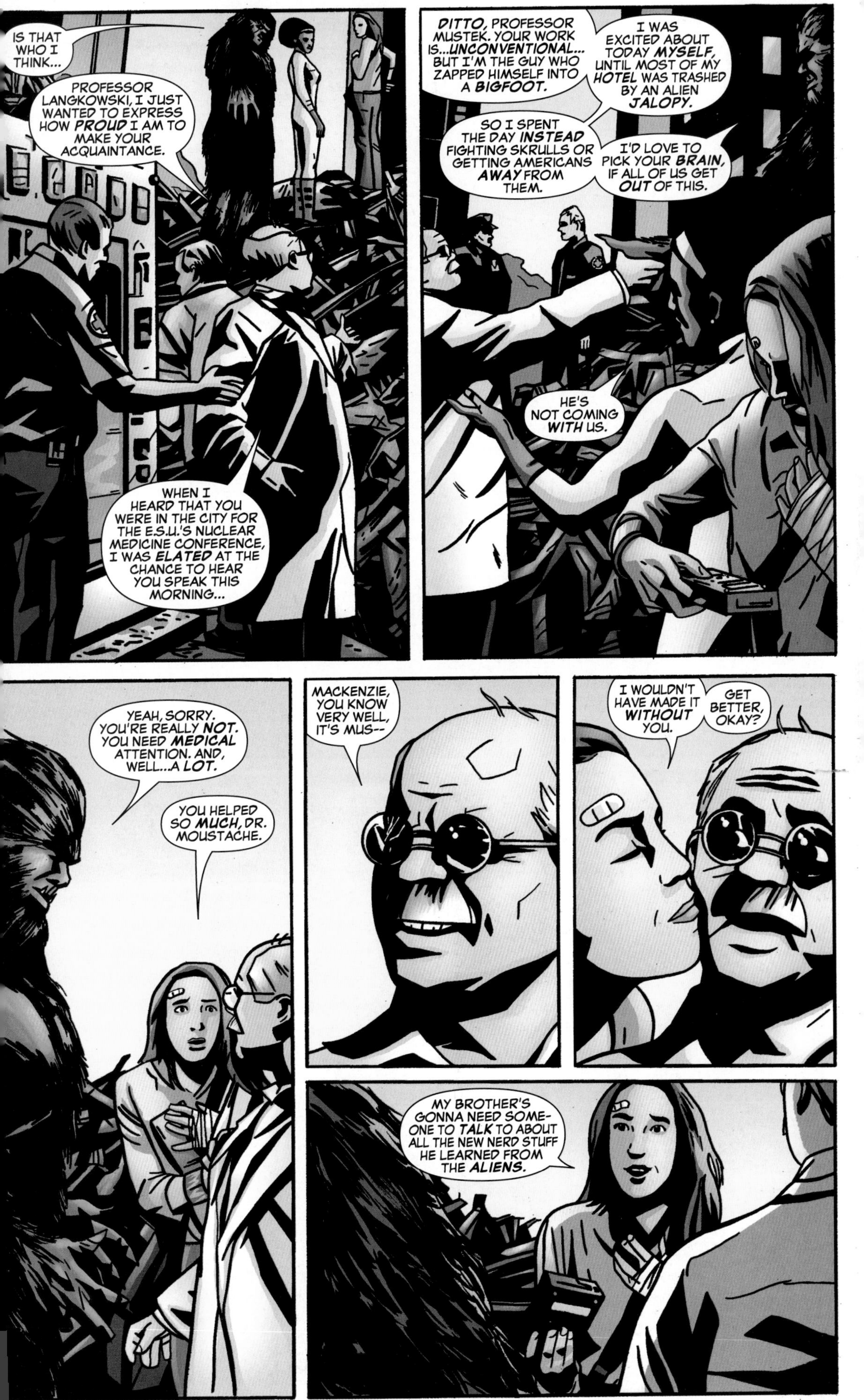
IS THAT WHO I THINK...
PROFESSOR LANGKOWSKI, I JUST WANTED TO EXPRESS HOW PROUD I AM TO MAKE YOUR ACQUAINTANCE.
WHEN I HEARD THAT YOU WERE IN THE CITY FOR THE E.S.U.'S NUCLEAR MEDICINE CONFERENCE, I WAS ELATED AT THE CHANCE TO HEAR YOU SPEAK THIS MORNING...
DITTO, PROFESSOR MUSTEK. YOUR WORK IS...UNCONVENTIONAL... BUT I'M THE GUY WHO ZAPPED HIMSELF INTO A BIGFOOT.
I WAS EXCITED ABOUT TODAY MYSELF, UNTIL MOST OF MY HOTEL WAS TRASHED BY AN ALIEN JALOPY.
SO I SPENT THE DAY INSTEAD FIGHTING SKRULLS OR GETTING AMERICANS AWAY FROM THEM.
I'D LOVE TO PICK YOUR BRAIN, IF ALL OF US GET OUT OF THIS.
HE'S NOT COMING WITH US.
YEAH, SORRY. YOU'RE REALLY NOT. YOU NEED MEDICAL ATTENTION. AND, WELL...A LOT.
YOU HELPED SO MUCH, DR. MOUSTACHE.
MACKENZIE, YOU KNOW VERY WELL, IT'S MUS--
I WOULDN'T HAVE MADE IT WITHOUT YOU.
GET BETTER, OKAY?
MY BROTHER'S GONNA NEED SOME-ONE TO TALK TO ABOUT ALL THE NEW NERD STUFF HE LEARNED FROM THE ALIENS.

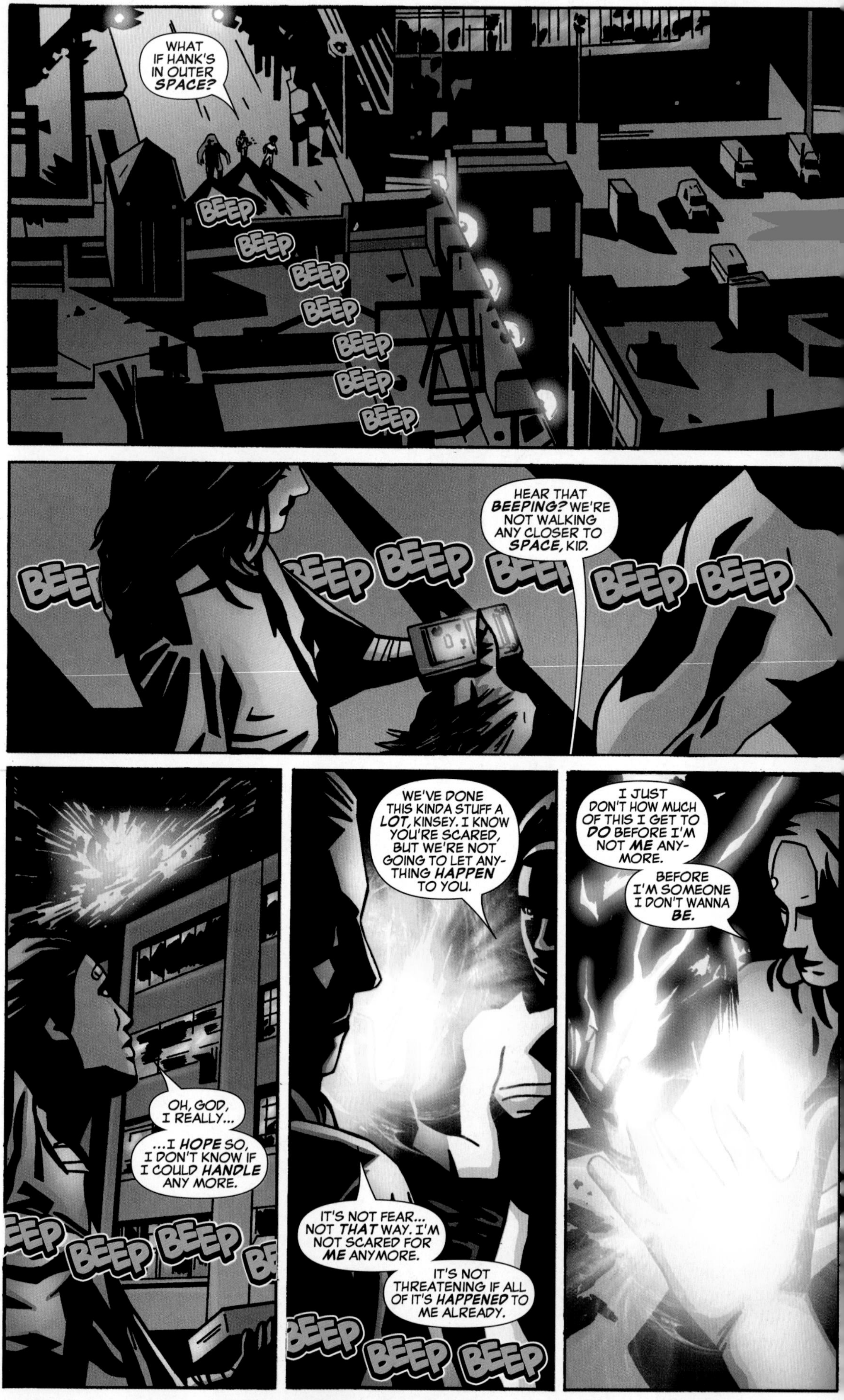

WHAT IF HANK'S IN OUTER SPACE?
BEEP
BEEP
BEEP
BEEP
BEEP
BEEP
BEEP
HEAR THAT BEEPING? WE'RE NOT WALKING ANY CLOSER TO SPACE, KID.
BEEP
BEEP
BEEP
BEEP
OH, GOD, I REALLY...
...I HOPE SO, I DON'T KNOW IF I COULD HANDLE ANY MORE.
BEEP
BEEP
WE'VE DONE THIS KINDA STUFF A LOT, KINSEY. I KNOW YOU'RE SCARED, BUT WE'RE NOT GOING TO LET ANYTHING HAPPEN TO YOU.
IT'S NOT FEAR... NOT THAT WAY. I'M NOT SCARED FOR ME ANYMORE.
IT'S NOT THREATENING IF ALL OF IT'S HAPPENED TO ME ALREADY.
BEEP
BEEP
BEEP
I JUST DON'T HOW MUCH OF THIS I GET TO DO BEFORE I'M NOT ME ANYMORE.
BEFORE I'M SOMEONE I DON'T WANNA BE.

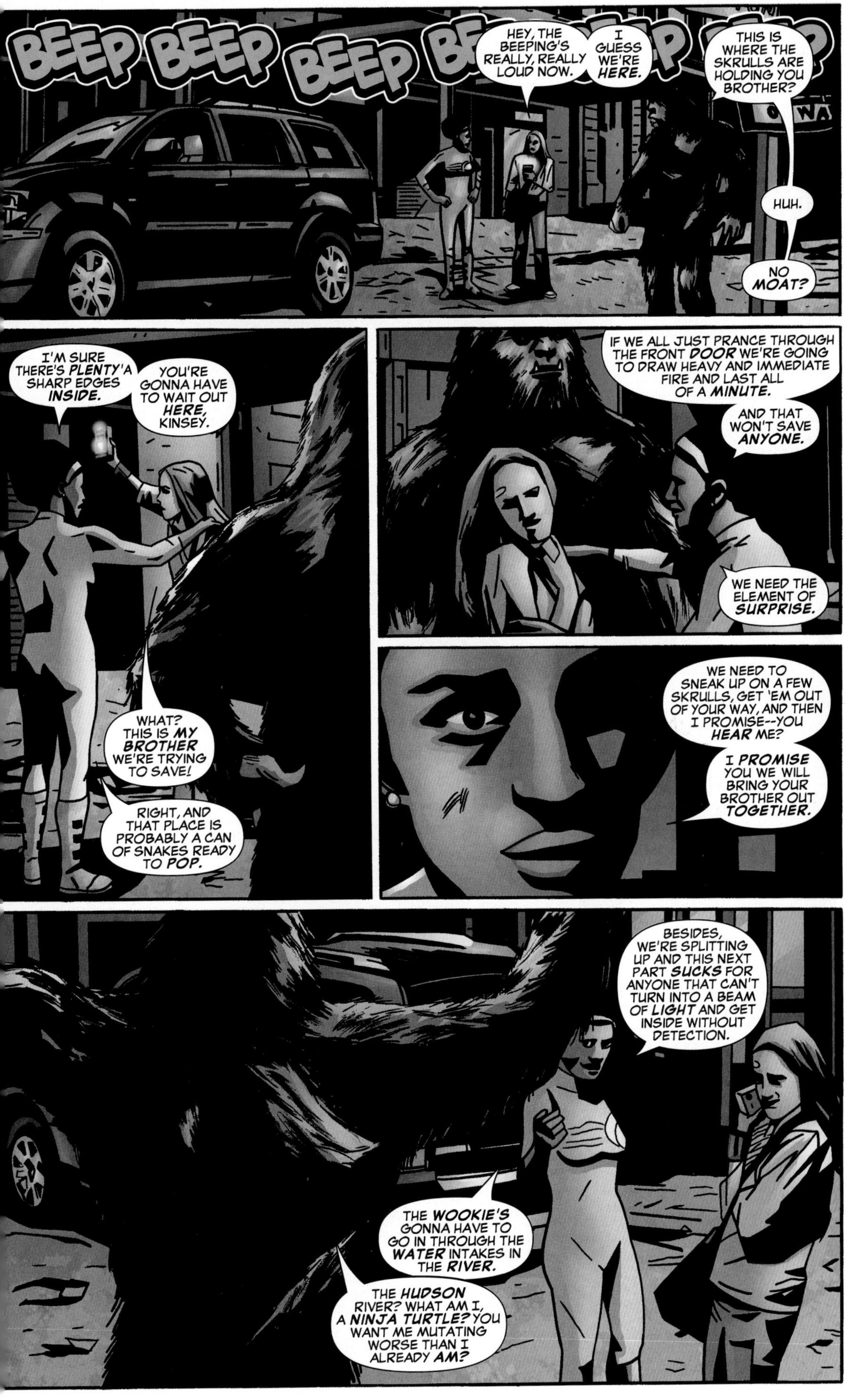
BEEP BEEP BEEP BEEP BEEP BEEP
HEY, THE BEEPING'S REALLY, REALLY LOUD NOW.
I GUESS WE'RE HERE.
THIS IS WHERE THE SKRULLS ARE HOLDING YOU BROTHER?
HUH.
NO MOAT?
I'M SURE THERE'S PLENTY'A SHARP EDGES INSIDE.
YOU'RE GONNA HAVE TO WAIT OUT HERE, KINSEY.
WHAT? THIS IS MY BROTHER WE'RE TRYING TO SAVE!
RIGHT, AND THAT PLACE IS PROBABLY A CAN OF SNAKES READY TO POP.
IF WE ALL JUST PRANCE THROUGH THE FRONT DOOR WE'RE GOING TO DRAW HEAVY AND IMMEDIATE FIRE AND LAST ALL OF A MINUTE.
AND THAT WON'T SAVE ANYONE.
WE NEED THE ELEMENT OF SURPRISE.
WE NEED TO SNEAK UP ON A FEW SKRULLS, GET 'EM OUT OF YOUR WAY, AND THEN I PROMISE--YOU HEAR ME?
I PROMISE YOU WE WILL BRING YOUR BROTHER OUT TOGETHER.
BESIDES, WE'RE SPLITTING UP AND THIS NEXT PART SUCKS FOR ANYONE THAT CAN'T TURN INTO A BEAM OF LIGHT AND GET INSIDE WITHOUT DETECTION.
THE WOOKIE'S GONNA HAVE TO GO IN THROUGH THE WATER INTAKES IN THE RIVER.
THE HUDSON RIVER? WHAT AM I, A NINJA TURTLE? YOU WANT ME MUTATING WORSE THAN I ALREADY AM?

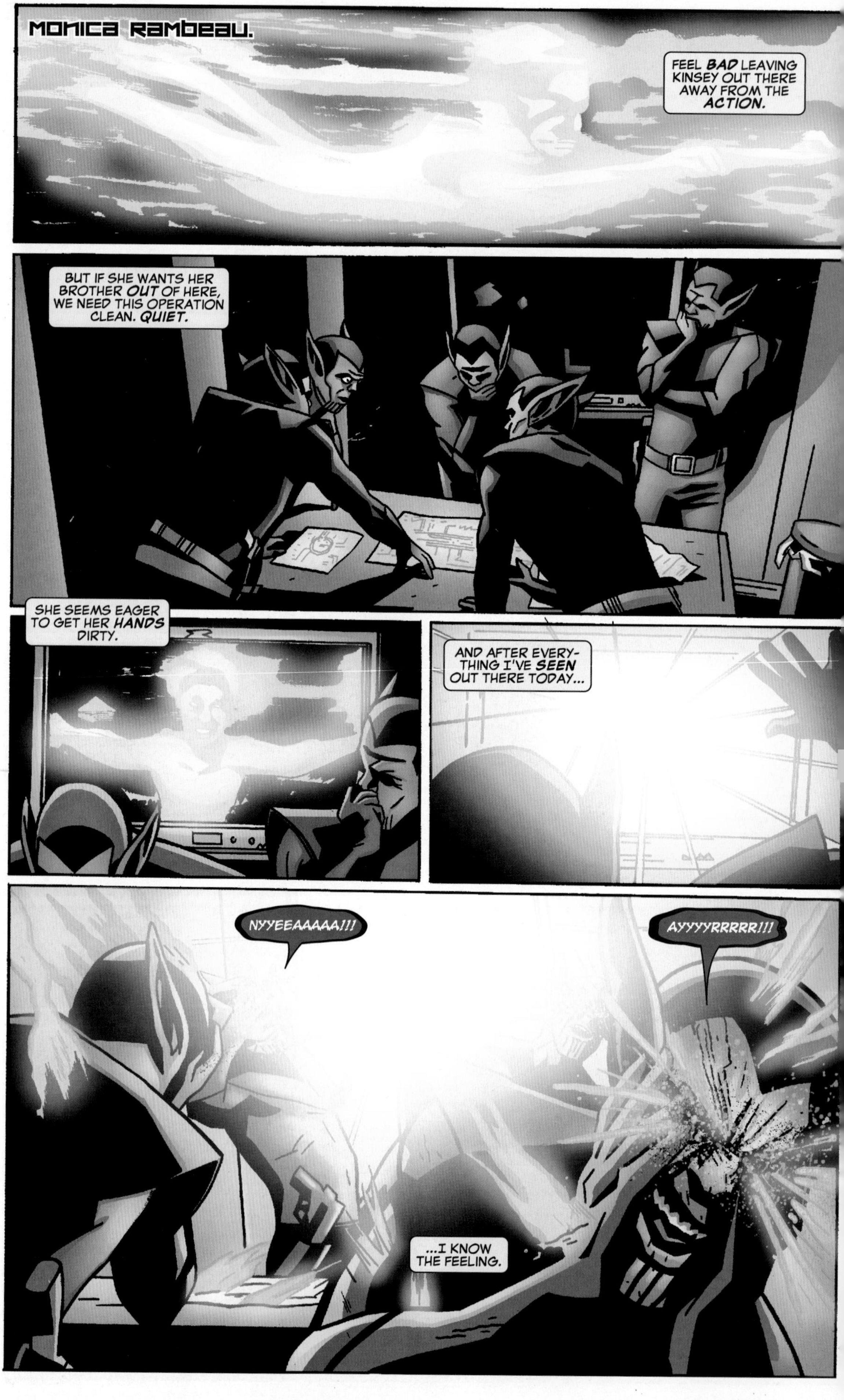

MONICA RAMBEAU.
FEEL BAD LEAVING KINSEY OUT THERE AWAY FROM THE ACTION.
BUT IF SHE WANTS HER BROTHER OUT OF HERE, WE NEED THIS OPERATION CLEAN. QUIET.
SHE SEEMS EAGER TO GET HER HANDS DIRTY.
AND AFTER EVERYTHING I'VE SEEN OUT THERE TODAY...
NYYEEAAAAA!!!
AYYYYRRRRR!!!
...I KNOW THE FEELING.

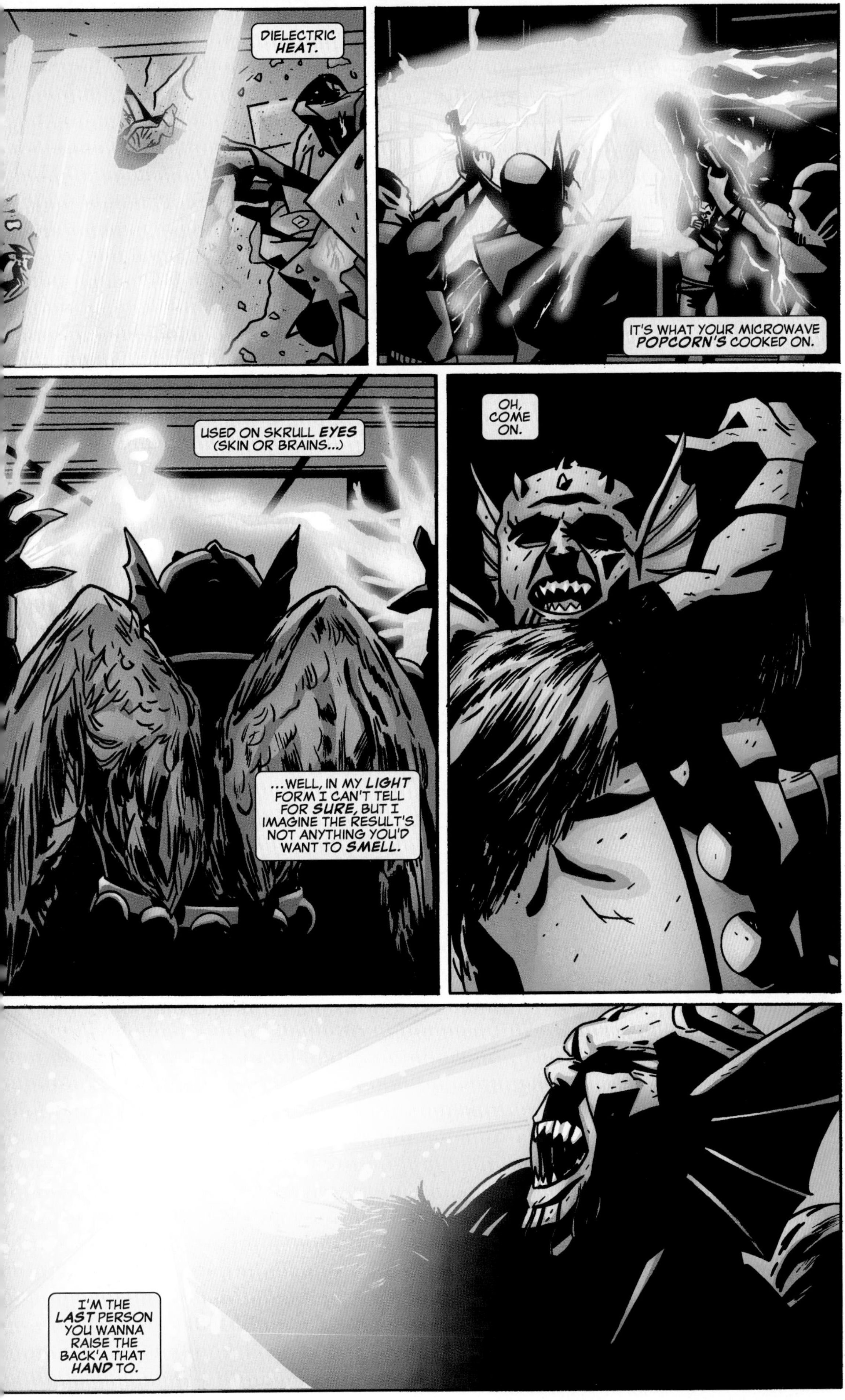
DIELECTRIC HEAT.
IT'S WHAT YOUR MICROWAVE POPCORN'S COOKED ON.
USED ON SKRULL EYES (SKIN OR BRAINS...)
...WELL, IN MY LIGHT FORM I CAN'T TELL FOR SURE, BUT I IMAGINE THE RESULT'S NOT ANYTHING YOU'D WANT TO SMELL.
OH, COME ON.
I'M THE LAST PERSON YOU WANNA RAISE THE BACK'A THAT HAND TO.

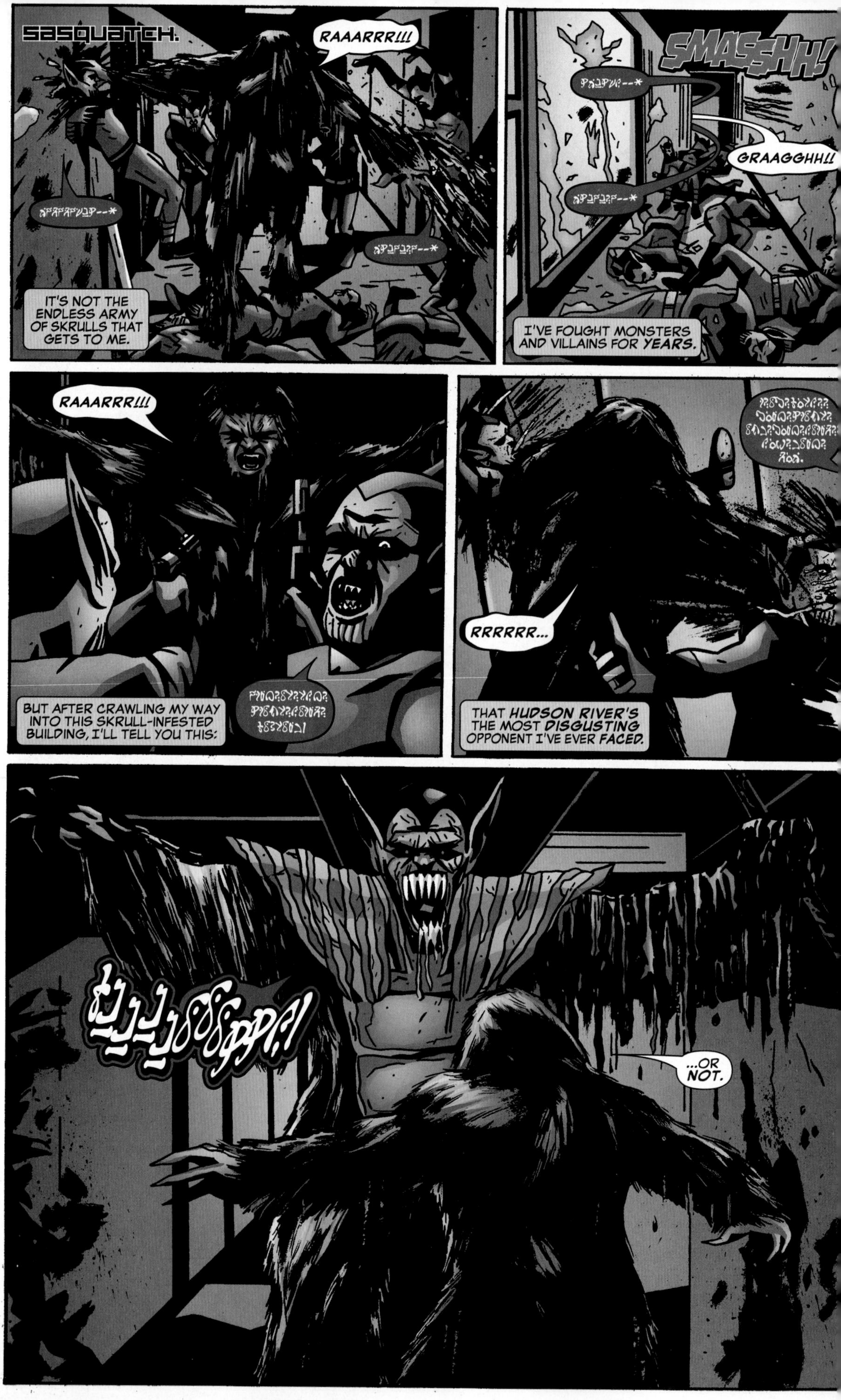
SASQUATCH.
RAAARRR!!!
IT'S NOT THE ENDLESS ARMY OF SKRULLS THAT GETS TO ME.
SMASSHH!
GRAAGGHH!!
I'VE FOUGHT MONSTERS AND VILLAINS FOR YEARS.
RAAARRR!!!
BUT AFTER CRAWLING MY WAY INTO THIS SKRULL-INFESTED BUILDING, I'LL TELL YOU THIS:
RRRRRR...
THAT HUDSON RIVER'S THE MOST DISGUSTING OPPONENT I'VE EVER FACED.
...OR NOT.

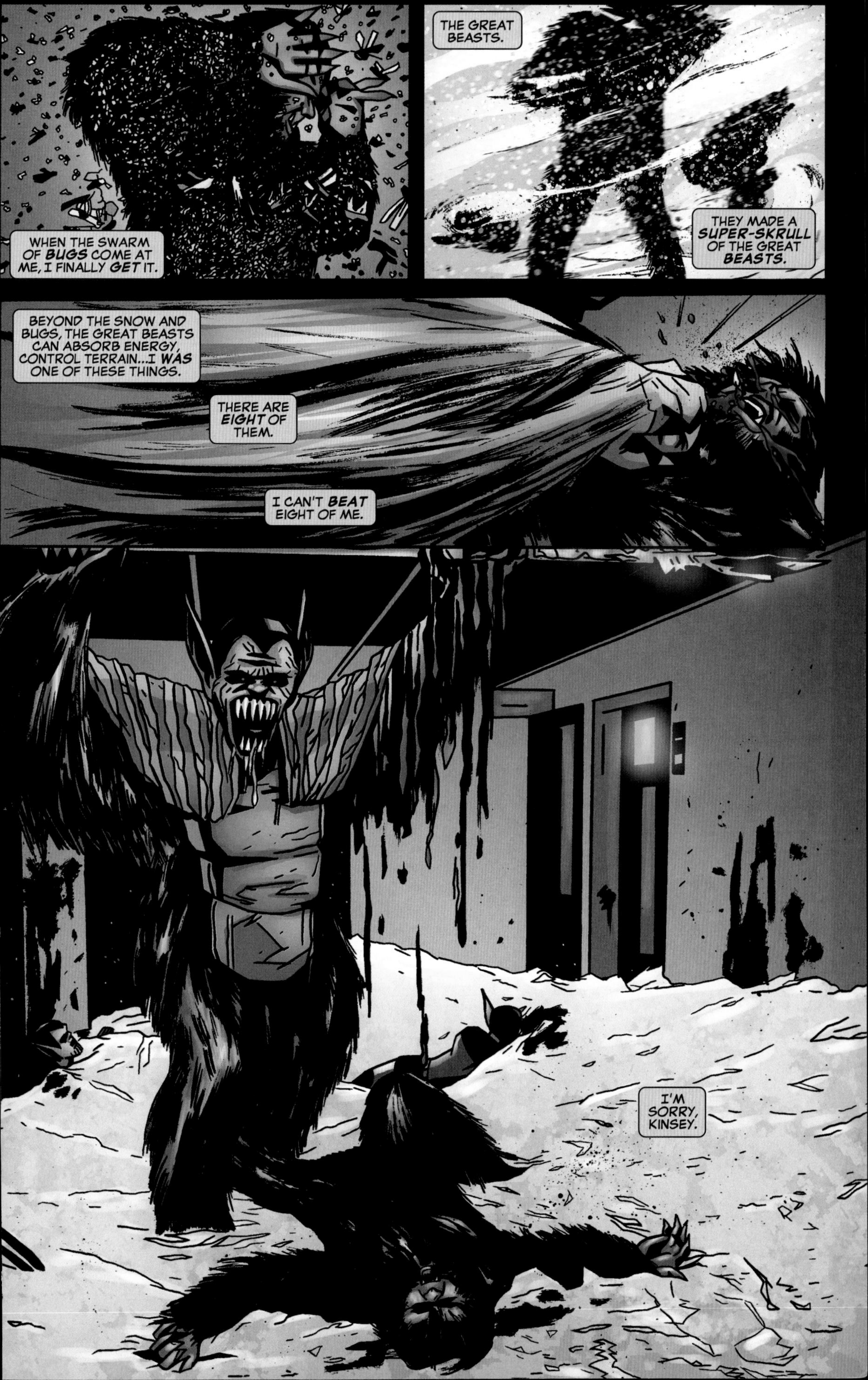

WHEN THE SWARM OF BUGS COME AT ME, I FINALLY GET IT.
THE GREAT BEASTS.
THEY MADE A SUPER-SKRULL OF THE GREAT BEASTS.
BEYOND THE SNOW AND BUGS, THE GREAT BEASTS CAN ABSORB ENERGY, CONTROL TERRAIN...I WAS ONE OF THESE THINGS.
THERE ARE EIGHT OF THEM.
I CAN'T BEAT EIGHT OF ME.
I'M SORRY, KINSEY.

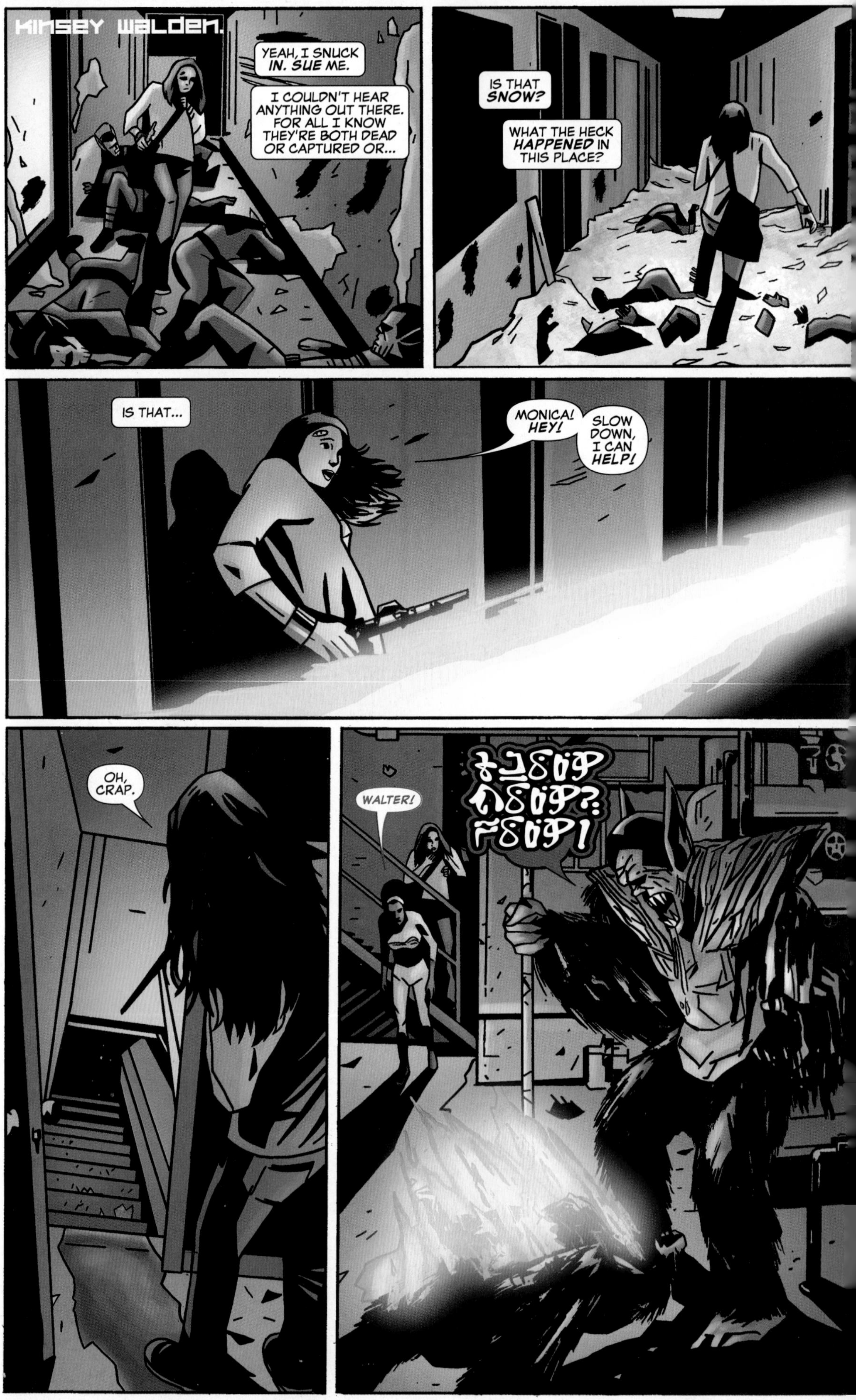
KINSEY WALDEN.
YEAH, I SNUCK IN. SUE ME.
I COULDN'T HEAR ANYTHING OUT THERE. FOR ALL I KNOW THEY'RE BOTH DEAD OR CAPTURED OR...
IS THAT SNOW?
WHAT THE HECK HAPPENED IN THIS PLACE?
IS THAT...
MONICA! HEY!
SLOW DOWN, I CAN HELP!
OH, CRAP.
WALTER!

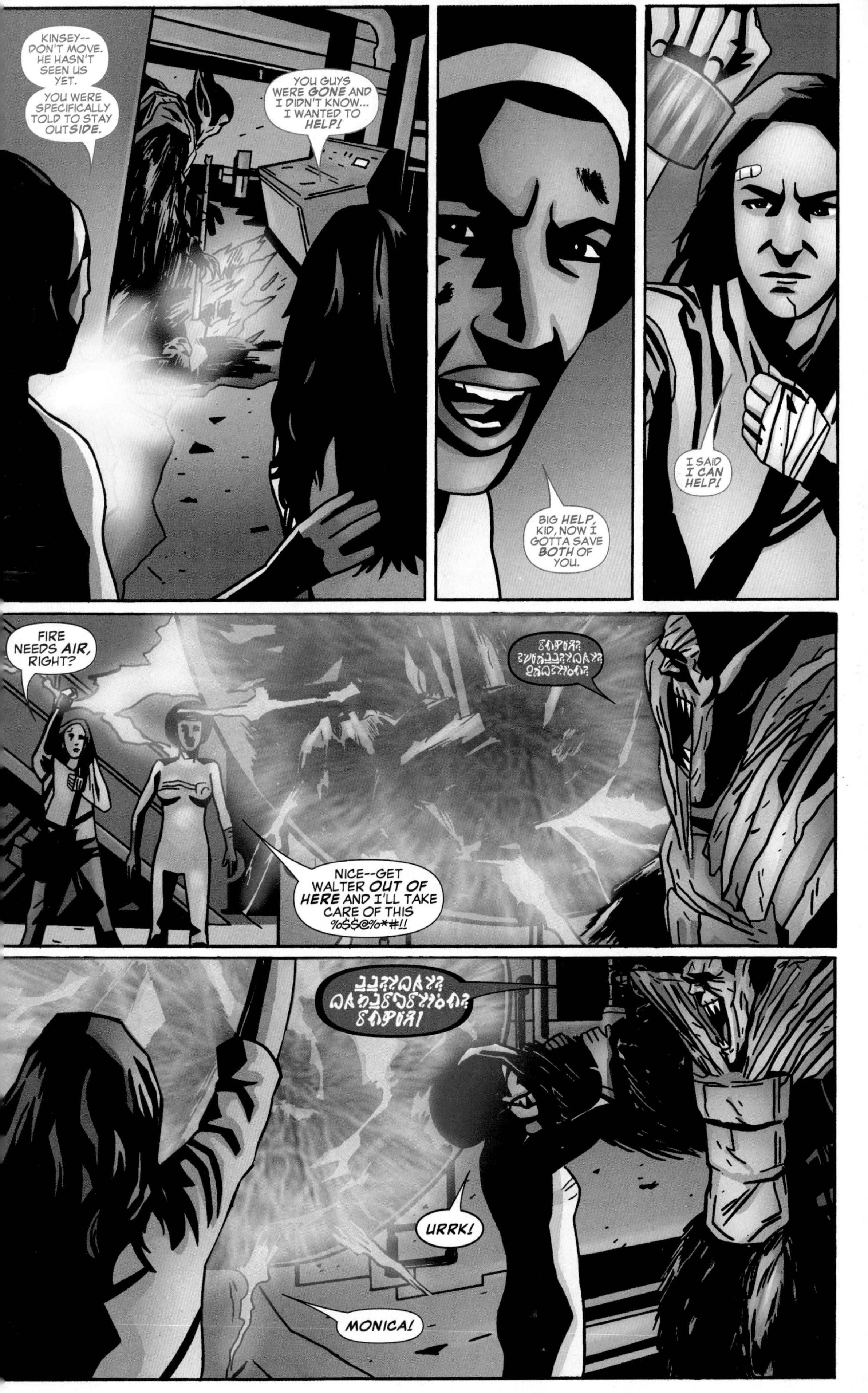
KINSEY-- DON'T MOVE. HE HASN'T SEEN US YET.
YOU WERE SPECIFICALLY TOLD TO STAY OUTSIDE.
YOU GUYS WERE GONE AND I DIDN'T KNOW... I WANTED TO HELP!
BIG HELP, KID, NOW I GOTTA SAVE BOTH OF YOU.
I SAID I CAN HELP!
FIRE NEEDS AIR, RIGHT?
NICE--GET WALTER OUT OF HERE AND I'LL TAKE CARE OF THIS %$$@%*#!!
URRK!
MONICA!

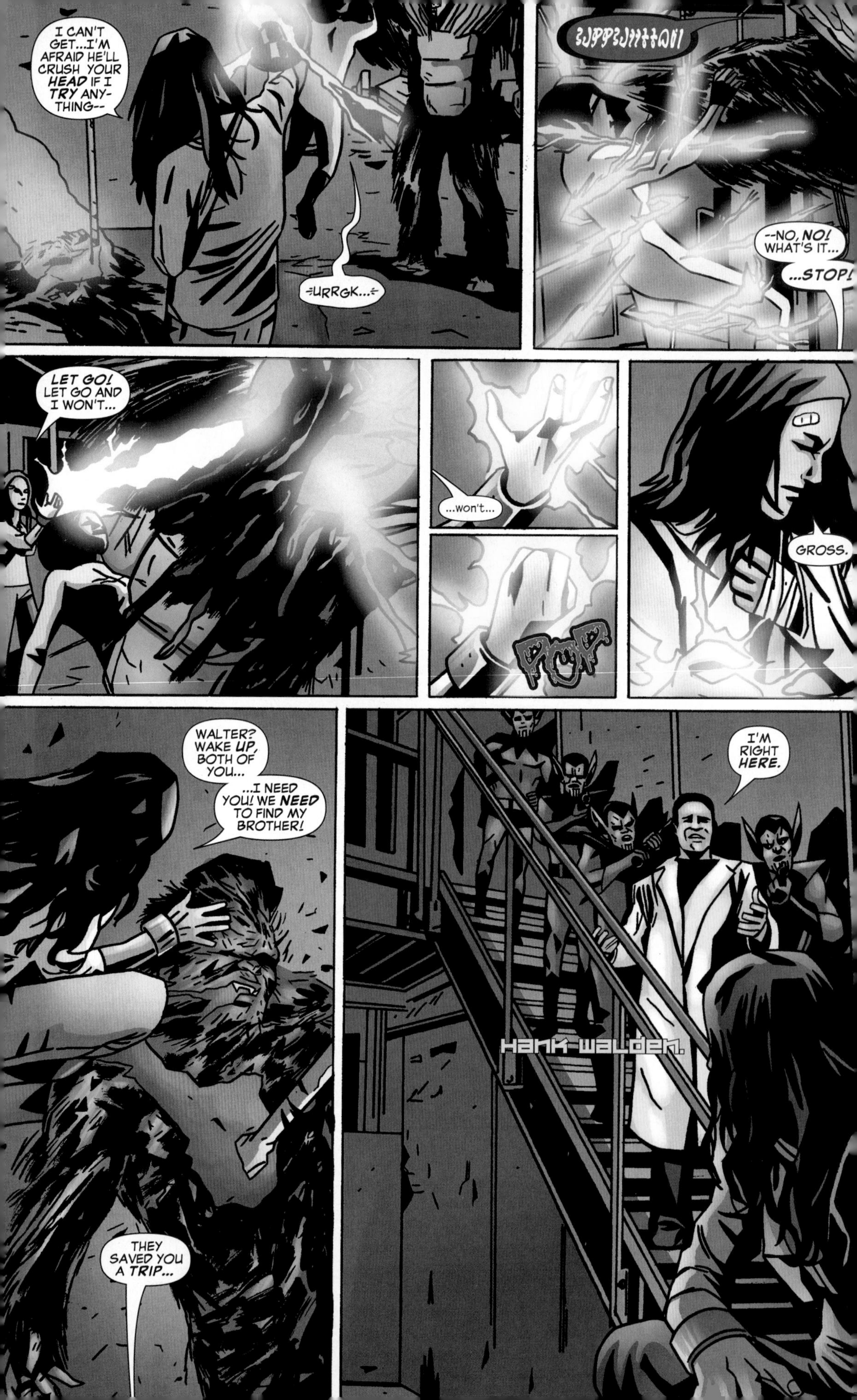

I CAN'T GET...I'M AFRAID HE'LL CRUSH YOUR HEAD IF I TRY ANYTHING--
URRGK...
--NO, NO! WHAT'S IT...
...STOP!
LET GO! LET GO AND I WON'T...
...won't...
POP
GROSS.
WALTER? WAKE UP, BOTH OF YOU...
...I NEED YOU! WE NEED TO FIND MY BROTHER!
THEY SAVED YOU A TRIP...
I'M RIGHT HERE.
HANK WALDEN.

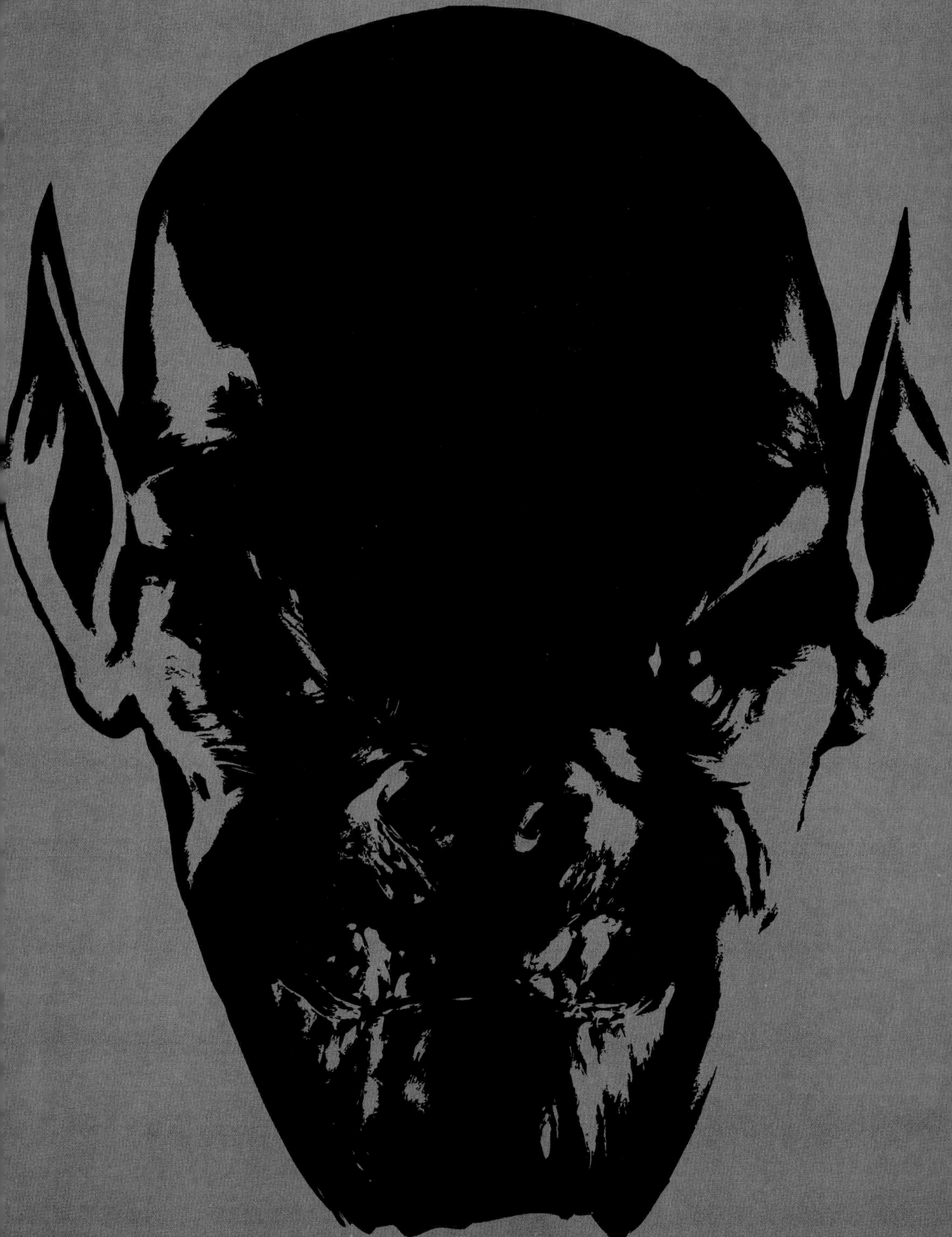

CHAPTER 8

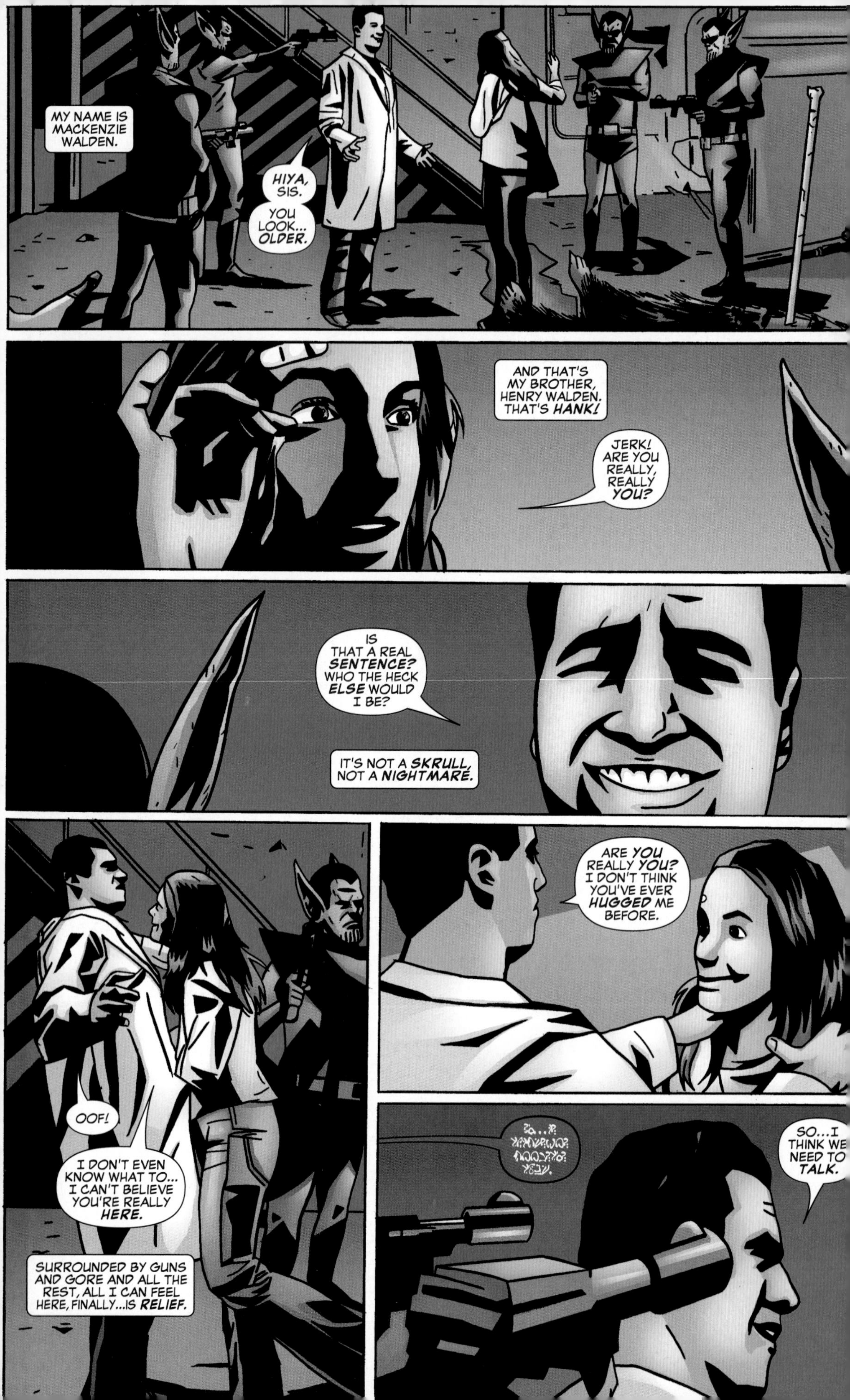

MY NAME IS MACKENZIE WALDEN.
HIYA, SIS.
YOU LOOK... OLDER.
AND THAT'S MY BROTHER, HENRY WALDEN. THAT'S HANK!
JERK! ARE YOU REALLY, REALLY YOU?
IS THAT A REAL SENTENCE? WHO THE HECK ELSE WOULD I BE?
IT'S NOT A SKRULL, NOT A NIGHTMARE.
OOF!
I DON'T EVEN KNOW WHAT TO... I CAN'T BELIEVE YOU'RE REALLY HERE.
SURROUNDED BY GUNS AND GORE AND ALL THE REST, ALL I CAN FEEL HERE, FINALLY...IS RELIEF.
ARE YOU REALLY YOU? I DON'T THINK YOU'VE EVER HUGGED ME BEFORE.
SO...I THINK WE NEED TO TALK.

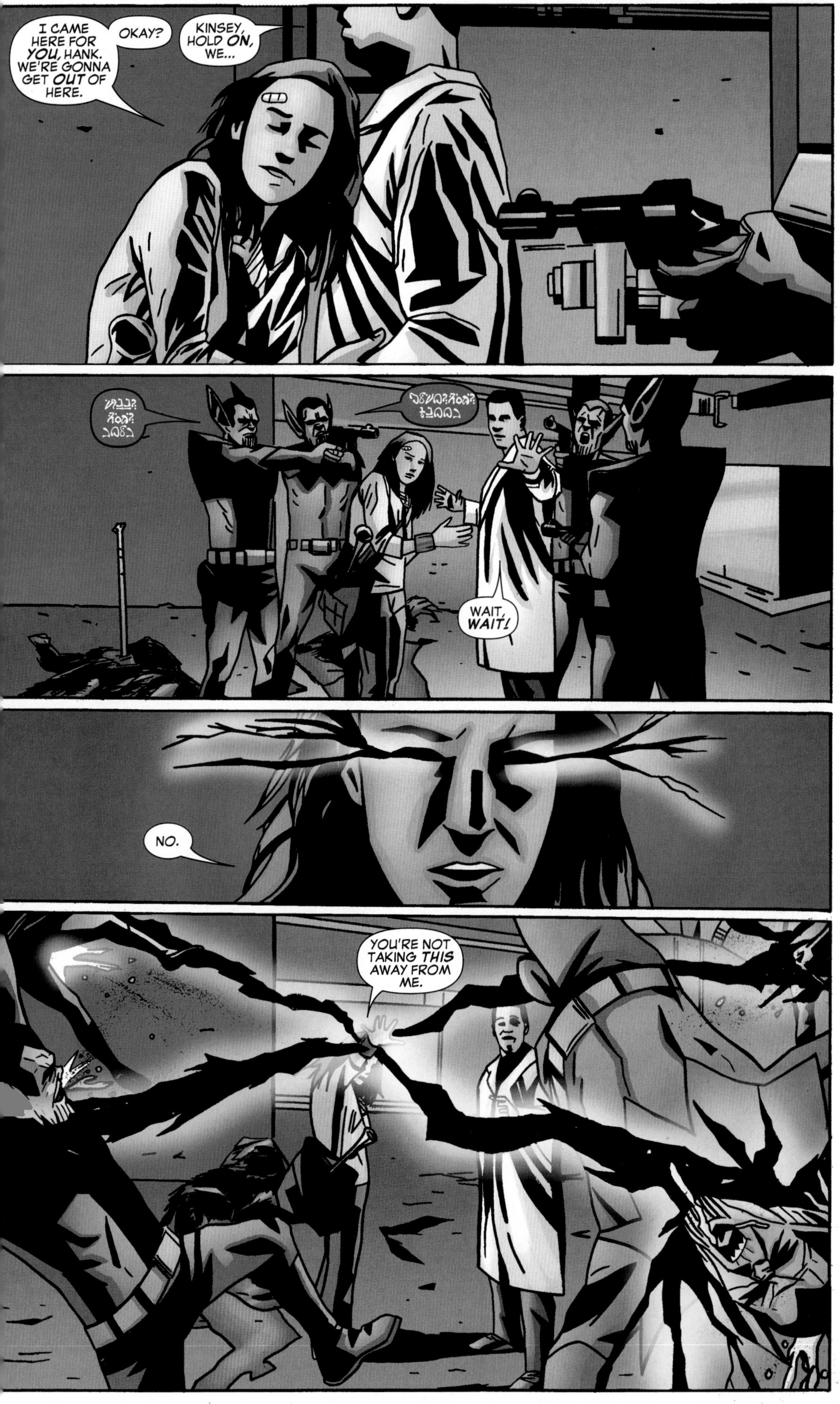
I CAME HERE FOR YOU, HANK. WE'RE GONNA GET OUT OF HERE.
OKAY?
KINSEY, HOLD ON, WE...
WAIT, WAIT!
NO.
YOU'RE NOT TAKING THIS AWAY FROM ME.

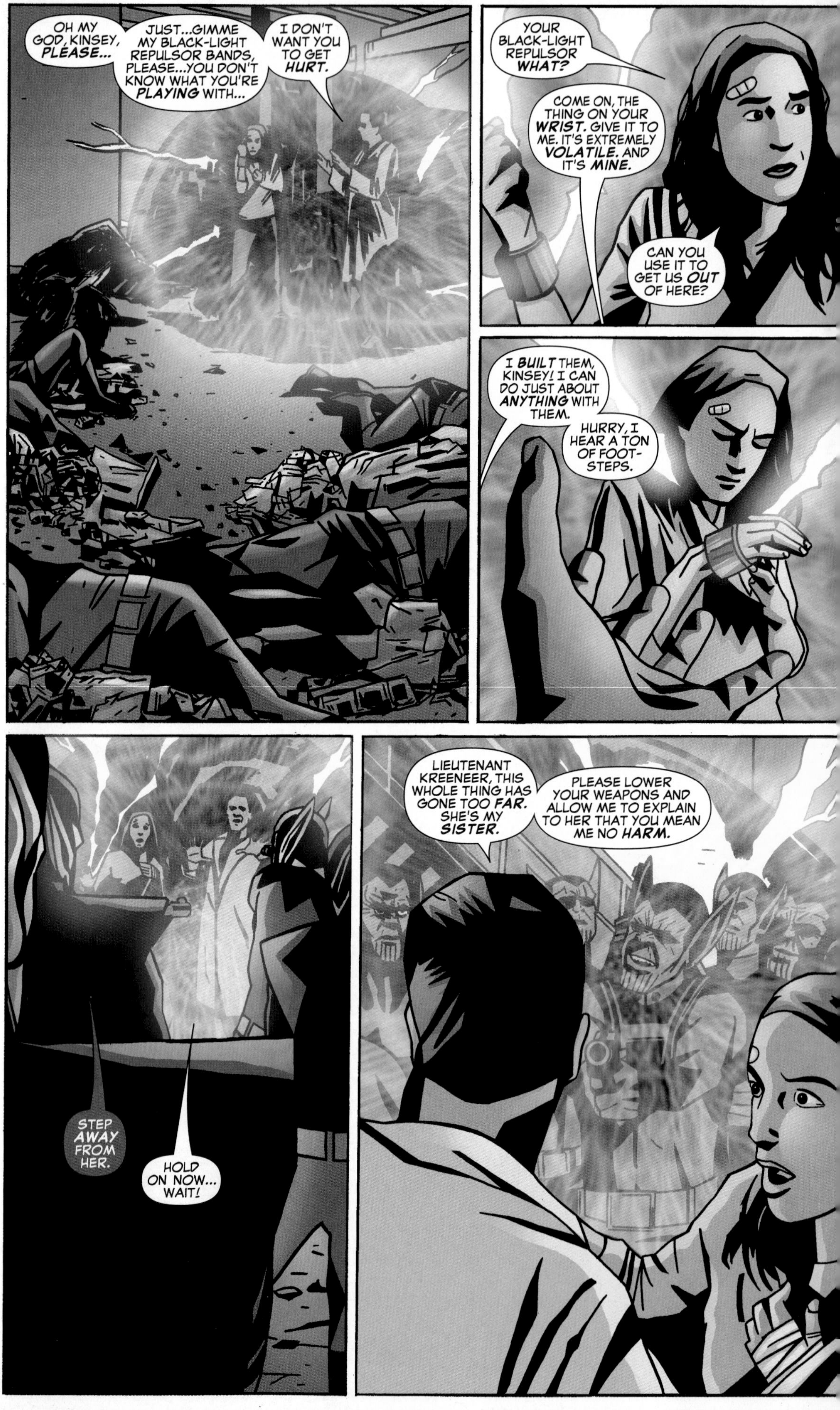
OH MY GOD, KINSEY, PLEASE...
JUST...GIMME MY BLACK-LIGHT REPULSOR BANDS, PLEASE...YOU DON'T KNOW WHAT YOU'RE PLAYING WITH...
I DON'T WANT YOU TO GET HURT.
YOUR BLACK-LIGHT REPULSOR WHAT?
COME ON, THE THING ON YOUR WRIST. GIVE IT TO ME. IT'S EXTREMELY VOLATILE. AND IT'S MINE.
CAN YOU USE IT TO GET US OUT OF HERE?
I BUILT THEM, KINSEY! I CAN DO JUST ABOUT ANYTHING WITH THEM.
HURRY, I HEAR A TON OF FOOT-STEPS.
STEP AWAY FROM HER.
HOLD ON NOW... WAIT!
LIEUTENANT KREENEER, THIS WHOLE THING HAS GONE TOO FAR. SHE'S MY SISTER.
PLEASE LOWER YOUR WEAPONS AND ALLOW ME TO EXPLAIN TO HER THAT YOU MEAN ME NO HARM.

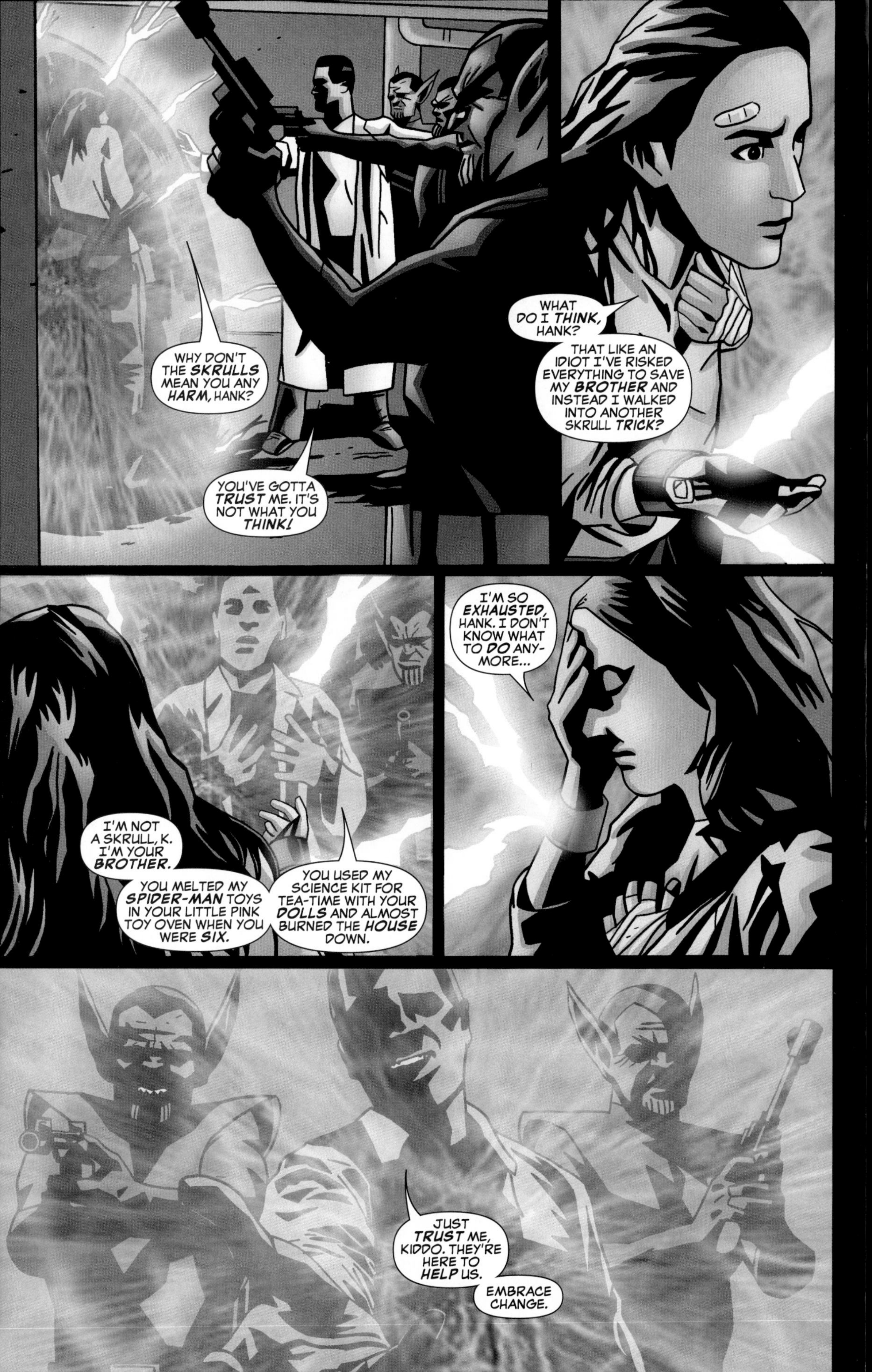
WHY DON'T THE SKRULLS MEAN YOU ANY HARM, HANK?
YOU'VE GOTTA TRUST ME. IT'S NOT WHAT YOU THINK!
WHAT DO I THINK, HANK?
THAT LIKE AN IDIOT I'VE RISKED EVERYTHING TO SAVE MY BROTHER AND INSTEAD I WALKED INTO ANOTHER SKRULL TRICK?
I'M NOT A SKRULL, K. I'M YOUR BROTHER.
YOU MELTED MY SPIDER-MAN TOYS IN YOUR LITTLE PINK TOY OVEN WHEN YOU WERE SIX.
YOU USED MY SCIENCE KIT FOR TEA-TIME WITH YOUR DOLLS AND ALMOST BURNED THE HOUSE DOWN.
I'M SO EXHAUSTED, HANK. I DON'T KNOW WHAT TO DO ANY-MORE...
JUST TRUST ME, KIDDO. THEY'RE HERE TO HELP US.
EMBRACE CHANGE.

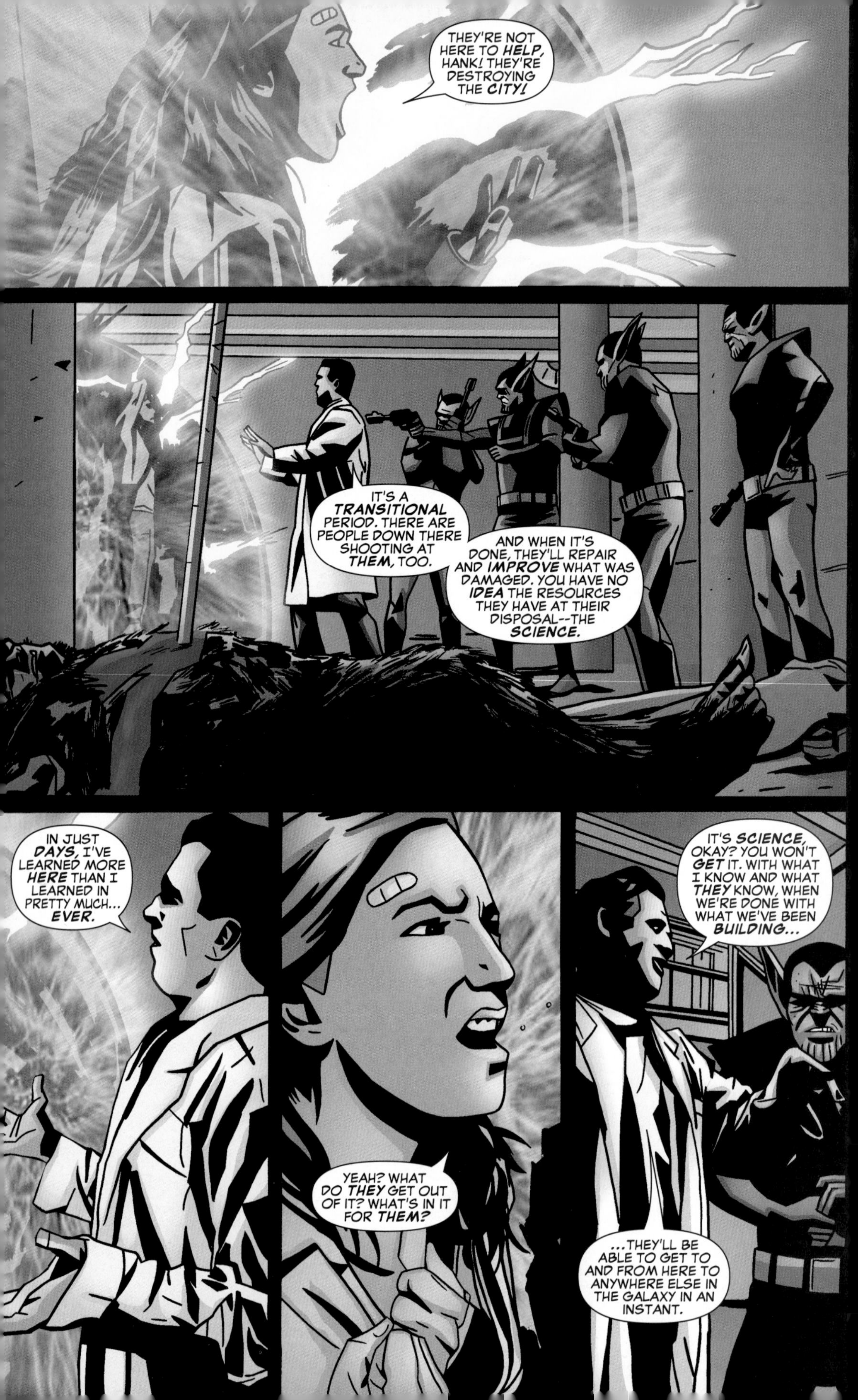
THEY'RE NOT HERE TO HELP, HANK! THEY'RE DESTROYING THE CITY!
IT'S A TRANSITIONAL PERIOD. THERE ARE PEOPLE DOWN THERE SHOOTING AT THEM, TOO.
AND WHEN IT'S DONE, THEY'LL REPAIR AND IMPROVE WHAT WAS DAMAGED. YOU HAVE NO IDEA THE RESOURCES THEY HAVE AT THEIR DISPOSAL--THE SCIENCE.
IN JUST DAYS, I'VE LEARNED MORE HERE THAN I LEARNED IN PRETTY MUCH... EVER.
YEAH? WHAT DO THEY GET OUT OF IT? WHAT'S IN IT FOR THEM?
IT'S SCIENCE, OKAY? YOU WON'T GET IT. WITH WHAT I KNOW AND WHAT THEY KNOW, WHEN WE'RE DONE WITH WHAT WE'VE BEEN BUILDING...
...THEY'LL BE ABLE TO GET TO AND FROM HERE TO ANYWHERE ELSE IN THE GALAXY IN AN INSTANT.

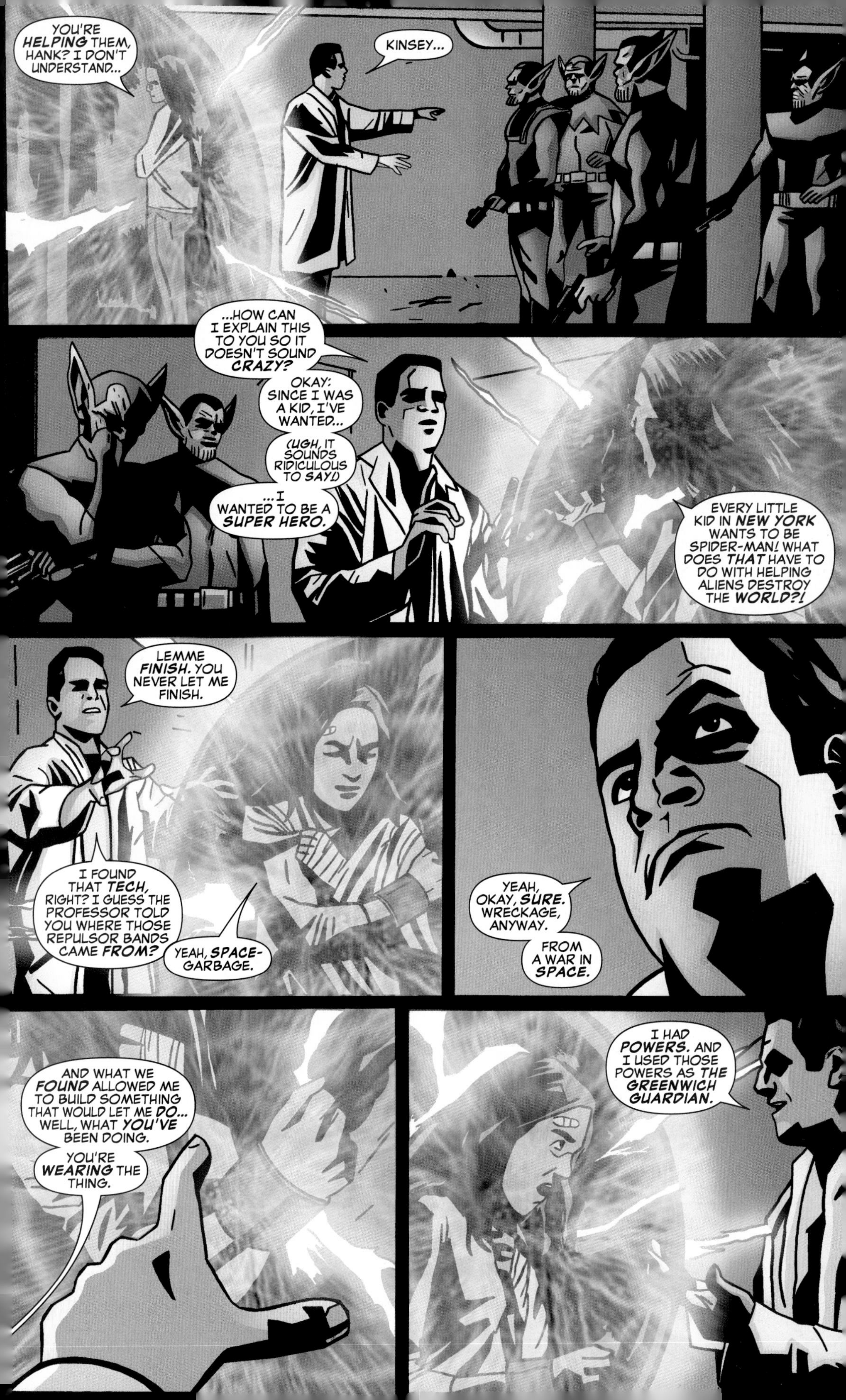
YOU'RE HELPING THEM, HANK? I DON'T UNDERSTAND...
KINSEY...
...HOW CAN I EXPLAIN THIS TO YOU SO IT DOESN'T SOUND CRAZY?
OKAY: SINCE I WAS A KID, I'VE WANTED...
(UGH, IT SOUNDS RIDICULOUS TO SAY!)
...I WANTED TO BE A SUPER HERO.
EVERY LITTLE KID IN NEW YORK WANTS TO BE SPIDER-MAN! WHAT DOES THAT HAVE TO DO WITH HELPING ALIENS DESTROY THE WORLD?!
LEMME FINISH. YOU NEVER LET ME FINISH.
I FOUND THAT TECH, RIGHT? I GUESS THE PROFESSOR TOLD YOU WHERE THOSE REPULSOR BANDS CAME FROM?
YEAH, SPACE-GARBAGE.
YEAH, OKAY, SURE. WRECKAGE, ANYWAY.
FROM A WAR IN SPACE.
AND WHAT WE FOUND ALLOWED ME TO BUILD SOMETHING THAT WOULD LET ME DO... WELL, WHAT YOU'VE BEEN DOING.
YOU'RE WEARING THE THING.
I HAD POWERS. AND I USED THOSE POWERS AS THE GREENWICH GUARDIAN.

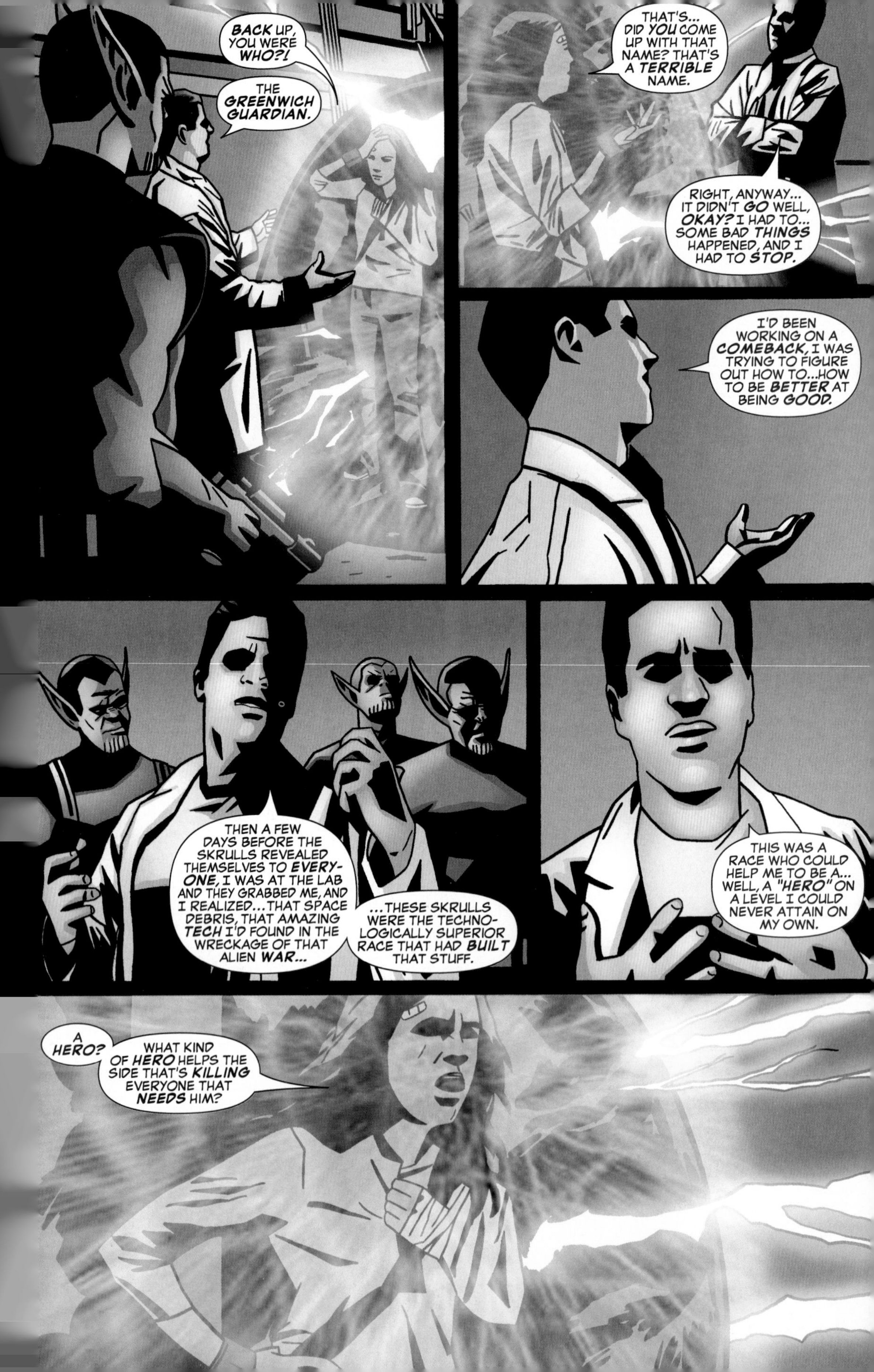
BACK UP, YOU WERE WHO?!
THE GREENWICH GUARDIAN.
THAT'S... DID YOU COME UP WITH THAT NAME? THAT'S A TERRIBLE NAME.
RIGHT, ANYWAY... IT DIDN'T GO WELL, OKAY? I HAD TO... SOME BAD THINGS HAPPENED, AND I HAD TO STOP.
I'D BEEN WORKING ON A COMEBACK, I WAS TRYING TO FIGURE OUT HOW TO...HOW TO BE BETTER AT BEING GOOD.
THEN A FEW DAYS BEFORE THE SKRULLS REVEALED THEMSELVES TO EVERY-ONE, I WAS AT THE LAB AND THEY GRABBED ME, AND I REALIZED... THAT SPACE DEBRIS, THAT AMAZING TECH I'D FOUND IN THE WRECKAGE OF THAT ALIEN WAR...
...THESE SKRULLS WERE THE TECHNO-LOGICALLY SUPERIOR RACE THAT HAD BUILT THAT STUFF.
THIS WAS A RACE WHO COULD HELP ME TO BE A... WELL, A "HERO" ON A LEVEL I COULD NEVER ATTAIN ON MY OWN.
A HERO?
WHAT KIND OF HERO HELPS THE SIDE THAT'S KILLING EVERYONE THAT NEEDS HIM?

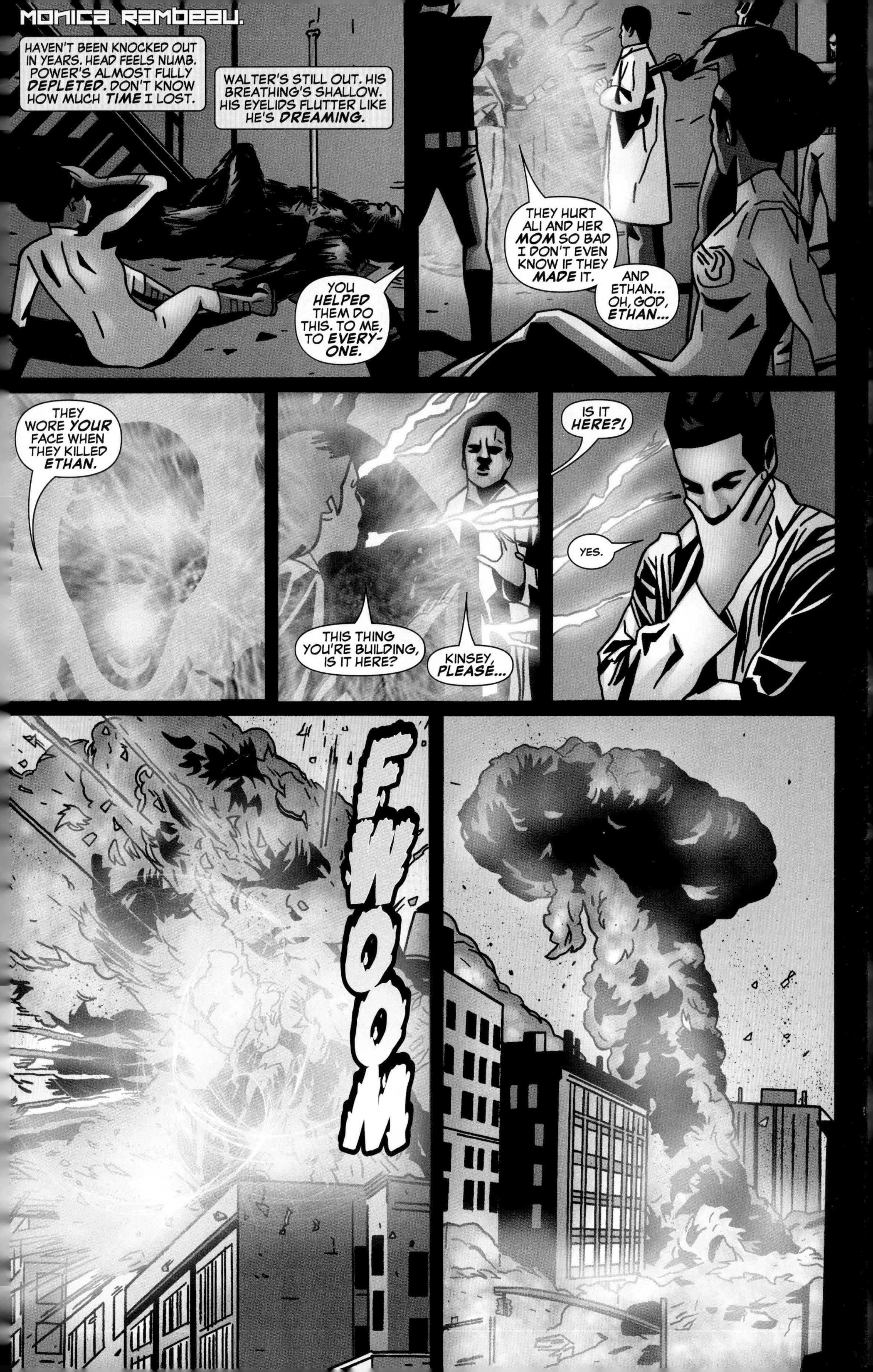
MONICA RAMBEAU.
HAVEN'T BEEN KNOCKED OUT IN YEARS. HEAD FEELS NUMB. POWER'S ALMOST FULLY DEPLETED. DON'T KNOW HOW MUCH TIME I LOST.
WALTER'S STILL OUT. HIS BREATHING'S SHALLOW. HIS EYELIDS FLUTTER LIKE HE'S DREAMING.
YOU HELPED THEM DO THIS. TO ME, TO EVERY-ONE.
THEY HURT ALI AND HER MOM SO BAD I DON'T EVEN KNOW IF THEY MADE IT.
AND ETHAN... OH, GOD, ETHAN...
THEY WORE YOUR FACE WHEN THEY KILLED ETHAN.
THIS THING YOU'RE BUILDING, IS IT HERE?
KINSEY, PLEASE...
IS IT HERE?!
YES.
FWOOOM

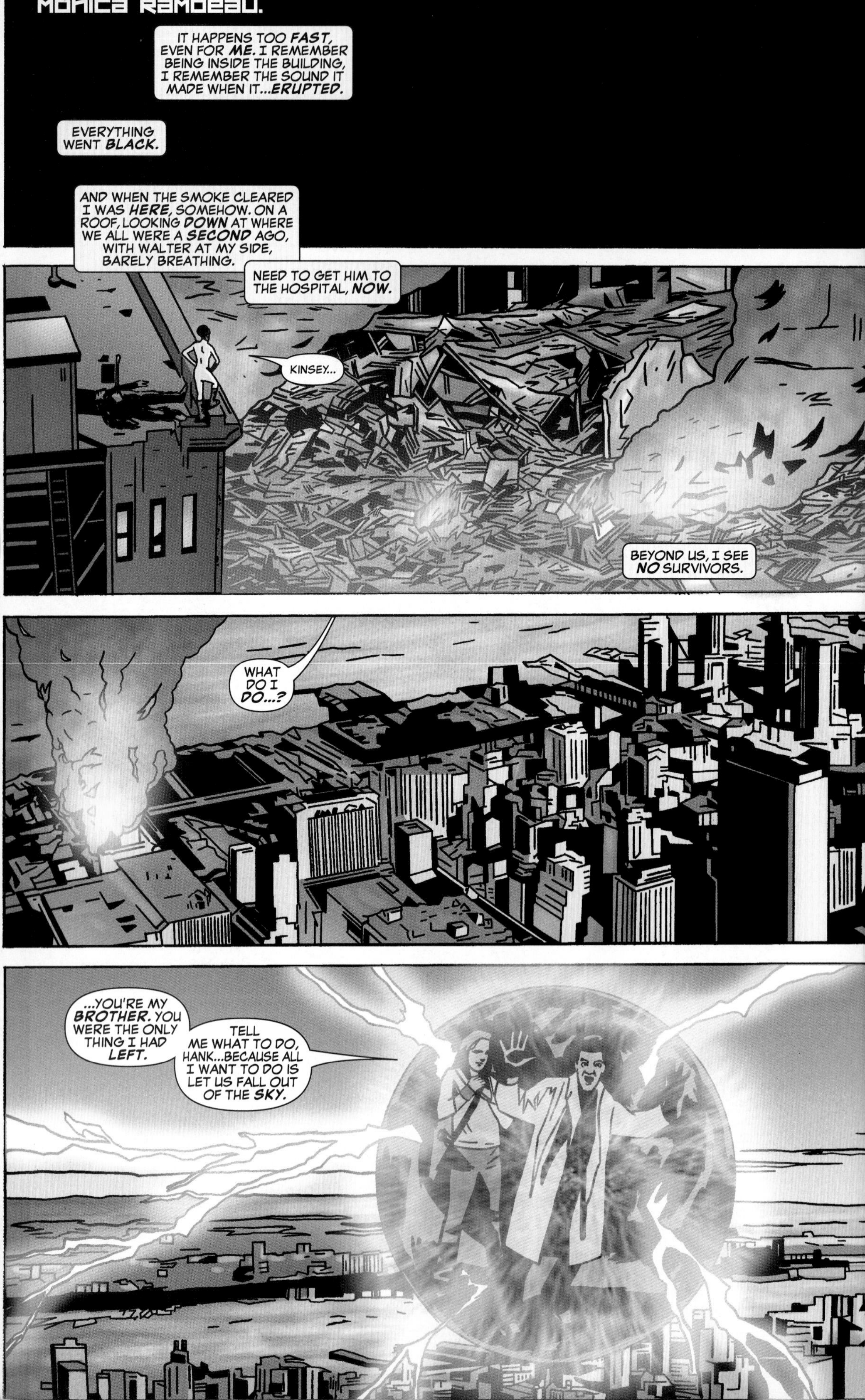
MONICA RAMBEAU.
IT HAPPENS TOO FAST, EVEN FOR ME. I REMEMBER BEING INSIDE THE BUILDING, I REMEMBER THE SOUND IT MADE WHEN IT...ERUPTED.
EVERYTHING WENT BLACK.
AND WHEN THE SMOKE CLEARED I WAS HERE, SOMEHOW. ON A ROOF, LOOKING DOWN AT WHERE WE ALL WERE A SECOND AGO, WITH WALTER AT MY SIDE, BARELY BREATHING.
NEED TO GET HIM TO THE HOSPITAL, NOW.
KINSEY...
BEYOND US, I SEE NO SURVIVORS.
WHAT DO I DO...?
...YOU'RE MY BROTHER. YOU WERE THE ONLY THING I HAD LEFT.
TELL ME WHAT TO DO, HANK...BECAUSE ALL I WANT TO DO IS LET US FALL OUT OF THE SKY.

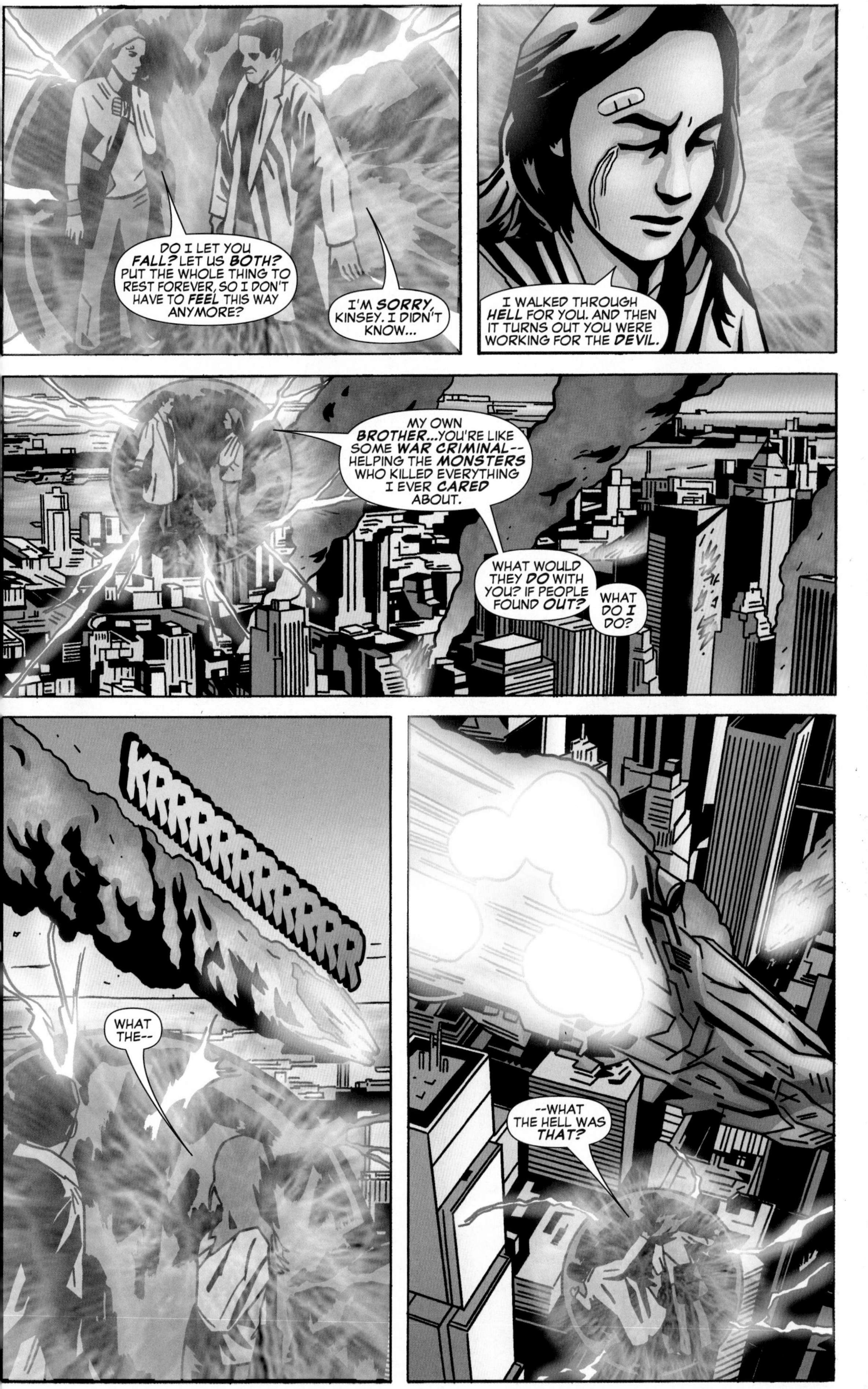
DO I LET YOU FALL? LET US BOTH? PUT THE WHOLE THING TO REST FOREVER, SO I DON'T HAVE TO FEEL THIS WAY ANYMORE?
I'M SORRY, KINSEY. I DIDN'T KNOW...
I WALKED THROUGH HELL FOR YOU. AND THEN IT TURNS OUT YOU WERE WORKING FOR THE DEVIL.
MY OWN BROTHER...YOU'RE LIKE SOME WAR CRIMINAL--HELPING THE MONSTERS WHO KILLED EVERYTHING I EVER CARED ABOUT.
WHAT WOULD THEY DO WITH YOU? IF PEOPLE FOUND OUT?
WHAT DO I DO?
KRRRRRRRRRRRRRRR
WHAT THE--
--WHAT THE HELL WAS THAT?

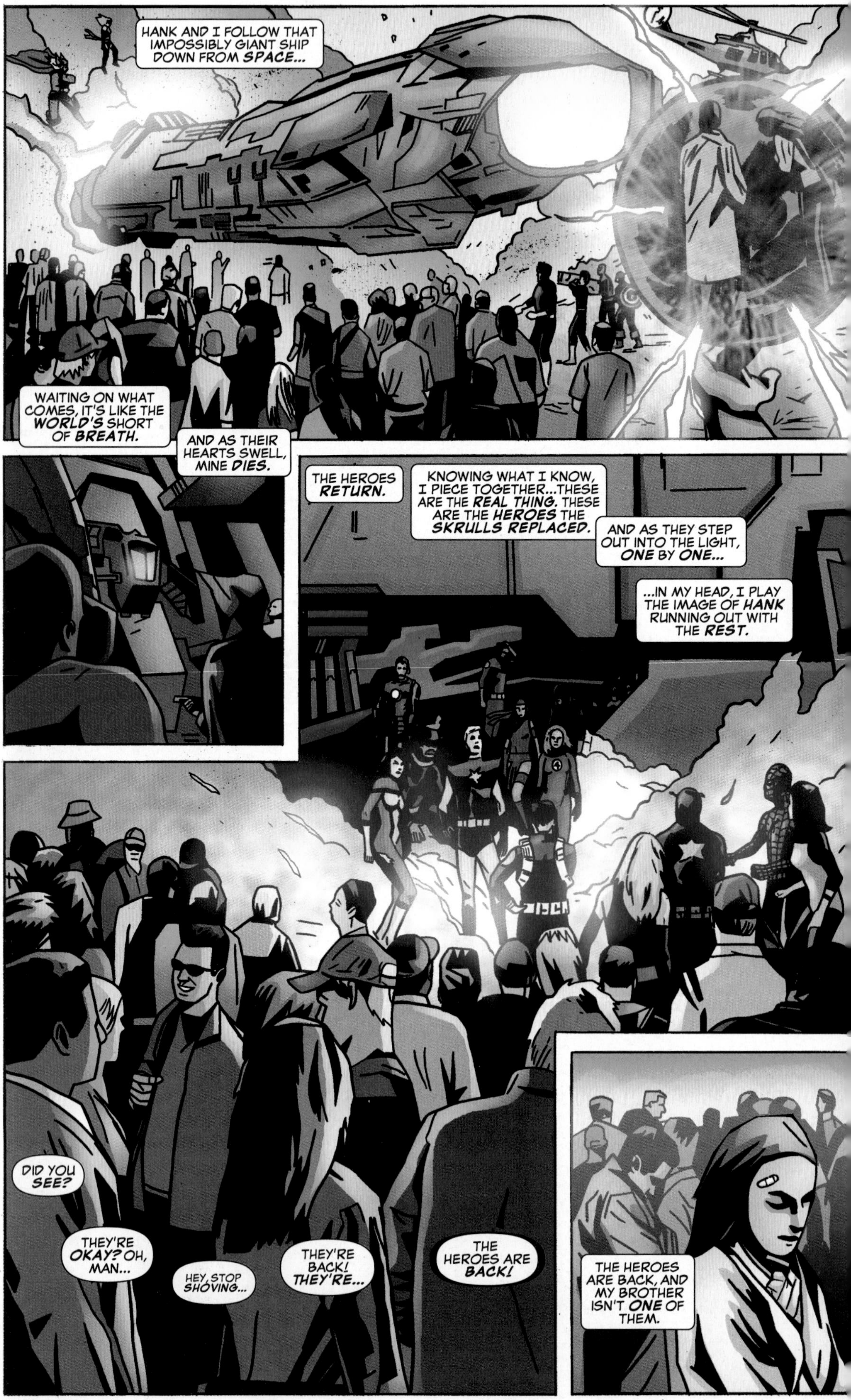
HANK AND I FOLLOW THAT IMPOSSIBLY GIANT SHIP DOWN FROM SPACE...
WAITING ON WHAT COMES, IT'S LIKE THE WORLD'S SHORT OF BREATH.
AND AS THEIR HEARTS SWELL, MINE DIES.
THE HEROES RETURN.
KNOWING WHAT I KNOW, I PIECE TOGETHER...THESE ARE THE REAL THING. THESE ARE THE HEROES THE SKRULLS REPLACED.
AND AS THEY STEP OUT INTO THE LIGHT, ONE BY ONE...
...IN MY HEAD, I PLAY THE IMAGE OF HANK RUNNING OUT WITH THE REST.
DID YOU SEE?
THEY'RE OKAY? OH, MAN...
HEY, STOP SHOVING...
THEY'RE BACK! THEY'RE...
THE HEROES ARE BACK!
THE HEROES ARE BACK, AND MY BROTHER ISN'T ONE OF THEM.

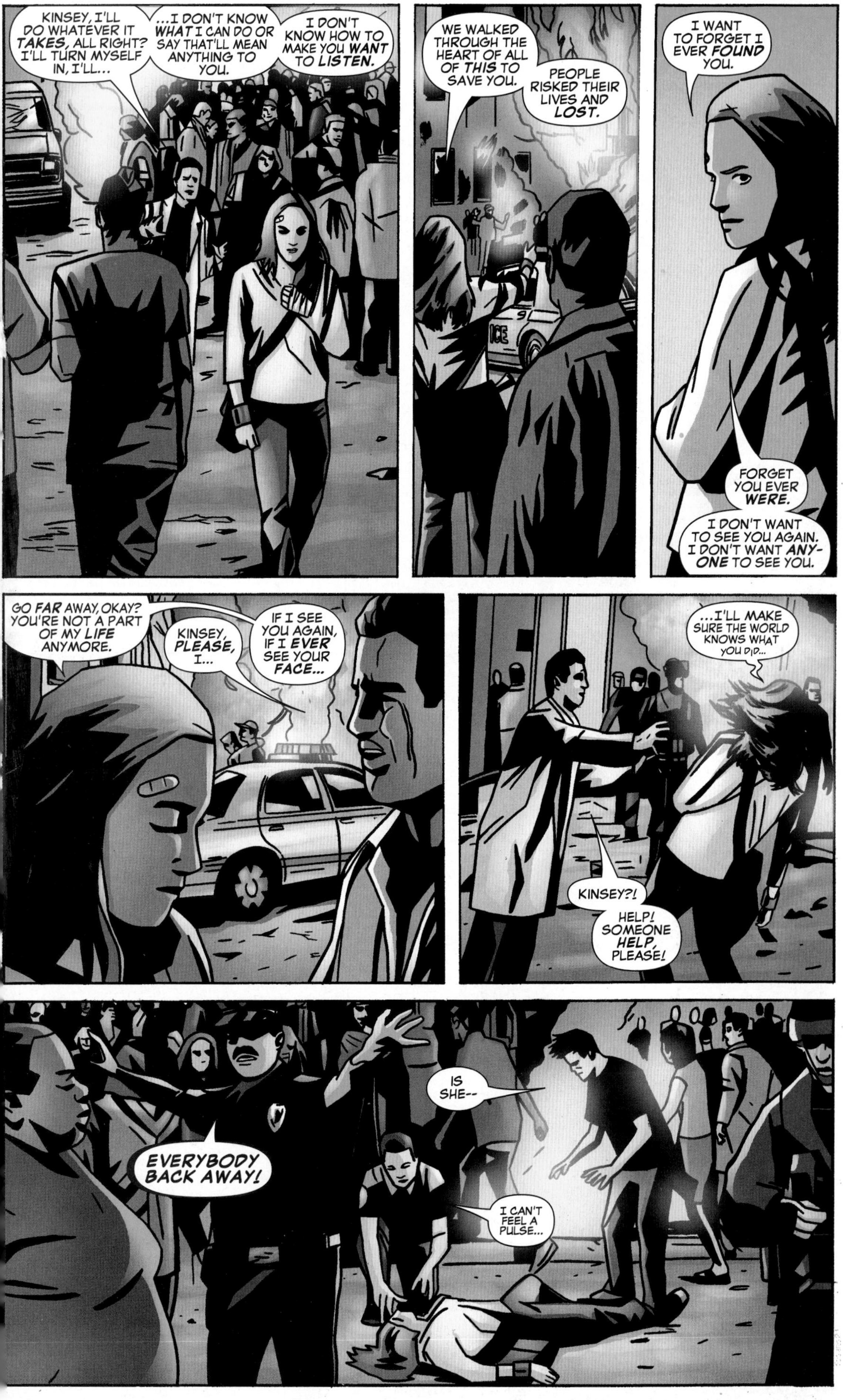
KINSEY, I'LL DO WHATEVER IT TAKES, ALL RIGHT? I'LL TURN MYSELF IN, I'LL...
...I DON'T KNOW WHAT I CAN DO OR SAY THAT'LL MEAN ANYTHING TO YOU.
I DON'T KNOW HOW TO MAKE YOU WANT TO LISTEN.
WE WALKED THROUGH THE HEART OF ALL OF THIS TO SAVE YOU.
PEOPLE RISKED THEIR LIVES AND LOST.
I WANT TO FORGET I EVER FOUND YOU.
FORGET YOU EVER WERE.
I DON'T WANT TO SEE YOU AGAIN. I DON'T WANT ANY-ONE TO SEE YOU.
GO FAR AWAY, OKAY? YOU'RE NOT A PART OF MY LIFE ANYMORE.
KINSEY, PLEASE, I...
IF I SEE YOU AGAIN, IF I EVER SEE YOUR FACE...
...I'LL MAKE SURE THE WORLD KNOWS WHAT YOU DID...
KINSEY?!
HELP! SOMEONE HELP, PLEASE!
IS SHE--
EVERYBODY BACK AWAY!
I CAN'T FEEL A PULSE...

WHEN I WAKE UP, *DAYS'VE* PASSED. MY BROTHER'S NOT AROUND. NO ONE'S *SHOOTING* AT ME.

WHATEVER THE HEROES DID IN *SPACE*, THE INVASION IS *OVER*.

NONETHELESS, THE CITY *SMOLDERS*.

EMERGENC

AND YEAH, THE ALIENS ARE GONE, BUT IT'S NOT *QUIET*.

ALI WAKES UP IN THE *ICU*, COVERED IN WIRES AND A MACHINE THAT HELPS HER BREATHE.

SHE WAKES LOOKING AT HER *MOTHER*, WHO CHECKED OUT OF THE SAME HOSPITAL THREE HOURS BEFORE THEY CALLED TO SAY HER *DAUGHTER'S* IN CRITICAL CARE.

ALI WILL *MAKE* IT.

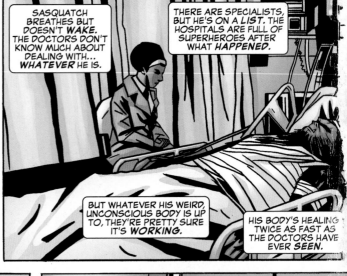

SASQUATCH BREATHES BUT DOESN'T *WAKE*. THE DOCTORS DON'T KNOW MUCH ABOUT DEALING WITH... *WHATEVER* HE IS.

THERE ARE SPECIALISTS, BUT HE'S ON A *LIST*. THE HOSPITALS ARE FULL OF SUPERHEROES AFTER WHAT *HAPPENED*.

BUT WHATEVER HIS WEIRD, UNCONSCIOUS BODY IS UP TO, THEY'RE PRETTY SURE IT'S *WORKING*.

HIS BODY'S HEALING TWICE AS FAST AS THE DOCTORS HAVE EVER *SEEN*.

LOT OF OTHER THINGS CAN'T *EVER* BE FIXED. NOT THE CRIPPLED, NOT THE *DEAD*...

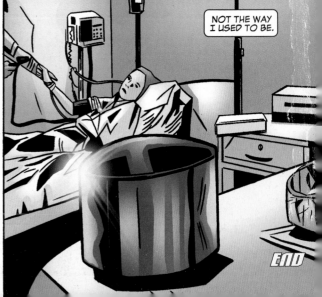

NOT THE WAY I USED TO BE.

END